Men's Health

Life Improvement Guides

Fight Fat

A Total Lifestyle
Program for
Men to Stay Slim
and Healthy

by Stephen C. George, Jeff Bredenberg
and the Editors of **Men'sHealth** Books

Rodale Press, Inc.
Emmaus, Pennsylvania

Printed in the United States of America

The graph in "Body Composition" on page 11 is from *Sensible Fitness* (page 30) by Jack H. Wilmore, Champaign, IL: Human Kinetics Publishers. Copyright 1986 by Jack H. Wilmore. Reprinted by permission.

"Mentally Fit" on page 69 is adapted from "Self-Motivation Assessment Scale" by Rod K. Dishman, from *Essentials of Fitness* by H. B. Falls, A. M. Baylor and R. K. Dishman (1988): pages 263–265. Used with permission.

Interview with John Candy on page 164 is excerpted from "20 Questions: John Candy," *Playboy* magazine (August 1989). Copyright © 1989 by Playboy. All rights reserved.

Library of Congress Cataloging-in-Publication Data

George, Stephen C.
    Fight fat : a total lifestyle program for men to stay slim and
healthy / by Stephen C. George, Jeff Bredenberg and the editors of
Men's Health Books.
        p.   cm. — (Men's health life improvement guides)
    Includes index.
     ISBN 0–87596–278–5 paperback
     1. Weight loss.   2. Men—Health and hygiene.   3. Lifestyle.
I. Bredenberg, Jeff.   II. Men's Health Books   III. Title.
IV. Series.
RM222.2.G4465   1995
613.2'5'081—dc20   95–20384

Distributed in the book trade by St. Martin's Press

  4   6   8   10   9   7   5   3   paperback

—— OUR MISSION ——
We publish books that empower people's lives.
—— RODALE BOOKS ——

Fight Fat Editorial Staff
Senior Managing Editor: **Neil Wertheimer**
Senior Editor: **Matthew Hoffman**
Food Editor: **Jean Rogers**
Writers: **Stephen C. George, Jeff Bredenberg, Brian Chichester, Jack Croft**
Book and Cover Designer: **John Herr**
Cover Photographer: **Mitch Mandel**
Photo Editor: **Susan Pollack**
Illustrators: **John Herr, Mark Matcho, David Smith**
Studio Manager: **Joe Golden**
Technical Artists: **J. Andrew Brubaker, Kristen Morgan Downey, David Q. Pryor, Liz Reap**
Assistant Research Manager: **Carlotta Cuerdon**
Researchers and Fact-Checkers: **Susan E. Burdick, Christine Dreisbach, Valerie Edwards-Paulik, Jan Eickmeier, Theresa Fogarty, Carol J. Gilmore, Deborah Pedron, Sally A. Reith, Sandra Salera-Lloyd, Anita Small, Bernadette Sukley, Michelle M. Szulborski, John Waldron**
Senior Copy Editor: **Susan G. Berg**
Copy Editor: **Kathy Diehl**
Production Manager: **Helen Clogston**
Manufacturing Coordinator: **Jodi Schaffer**
Office Staff: **Roberta Mulliner, Julie Kehs, Bernadette Sauerwine, Mary Lou Stephen**

Rodale Health and Fitness Books
Vice-President and Editorial Director: **Debora T. Yost**
Art Director: **Jane Colby Knutila**
Research Manager: **Ann Gossy Yermish**
Copy Manager: **Lisa D. Andruscavage**

Contents

Introduction

Diets, Bad Videos and the Truth about Fat

I grew up thinking there was a pill for everything. That was how you thought back in the 1960s and 1970s, when high-tech medicine was taking hold and new drugs and treatments were in the headlines almost every day.

I worked in a drugstore in my early teens, and I remember stocking diet pills—and restocking, and restocking. Boy, did those things sell. As the old pop tune goes, we were blinded by science.

Certainly I was. Like a lot of skinny guys, I wanted to gain weight. So I applied my worker's discount to a huge canister of weight-gain tablets. Forty a day, chew 'em up and try not to gag. A week later, I read the label.

Turns out those 40 pills were the caloric and nutritional equivalent of two glasses of milk, but cost about ten times as much—even with my employee discount. I immediately broke away from the Church of Quick Medical Fixes, and I'm proud to say I have never rejoined.

But nearly 30 years later, a lot of men still aren't convinced. They're still looking for quick fixes, particularly to weight problems. Medical professionals, meanwhile, have moved light-years ahead. Today, we know that when it comes to weight control, quick fixes (1) don't work and (2) still taste awful.

It's time to be convinced, once and for all, that weight control is a lifestyle, not a diet program. That you can regularly eat large amounts of great-tasting chow without putting on the pounds—if it's the right chow. That effective, high-powered exercise can be an enjoyable part of your life without taking it over. That like washing your hands, fat-fighting habits can be seamlessly added to your daily routine so that after a while, you never even have to think about being lean to be lean.

The benefits are far more than mirror vanity. The lean lifestyle energizes you around the clock; it improves your attitude; it invigorates your sex life. Not to mention that you'll be fighting off the top men-killers like heart disease and diabetes.

Fight Fat was written to be the definitive guide to achieve the lean lifestyle. But there's another reason we wrote it. Virtually all mass-market weight-loss products—diet books, aerobics videos, frozen dinners, even odd-shaped exercise gizmos—are aimed at women. Well, this book is unabashedly male. Not in a macho, swaggering kind of way, but by acknowledging that men eat, work, play, talk and solve problems in their own ways. No apologies, either. We like being who we are.

In fact, that is the spirit behind the entire series that *Fight Fat* is part of. Each book in the *Men's Health* Life Improvement Guides offers practical health information researched and written entirely for guys. Fast, fun and reliable, the series delivers smart information on the things that matter most.

We know that two-thirds of you consider yourselves overweight. Now you have the perfect tool to fix it. It's called *Fight Fat*, and you're reading it now. Happy fixing.

Neil Wertheimer
Senior Managing Editor, *Men's Health* Books

Part One

What's the Problem?

Defining Fat

What It Is—And How It Can Kill You

If you were to train a high-powered microscope on the inside of the belly of the typical overweight male, you'd probably be reminded of those low-budget sci-fi flicks of the 1950s. Seen up close, it resembles the voracious, man-eating plant from Roger Corman's *Little Shop of Horrors* cross-pollinated with *The Blob*. Only Steve McQueen isn't around anymore to save the day. Behind the belt of every man are billions of tiny blobs, each one emitting the same primal plea as Corman's campy carnivore.

"They're saying 'Feed me. Feed me,' " says John P. Foreyt, Ph.D., director of the Nutrition Research Clinic at Baylor College of Medicine in Houston and author of *Living without Dieting*. "They're waiting to be filled."

They probably won't have to wait long. These blobs are fat cells, aptly described by Phillip M. Sinaikin, M.D., a psychiatrist who specializes in the treatment of obesity in Longwood, Florida, and author of *Fat Madness: How to Stop the Diet Cycle and Achieve Permanent Well-Being*, as "kind of like a Baggie filled with oil." It's not a pretty picture.

The Incredible Mr. Lipid

The average man has about 30 billion fat cells that can fluctuate wildly in size, depending on the amount of fat they contain. They may not be visible to the naked eye. But if you lump a few billion fat cells together, you'll wind up with one lumpy

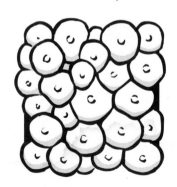

naked guy eyeing you contemptuously from the bathroom mirror.

The oily substances stored in fat cells are called lipids. But don't get confused. The term comes from the Greek word *lipos*, which means—you guessed it—fat.

We get fats from two sources: our bodies and our diets. "They're an integral part of all living systems," says Paul Saltman, Ph.D., professor of biology at the University of California, San Diego, and co-author of *The University of California San Diego Nutrition Book*. "All creatures have fats. They're naturally produced and they're naturally a part of all the membranes and cells of our bodies."

Each of us seems to be born with a genetically determined capacity to make fat cells, which answer to the scientific name of adipose tissue. Despite the way it may seem, they were not created solely to embarrass you with a middle-age paunch. "The primary purpose for which God or nature put fat cells in our bodies was to be a reservoir for energy," says R. Paul Abernathy, Ph.D., professor in the Department of Foods and Nutrition at Purdue University in West Lafayette, Indiana. "They're a place to put the energy until we need it. And when we need it, we get it out."

The problem is that most of us deposit far more than we withdraw. Now that's a great idea if you're talking about banking. But not with fat. Like the big-screen Blob, individual fat cells can expand to frightening proportions. "They can increase a thousandfold in volume," says Dr. Sinaikin.

They can also multiply. When fat cells expand to their outer limits—something Dr. Foreyt says occurs after a significant weight gain—they divide, forming new fat cells. And once a new fat cell is created, you have it for life. That is one of the primary reasons that it's so difficult to lose weight once you've ballooned up.

"A person with more fat cells has greater difficulty maintaining a lower body weight than a person with fewer fat cells," Dr. Foreyt says. "So you don't want to gain more fat cells. That's the bottom line. If you've got them, you can't get rid of them."

Trouble in the Cell Block

While a fat cell's main function is storing energy for future use, it also serves as a "buffer" that keeps excess blood sugar (glucose) and wayward globs of fat out of the bloodstream. But when fat cells are filled, they get less efficient. This means they no longer can adequately keep harmful substances out of circulation.

"The problems come not only from the fat cells but also from the things the fat cells can't do," Dr. Abernathy says. He likens the situation to overcrowded prisons. "It's not who's in the prison that's causing the damage. It's who's out on the streets," he says.

In society, we've got two choices: Either we can take steps to prevent crimes from being committed or we can build new cells to hold criminals. The body is faced with the same choice when exposed to a high-fat diet. If you won't take preventive steps to cut down the amount of fat circulating through your system, the body will build new cells to store it.

By continuing to take in more energy than you can use, you'll soon fill up the new fat cells and then return even more fat and sugar to your bloodstream. This causes more insulin to be produced, which signals your body to make additional fat cells. At the same time, the excess fat and sugar in your bloodstream can eventually

Lipid Lingo

Cholesterol must have a great agent. In the world of fat and fatlike substances, it always gets star billing. So it might surprise you to learn that other forms of fat account for most of the lipids in your body. Here's a quick guide to the three major classes of lipids.

Triglycerides. Found in both animal and plant foods, this is the form in which almost all of the fat in your body is stored. About 95 percent of lipids in fat cells are triglycerides, which occur when three fatty acids glom on to a molecule of glycerol. Your triglyceride level should register under 200 on a fasting test. If it's higher than that, you may be at risk for heart disease.

Phospholipids. These compounds mix fat with water, making them key players in the structure of cell membranes. They're similar to triglycerides, with one notable exception: One of the three fatty acids is traded for a molecule containing phosphorus. The best-known member of the phospholipid family is lecithin, which can be found in oatmeal, soybeans, cauliflower, peanuts, eggs, milk and chocolate, among other foods. Proponents say it may have health benefits ranging from improving memory to preventing liver damage from alcohol. But the jury is still out, and dietary supplements cannot be recommended.

Sterols. The most famous—and infamous—member of this lipid clan is cholesterol, which is found in animal tissues but not in plants. It serves many essential functions in the body. Too much cholesterol in the blood, however, increases the risk of heart disease. A level below 200 is considered desirable. Eggs and organ meats are particularly rich in cholesterol.

put you at greater risk for a raft of serious, often fatal health problems, like heart disease, high blood pressure and stroke.

Where Fat Comes From

Hint: Look on Your Plate

In the most widely quoted line from the movie *Forrest Gump*, the lovable main character remarks, "Life is like a box of chocolates. You never know what you're going to get."

That's not entirely true. If you eat that box of chocolates, you know exactly what you're going to get—fat. Because to paraphrase another oft-quoted Gumpism, fat is as fat does.

Although the human body manufactures some fat internally, the vast majority comes from food—specifically from things such as nuts, steaks, candy bars and corn dogs. Dietary fat in turn breeds body fat. The reason is simple: Fat is more than twice as, well, fattening as carbohydrates and protein. Specifically, one gram of fat packs a whopping nine calories, while a gram of carbohydrates or protein carries only about four calories.

"The real curse of fat, when push comes to shove, is that fat makes food taste good," says Dr. Paul Saltman of the University of California, San Diego. "When food tastes good, you eat more and you get more calories."

Fat to Fat

The average person needs to get between 2 and 5 percent of total calories from fat. Anything over that small amount gets stored as body fat.

Dietary fat isn't the only stuff that goes into storage, of course. The body also stores carbohydrates and protein. But in the process of converting them into fat—which acts as the body's

energy warehouse—your metabolism burns off about a quarter of their calories. Compare that with dietary fat, which zips straight into storage virtually untouched, calories and all.

"So if you eat the same number of calories but more come from fat, you're going to get fatter, because fat is nine calories per gram, and that fat is directly stored," says Dr. John P. Foreyt of the Nutrition Research Clinic at Baylor College of Medicine. "Fat is laid down first."

The Fat Factor

For years it was believed that overweight people simply ate too much. But research suggests that what you eat can be a lot more important than how much you eat.

A study that looked at 23 lean men and 23 obese men, for example, found little difference in their total sugar intake or the number of calories they consumed. But the overweight men got an average of 33 percent of their total calories from fat, compared with 29 percent for their lean counterparts.

The study, led by Wayne C. Miller, Ph.D., assistant professor of kinesiology at Indiana University in Bloomington and director of the university's weight-loss clinic, adds more credence to the message preached for years by health experts: No more than 25 to 30 percent of your total daily calories should come from fat—ideally with fewer than 10 percent coming from saturated fat, the most dangerous form.

Trimming the Fat

The message doesn't appear to be getting through. The National Health and Nutrition Examination Survey conducted from 1988 through 1994 found that men between the ages of 20 and 70 are still getting 33 to 34 percent of total calories from fat.

"There's nothing wrong

with a high-fat meal," adds Dr. Foreyt. "You just have to balance it with a low-fat meal."

Reducing the amount of fat in your diet does not require starvation or even deprivation. Here are a few ways to get started.

Three grams keeps you out of a jam. "If you're looking at food labels, one rule of thumb is that if it has three grams of fat or less per serving, that would be acceptable," Dr. Miller says. "Not that you're not ever going to have anything that has more than that in it, but that's a good rule to follow."

Size matters. Even if you're strict about following the three-gram rule, "you can get into trouble with quantities," says Paul R. Thomas, R.D., Ed.D., a staff scientist with the Food and Nutrition Board of the National Academy of Sciences in Washington, D.C. Suppose you're eating low-fat ice cream and the single serving size is a half-cup. Don't routinely scarf down a pint at one time and then wonder why you haven't lost weight.

Keep on top of toppings. Even if you normally eat a lot of low-fat foods—potatoes, pasta and bread, for example—you can lob a dietary bomb into the menu by piling on add-ons such as butter and sour cream. By all means, have a baked potato—but hold the butter and maybe substitute salsa.

Trim the fat. When shopping for red meat, look for cuts with the least fat. "Well-marbled meat with thick white streaks is going to be fattier than many other cuts," Dr. Thomas says.

In general, cuts with *loin* or *round* in the name are among the least fatty. And once you get the meat home, take a minute to trim away visible fat. Better to leave it on your plate than see it on your waist.

Mooo-ve to low-fat dairy products. Most cheeses derive more than 70 percent of

---

Fat Facts

Not all fats are created equal. While all are calorie-dense and can make you gain weight, some are better for you than others. Here's a quick primer.

Monounsaturated. Found mainly in vegetable and nut oils, such as olive and canola, these are often referred to as good fats. They help reduce blood cholesterol levels and protect against heart disease.

Polyunsaturated. These contain the essential nutrient linoleic acid and are found in the fat from plants, such as safflower and corn oils. Like the monounsaturated variety, these also tend to reduce blood cholesterol levels.

Hydrogenated. These are liquid oils that have been chemically altered to a semisolid state. Margarine and vegetable shortening are prime examples. Hydrogenated fats are thought to clog coronary arteries, which places them in the "bad" category.

Saturated. These fats are found in all foods that come from animal sources, including meats and dairy products. They are also in oils such as coconut and palm-kernel oil. Saturated fats pose the highest risk for heart disease and some types of cancer. They are found not only in meats and butter but also in things such as coconut, cheese and nondairy dessert toppings and creamers.

---

their calories from fat. So a one-ounce chunk of Cheddar cheese contains more fat than a three-ounce cut of T-bone steak.

White cheeses, such as Parmesan and mozzarella, are usually lower in fat than their yellow counterparts, such as Cheddar and American. Reduced-fat versions of the white cheeses can make an even bigger difference in any cheese-lover's diet. And switching from whole milk to low-fat or skim can also cut your fat intake substantially.

Genetics versus Lifestyle

"Bad" Genes Don't Necessarily Mean Big Jeans

Talk about the American dream. When researchers announced that they'd identified and cloned a "fat gene" in mice, there was immediate speculation that someday scientists might come up with a pill to cure obesity. Fat chance. Experts say you'd be better off holding the mayo than holding your breath waiting for a magic pill.

While it seems clear that genetics plays a role in the amount of body fat we carry around with us, don't blame your parents if you have too much. Ultimately, tight jeans aren't the fault of your genes.

Biology or Behavior?

The discovery of the obesity gene in mice revived a debate that has raged in scientific circles for decades. Does biology determine how fat we are, or does behavior? The answer, experts say, is both.

The role genetics plays in determining weight seems to vary greatly from individual to individual. But even if you are born with a genetic predisposition to overweight, the way you live is what will ultimately determine whether you get fat. If you're living large, odds are you'll be large.

"Clearly, the genes play a major role," says Dr. John P. Foreyt of the Nutrition Research Clinic at Baylor College of Medicine. "The genes, however, do not determine what you're going to have for dinner tonight or how much you're going to exercise."

Out of the Feedback Loop

The discovery of what was dubbed the ob gene by a team of researchers from the Howard Hughes Medical Institute at Rockefeller University in New York City significantly bolsters the long-held theory that there is a feedback loop between fat cells and the brain.

Researchers believe the ob gene makes fat cells secrete a protein that tells the brain when the body has had enough fat. Theoretically, once the brain receives that signal, it attempts to maintain constant body weight by suppressing appetite or speeding the rate at which your body burns calories.

In some cases, however, this feedback loop appears to short-circuit. In mice, for example, researchers found that those with a defective copy of the ob gene do not produce the signal-sending protein and so eat themselves into obesity. Experts believe that a similar pattern may occur in humans.

Genetics does more than tell us how much to eat. It controls our metabolism as well. In mouse studies, for example, researchers have found that some animals that don't overeat still have a tendency to gain weight.

Putting Fat in the Fire

Some guys can eat more and exercise less than others and not gain weight. To those who complain they got dealt a bad hand, Morton H. Shaevitz, Ph.D., associate clinical professor of psychiatry at the University of California, San Diego, School of Medicine and author of *Lean and Mean: The No Hassle Life-Extending Weight Loss Program for Men*, agrees: "You did. You got dealt bad genes. So in order to not get fat you may have to watch what you eat more and exercise more than the other guy. So you either play your hand or ignore it."

How do you play your hand if you were dealt, say, a pair of treys instead of aces-full? Here are some tips recommended by experts to help burn off the excess before it settles on your waist.

Exercise late. It's every man's dream workout—literally. Researchers at the Human Energy Laboratory at Colorado State University in Fort Collins have found a way to burn more calories while you sleep. The key is exercising in the evening. Men who performed a 90-minute strength-training session in the evening woke up the next morning—15 hours after working out—with their metabolism still as much as 10 percent above normal.

Eat early. "Most people with weight problems eat 60 to 70 percent of their food between 6:00 P.M. and midnight and eat very little during the day," says Dr. Shaevitz. You need most of your calories during the day while you're active, so you should eat 70 percent of your day's food during those hours, Dr. Shaevitz says.

Spice up your life. Spicy condiments such as hot peppers, horseradish and chili powder serve double duty in the fight against fat. They fill you up more quickly and they speed up your metabolic rate. So if you're looking for something quick and easy to spice up that drab grilled chicken breast, forget the salt and try this: Stir a small amount of chili powder, cumin, chopped cucumber and green onions into nonfat sour cream or plain yogurt. *Olé*—an instant Mexican topping.

Build up your bulk. When you get pumped up, you also pump up your metabolism. Studies have shown that for each extra pound of muscle you put on, you'll burn as many as 30 to 50 more calories a day, because it takes more energy to sustain lean body mass than fat.

Feeding Frenzy: Is It Hunger or Appetite?

Scientists believe there's a "circuit" between fat cells and the brain. When the cells are full they signal the brain, which says, "No more, thanks."

But humans are not automatons. There is a big difference between *hunger* and *appetite*. Hunger is what goes on in your belly—the physiological need to eat. Appetite refers to what's going on in your head—the psychological desire to eat.

For animals, at least in the laboratory, hunger is the key issue. "Mice, when you give them a cafeteria diet where they can pick and choose, will gorge for a while on one type of thing and then go back to eating a balanced diet over the period of a week," says Douglas L. Coleman, a biochemist and senior staff scientist emeritus at the Jackson Laboratory in Bar Harbor, Maine.

But people eat for reasons that have nothing to do with hunger. We eat when we're bored. We eat when we're depressed or under stress. Or we eat for the same reason people conquer a mountain: because it's there.

Appetite can also be driven by cravings—overpowering, not-to-be-denied yearnings for a special, usually high-fat, food, says Marcia Levin Pelchat, Ph.D., a food cravings expert at the Monell Chemical Senses Center in Philadelphia.

While hunger and appetite roar full throttle for most of our lives, cravings appear to diminish. "One thing men can look forward to is that as they get older, they get fewer cravings and can resist them better," Dr. Pelchat says.

Where Fat Accumulates

It's Abominable, It's Abdominal

When excess dietary fat hits your system, it acts like an out-of-town conventioneer at an overbooked hotel, except without the funny hat. Instead of doing the sensible thing and leaving town, the fat lurches off in search of a room for the night. Chances are it will wind up in Fat City—that section of the body known as the abdomen. And there's always a neon sign out front, blinking "Vacancy."

But unlike obnoxious conventioneers, who eventually sober up and go home, the fat you eat tends to stick around. Once it's stored as body fat, it will establish permanent residency in your gut unless you forcibly evict it.

The First Shall Be Last

Most men consider fat to be simply abominable. But the real problem is that it's mainly abdominal.

Experts aren't sure why, but men tend to store fat in the abdominal region first. "Most men store their fat between the nipples and the navel. And most women store it between the navel and the knees," says Dr. Morton H. Shaevitz of the University of California, San Diego, School of Medicine.

And when it comes to getting rid of unwanted fat, the body is strictly a union shop: first hired, last fired. In other words, the fat in the abdomen is often the last fat to go, since it's the first fat put on, says Dr. Phillip M. Sinaikin, a psychiatrist who specializes in the treatment of obesity.

Fat settles on the body in two patterns. When fat groups in the abdomen and lower chest, it's known as apple-type distribution. When fat congregates in the hips, buttocks and thighs, it's called the pear type.

"Men mostly fall into the apple type, which is the most dangerous," says John Erdman, Ph.D., professor of food science and director of the Division of Nutritional Sciences at the University of Illinois at Urbana.

Forbidden Fruit

Maybe it goes back to the Garden of Eden. Man bit the apple; now, whenever he eats too much, he starts to look like one. Who said God doesn't have a sense of humor?

But the health risks associated with the apple-type storage of fat are anything but funny. According to a review published by the President's Council on Physical Fitness and Sports, this fat pattern is "a risk factor for heart disease, high blood pressure, stroke, elevated blood lipids and diabetes."

In fact, where fat accumulates may pose a greater health risk than how much fat you have, says Jack H. Wilmore, Ph.D., professor in the Department of Kinesiology and Health Education at the University of Texas at Austin.

By contrast, the Widettes—those grotesquely wide-bottomed misfits portrayed by Dan Aykroyd, Jane Curtin and John Belushi in the early years of *Saturday Night Live*—apparently would be in no great danger. "People could probably weigh more if most of that fat was in their behinds," says Dr. John P. Foreyt of the Nutrition Research Clinic at Baylor College of Medicine. That isn't to say there's no risk at all, he adds. But research suggests fat stored above the waist is far more dangerous than that stored below.

Experts aren't sure why abdominal fat is more dangerous. Perhaps it's because people with large amounts of belly fat have large concentrations of fat near vital organs and the hepatic portal circulatory system—the network of blood vessels that directly links the intestines to the liver.

"More recent evidence indicates that high levels of visceral fat—fat stored within the abdominal cavity—puts you at the highest risk," Dr. Wilmore says. "Not the fat that's directly under the skin, but the deep fat."

The Gatekeeper

How does excess dietary fat know where to go? Fat cells in certain areas are programmed for storing fat, Dr. Wilmore says. More specifically, an enzyme called lipoprotein lipase is thought to serve as a "gatekeeper enzyme," which steers fat into waiting fat cells.

"It's sort of like a traffic cop. It sees fat and says 'Stop, come in here,'" Dr. Wilmore says.

In men, the enzyme waves fat into adipose tissue in the abdomen, experts believe. "Why do you get big beer bellies in men? I suppose that's just where the fat is laid down," Dr. Foreyt says. "That's normal."

One theory is that the body stores fat in the gut because abdominal fat is more readily mobilized and put into action than fat from other parts of the body, Dr. Wilmore says. In women, however, fat is generally directed away from the abdomen to the hips and buttocks—probably so it can be safely stored for use during pregnancy.

The tendency for women to store fat in the pear pattern makes sense not only for reproductive purposes but also for their own survival. "If women had weight above the waist as young adults, that would set them at risk for heart disease," Dr. Foreyt says. "So it makes sense that you do not get 'apple' women, at least pre-menopausally. It would be detrimental to the species from an evolutionary point of view if the woman had fat above the waist."

Hidden Danger

Jean-Pierre Despres, Ph.D., isn't overweight, but inside his abdominal cavity is a store of fat that increases his risk for heart disease and diabetes.

It's called visceral fat, and Dr. Despres, professor of exercise and physiology at the Laval University Lipid Research Center in Quebec, says what you can't see can harm you.

"Some normal-weight individuals will not show an obvious accumulation of abdominal fat, but they might have too much of this internal, visceral fat," Dr. Despres says.

This may help explain why Old St. Nick has been around for so long. Having a belly that shakes like a bowl full of jelly is far less of a risk than having an expansive waistline and a hard belly, Dr. Despres says.

If you can grab the flab, that means it's subcutaneous fat, located just underneath the skin, he says. "If it's a hard belly and you pinch the skin with your fingers and measure very little accumulation of subcutaneous fat, this individual is at very high risk because all the fat is in the abdominal cavity," explains Dr. Despres.

Men who are susceptible to this type of internal fat storage need to be particularly vigilant about exercising regularly and avoiding excessive fat in the diet.

When Weight Becomes a Problem

The Naked Truth Is in the Mirror

There are all kinds of gizmos, charts and computations that will tell you if you're fat. You can consult a height/weight table. You can calculate your body mass index. You can even have your body fat percentage tested by calipers or electrodes—take your pick.

Each of these methods can help you understand how big your weight problem is. But if you're wondering whether you even have a weight problem, there's an easier way.

Get a mirror. And get naked.

"If you look at yourself in the mirror nude and you look overweight or obese, you probably are—and you probably ought to do something about it," says Dr. Paul R. Thomas of the Food and Nutrition Board of the National Academy of Sciences. "The vast majority of people can look at themselves and get a fairly honest assessment of whether or not they could stand to lose some weight."

Why We Need Fat

By itself, fat isn't all bad. In addition to storing energy so we can survive tough times, fat helps regulate the body's thermostat and protects vital organs, says Dr. Thomas. Cholesterol—another fat with a bad reputation—aids the formation of important hormones and also is involved in the formation of vitamin D and bile.

"It's false to say fat is bad,

in and of itself," Dr. Thomas adds. "The problem is how much you eat and how much is on your body."

How Much Is Too Much?

Obesity has been linked to an enormous range of health problems, from heart attacks and cancer to impotence. Experts define obesity as being 20 percent above your optimum weight or having more than 25 percent body fat. So if that spare tire is getting big enough to fit your car, you know it's time to start slimming down.

Even guys who are just starting to pudge out can benefit from trimming back. In one study, researchers followed a group of Harvard University alumni for 27 years. They found that men who were only 2 to 6 percent over their desirable weights still had a significantly greater chance of dying from heart disease than their slimmer counterparts.

The worst thing is that fat creeps up on you. By your early twenties the aging process makes it easier for fat to accumulate. Most muscles and organs become smaller, so the body needs fewer calories to keep itself going. Your metabolism slows down—and if you're like most men, so does the rest of you. And you keep eating the same amount of food. Your body burns less and stores more. Which is why it seems like you go to bed slim, only to wake up with a bulge you never had before.

How Much Is Enough?

With apologies to Thomas Jefferson, not all men are created equal—at least not when it comes to fat. "We can't all be Arnold Schwarzenegger," says Dale L. Anderson, M.D., head of the complementary medicine department at Park Nicollet Medical Center in Minneapolis.

Government health experts have abandoned the old insurance weight tables, which offered one-size-fits-all "ideal" weights based on height. Experts today emphasize what they call "healthy weight"—a broader, gentler standard that better reflects reality.

"All of us cannot be skinny. But certainly, all of us can be healthy," says Dr. John P. Foreyt of the Nutrition Research Clinic at Baylor College of Medicine. "By focusing on what you're eating and how much you're exercising, you'll achieve optimal wellness, even though you may not achieve optimal skinniness. You still may want to be skinnier than you are, but at least you're going to feel great."

Genetics plays a key role in how much you weigh and how much body fat you naturally carry around. "One thing I ask people is, do they come from a family of greyhounds or St. Bernards?" says Dr. Morton H. Shaevitz of the University of California, San Diego, School of Medicine.

"Take a look at animal husbandry. You take some animals and give them a pound of feed and they put on a pound of meat. You give other animals a pound of feed and they put on a half-pound of meat."

If your waistline is going out to pasture, you may have a genetic predisposition to gain weight. But that doesn't mean you have to get fat. "Obviously, you'll have to work harder than somebody who's genetically programmed to be thin," Dr. Shaevitz says. "Those without that programming need to be very active. They also have to be really smart, because in order not to feel hungry all the time they have to learn to eat foods that are not calorically dense."

What You Should Weigh

Unlike earlier weight tables that assumed everyone has more or less the same body type, modern guidelines allow for a wide range of "healthy" weights. Someone who's five feet ten

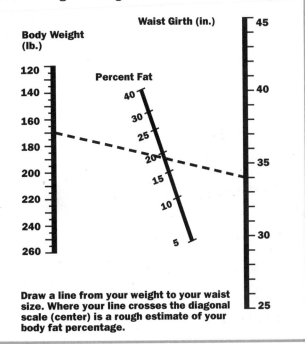

Body Composition

Experts have a variety of tools and techniques for determining your percentage of body fat. Here's a simple chart that brings it all together.

Draw a line from your weight to your waist size. Where your line crosses the diagonal scale (center) is a rough estimate of your body fat percentage.

inches tall and over age 35 should tip the scales somewhere between 146 and 188 pounds. The range is wide because it covers men and women (men are typically at the higher end of the scale) and because it also includes those who are naturally thick, thin or in between.

In addition, the maximum weights allowed for guys between ages 19 and 34 run roughly 12 to 16 pounds lighter than those for their grizzled counterparts, who naturally tend to get heavier with age.

Are you satisfied with your weight? "Get a bathroom scale and stand on it in the morning," recommends Dr. Paul Saltman of the University of California, San Diego. "If it's too high, what do you do? You eat less food and you exercise more. It's that simple."

When Fat Becomes Dangerous

Excess Pounds Pose Serious Health Problems

Not that this will come as a shock to most of you, but Andre Agassi was wrong. Image isn't everything—and nowhere is that more true than in how much you weigh.

The main reason to lose weight is not to impress the old gang at your 20th high school reunion—although that would surely be fun. If you're overweight, you should shed pounds purely for the health of it.

Being overweight can kill you. Excess body fat contributes to several types of cancer, heart disease, stroke and diabetes. It has also been linked to high blood pressure, gall-bladder disease, sleep apnea, osteoarthritis and even sexual dysfunction.

The costs are enormous. Experts estimate that obesity accounts for 19 percent—or $22.2 billion—of the $116.9 billion spent each year on cardiovascular disease. Similarly, 20 percent of the $7.6 billion spent annually on high blood pressure stems from obesity.

A Test You Can Pass

If you're like most men, you're still eating a high-fat diet. And odds are that plaque is building up in your arteries, making it more difficult for blood to flow smoothly and greatly increasing your risk for heart disease. Losing even a small amount of weight can boost levels of high-density lipoprotein (HDL) cholesterol, the "good" cholesterol that helps clean arteries.

If you want to find out your health risk, have a blood lipid profile done. It will check the levels of cholesterol—including HDL and its evil, artery-clogging cousin, LDL (low-density lipoprotein)—as well as triglycerides. In general, your cholesterol level should check in below 200. Your HDL reading should be around 60 or higher. If it's below 35, you're considered at risk for heart disease. An LDL level of under 130 is considered healthy. If it climbs to 160 or above, it's risky.

Check the Padding

"The primary thing is to reduce your fat mass percentage, because increased body fat has significant health risks, including your potential for developing non-insulin-dependent (Type II) diabetes, cardiovascular disease, sleep apnea and other medical problems," says Dr. Morton H. Shaevitz of the University of California, San Diego, School of Medicine.

If your blood lipid levels and body fat are high, don't despair. You can dramatically improve your health with even a relatively small weight loss. "For most of us, a 10 percent drop is reasonable," says Dr. John P. Foreyt of the Nutrition Research Clinic at Baylor College of Medicine. "And a 10 percent drop will lead to significant medical benefits."

At the University of Pittsburgh, researchers studied 159 people under age 45 who were 30 to 70 pounds overweight as they  followed a weight-loss program. The result: Those who were able to shed just 10 to 15 percent of their initial body weight and keep it off during the 18-month study showed significant improvements in HDL cholesterol and triglyceride levels, waist-to-hip ratios and blood pressure.

An American Epidemic

*Another Year Older,
Another Pound Heavier*

The Institute of Medicine of the National Academy of Sciences in Washington, D.C., has called obesity an American epidemic. The National Health and Nutrition Examination Survey found that one in three Americans is overweight. More than one in ten is severely overweight. And by the time men hit their sixties, 42 percent are overweight.

According to Dr. Jack H. Wilmore of the University of Texas at Austin, the average American gains one pound a year after age 25. Do the math: By the time he reaches his fifties, the average person has probably gained about 30 pounds—or more—in fat.

Heavy Trends

Throughout most of history, corpulence was a sign of opulence. After all, only the wealthy could afford to eat enough to grow fat. But if you look at the rich and famous today, you won't see many who could be called fat cats.

"If you look at demographic trends, the rich—those in the highest socio-economic classes—tend to have a lower prevalence of obesity than those in the lower classes or middle class," says Dr. Paul R. Thomas of the Food and Nutrition Board of the National Academy of Sciences.

Dr. Thomas says education accounts for some of the differences. Researchers have found that those with less than a high school education have the highest incidence of obesity--39 percent. Only 29 percent of those who attended college are similarly overweight.

Paradoxically, while experts have long called obesity a by-product of our affluent society, it's typically the poor and disadvantaged who are most at risk.

Loud and Clear—And Ignored

For years, experts have pleaded with us, rich and poor alike, to eat less fat and exercise more. But we keep getting fatter. In the early 1960s, for example, 24.4 percent of Americans were overweight. Today it's about a third, and there's no sign that we're slowing down. Clearly, the message hasn't gotten through—or at least is meeting stiff resistance.

"There comes a point when experts talk to you too long, too hard, and it becomes numbing," concedes Dr. Thomas. "You almost feel like doing things just to get their goat."

To keep the nation's combined tonnage within reasonable, healthful levels, government health officials have urged Americans to change their eating habits so that no more than 30 percent of total calories come from fat. Many experts say we should aim to go even lower, to below 25 percent.

Surveys, however, show that men continue to eat too much fat. Men in their fifties get almost 36 percent of calories from fat, while men in their twenties are at 34 percent.

"We're eating a little bit less, but we're not down in the range that's good for us," says Purdue University's Dr. R. Paul Abernathy.

Compounding the problem is the fact that few of us exercise in any significant way. The President's Council on Physical Fitness and Sports estimates that only one in five Americans exercises for at least 20 minutes three or more days a week. Meanwhile, two in five Americans are completely sedentary.

Alcohol and Weight

They Don't Call It a Beer Belly for Nothing

If you like to drink, you're going to have a tough time losing weight.

The reason is simple, although it was only recently discovered by health experts: Drinking alcohol has essentially the same effect on your weight as eating fat.

"We used to consider it liquid bread," says Dr. John P. Foreyt of the Nutrition Research Clinic at Baylor College of Medicine. "In other words, it was counted as a carbohydrate when doing food groups."

While alcohol owes its existence to grains, via the fermentation process, chemically it's closer to fat. "Alcohol may not show itself as a layer of oil on top of a glass, but metabolically, it's more like fat than sugar," says J. P. Flatt, Ph.D., professor of biochemistry at the University of Massachusetts Medical School in Worcester.

And like fat, alcohol has a high calorie content: about seven calories per gram. A gram of fat has nine calories, while carbohydrates and protein have about four calories per gram. In addition, when alcohol is consumed at the same time as food, the body tends to burn the alcohol first, sparing the fat.

"That helps explain why people get beer bellies," says Dr. Foreyt. "And it helps explain why you really have trouble losing or maintaining weight if you do a lot of drinking."

The bottom line, when you're trying to cut back on fat, is

to factor in the alcohol you drink. Suppose, for example, you cut your calories from fat down to the 25 to 30 percent level recommended by experts. If you continue to consume 10 percent of your daily calories—which is about two drinks for most people—from booze, it's as though your diet had 40 percent fat.

"If your dietary approach is to go to a very low fat diet, it won't work if you drink too much alcohol," Dr. Flatt says.

This isn't to say you have to cut out alcohol entirely. It does mean that if you're going to drink and not gain weight, you had better cut a little more fat from your diet than you otherwise would.

But there's a catch. Even if you cut back on fat and drink moderately, your weight-loss efforts may prove futile. First, there's the calorie issue: Drinking two 12-ounce cans of beer each day for a month is about the same as eating 550 grams of fat—or about 65 filet mignons. Then there's the small—or not so small—matter of appetite. "The circumstances under which you might enjoy alcohol are also conducive to eating more," Dr. Flatt says.

While some experts advocate giving up drinking, at least during the initial stages of trying to lose weight, Dr. Foreyt warns that abstinence could make the heart grow fonder.

"If you like a glass of wine at dinner, the worst thing you can do is give that up," Dr. Foreyt says. "You'll start thinking about it more. And psychologically, you're just setting yourself up for failure.

"If you do drink, you may have to cut back, that's true," he says. "If you're drinking a six-pack a day, you're not going to lose weight. You're going to have to gradually cut back to one beer every other night, or cut it back to weekends, or something like that. But you don't want to cut beer out completely or wine out completely if you like it."

Skip the Diets

Why Quick-Fix Programs Almost Always Fail

At any given time, the Institute of Medicine says, "tens of millions of people in this country are dieting." Americans shed pounds the way Madonna sheds clothes. There's only one big difference: Madonna's clothes tend to stay off.

According to the institute, which is part of the National Academy of Sciences in Washington, D.C., those who complete weight-loss programs will lose about 10 percent of their body weight—"only to regain two-thirds of it within one year and almost all of it within five years."

Losing Weight: It's a Way of Life

Most men view losing weight the same way college students approach studying for exams: Rather than working at it a little each night, they try to cram it all in at the last minute.

Taking a short-term approach to weight loss is shortsighted. And any results will almost certainly be short-lived, says Dr. Paul R. Thomas of the National Academy of Sciences' Food and Nutrition Board. "You do what's needed to be done to lose the weight, then you slowly go back to the old habits of eating and activity that got you into the problem in the first place," Dr. Thomas says.

Dieting can never be a quick fix, says Dr. Dale L. Anderson of the Park Nicollet Medical Center. Indeed, the word *diet* hails from the Greek word for "mode of life." And that, experts

say, is what we have to work on—not a temporary goal of losing 30 pounds for an upcoming high school reunion, for example, but keeping weight off for the long haul.

According to Dr. Morton H. Shaevitz of the University of California, San Diego, School of Medicine, when men come to him for help, they usually ask: "Doc, how much weight can I lose in the next three months?"

It's the wrong question. "The issue is, how much are you going to weigh in the next 3 years? The next 30 years? The next 50 years? That's very difficult for people to get a hold of," Dr. Shaevitz says.

Dieting Is Dead

The problem with most diets is that they are based on deprivation, experts say. You may be able to deny yourself certain favorite foods for a short period of time, but sooner or later you're going to crave them again.

"The abstinence theory does not work in eating," says Dr. John P. Foreyt of the Nutrition Research Clinic at Baylor College of Medicine.

Another major problem is that most books, videos and weight-loss products dictate exactly what you can and cannot eat. They don't leave a lot of room for flexibility and creativity.

"I call it 'no-brain dieting,' " says Martin Yadrick, R.D., a Los Angeles dietitian and spokesman for the American Dietetic Association. "You follow the orders and lose weight, but then when you're out in the real world, you don't know what to do and you gain it all back because you didn't learn anything."

If a basketball player who shoots 90 percent from the foul line stops practicing, his free-throw percentage will plummet. That's the way it is with dieters who regain weight, Dr. Shaevitz says. "You stop the behavior that was consistent with your success," he says.

Don't Count Calories

Why You Lose at the Numbers Game

You would think that Dr. Paul R. Thomas, a staff scientist with the Food and Nutrition Board of the National Academy of Sciences, would be a nut for fine print. The board has been a key player in developing and promoting the use of nutrition labels for a huge variety of foods, from canned beans and frozen ravioli to the latest in chocolate-frosted sugar bombs.

But when it comes to actually reading the labels he helped create, Dr. Thomas is like most men. "I'll admit I rarely look at nutrition labels outside of my professional life," he says.

It's not that Dr. Thomas doesn't care what's in his food. Just the opposite. But he knows that if he follows a few basic rules, he doesn't have to get caught up in calorie-counting or complicated nutritional analyses. His diet will still be healthy.

You can do the same.

Counter Intelligence

When you talk about losing weight or cutting down on fat, the first thing people think of is calorie-counting. That's all wrong. You can think about Count Dracula or Counting Crows or even counteroffensives, but do not—repeat, not—think about counting calories.

Studies show it's far more important to cut fat than calories. Eating fat, as you know, will make you fat. Researchers at Cornell University in Ithaca, New York, found that cutting fat intake can make people lose weight no matter how much food or how many calories they consume.

In one study, all subjects ate the same kinds of foods, but people in a low-fat group went without mayo on their turkey sandwiches, for example, or had low-fat yogurt instead of regular yogurt. After 11 weeks, the low-fat eaters lost twice as much weight as people who ate more fat, even though there was no restriction on the total calories they consumed and the high-fat eaters limited calories to 2,000 per day.

So rather than trying to keep track of the calories you eat each day and the specific nutrient content of every item you buy, focus on the big picture. This means cutting back on fat generally by selecting mainly low-fat, minimally processed foods and not getting hung up on the minutiae.

"Nutrition labels are primarily useful in the beginning stages of making changes, particularly if you're going to be making changes by using low-fat or lower-fat alternatives to common products," Dr. Thomas says. "But once you establish your overall dietary pattern, the kinds of foods you're going to buy, it's no problem."

Dr. Paul Saltman of the University of California, San Diego, agrees. "I never count calories. And I tell people not to. It's compulsive-neurotic, and they'll lose track and eat too many."

In stressing calorie-counting, Dr. Thomas says, some health experts have been guilty of promoting a strategy that can't possibly work. "The nutrition profession, by being so focused on the components of foods rather than the foods themselves, has led to unanticipated problems in how the general public thinks about eating," Dr. Thomas says. "When you're focusing on these individual parts, it does two things. Number one, it tends to take focus away from the whole. And second of all, it makes eating right seem incredibly complicated to do. And it's not."

What You Need to Know

All your life you've been told to eat a balanced diet. But if you're like most American men, you probably need to tip the balance away from calorie-dense fats to carbohydrates to avoid tipping the scales.

It's important to stress, though, that when it comes to your favorite foods, we're talking about cutting back, not cutting out.

"Think about a panorama of foods that gives you pleasure and a diversity that gives you nutrients," says Dr. Saltman. "Don't think of a single food, a single meal or a single day in your life. Think of a four- to six-day integrated dietary program."

Here's what that diet should include.

Be a complex eater. If you're a meat-and-potatoes kind of guy—and let's face it, a lot of us still are—the last thing you want to hear is someone telling you to cut out the meat. But you probably need to think about eating more potatoes—and hold the sour cream, butter or bacon bits—and less meat.

Carbohydrates can fill you up, so you crave less fat. At the same time, they burn fastest of all the body's energy sources and aren't easily converted into fat.

Nutrition experts recommend that at least 55 percent of your calories come from carbohydrates. However, the average U.S. male gets only about 46 percent of his calories from carbohydrates.

One important distinction needs to be made, though: Not all carbohydrates are created equal. If you're looking to cut fat and increase carbohydrate consumption, the emphasis should be on eating more complex carbohydrates such as fruits and vegetables, which are also rich in fiber. Eating simple carbohydrates such as sugar can make losing weight harder.

Experts are well-aware, however, that men are especially resistant to making changes when meat is on the table for discussion.

"What I try to do is have them visualize a plate of food," says Sandra Mowry, an applied clinical nutritionist in Wayne, Pennsylvania, who counsels individuals and corporate clients. "And where we used to think about having a big piece of steak and then a little bit of rice and a little bit of vegetables, I try to have them visualize a lot of rice and vegetables instead, with pieces of meat throughout."

Cut back on fat. Just as we eat too few carbohydrates, we generally consume too much fat. While the government sets 30 percent as the target, many health experts say we should aim to get 25 percent or less of our total calories from fat to attain maximum health benefits. The average man is still getting about 34 percent of his calories from fat.

If men will follow four simple steps, they can easily keep their fat consumption within those guidelines, says Dr. Wayne C. Miller of Indiana University. As part of the Non-Diet Diet he helped develop, Dr. Miller offers the following tips:

• Don't cook in oil or fry in grease.

• Don't add butter or oil-based products to your foods.

• Make all of the dairy products you eat or drink low-fat.

• Eat only lean red meat, or fish and poultry without the skin.

"I'm not counting fat grams. I'm not weighing this, that and the other," Dr. Miller says. "I'm not going to charts and tables and food exchanges. I'm just making some simple changes."

Don't be too pro-protein. High-protein foods, especially meats, are often rich in calories and loaded with fat. If you eat excessive amounts of protein, what your body doesn't burn for fuel it will store as fat.

Experts say you should limit your protein consumption to less than 15 percent of your total calories. It probably won't be too hard, since surveys show the average man is already in that ballpark.

Sane Ways to Lose Weight

It's about Food—And Exercise

While it's easy to lose some weight fast, keeping it off is hard. Dr. Dale L. Anderson of the Park Nicollet Medical Center jokingly refers to our pattern of gaining and losing weight as "the rhythm method of girth control."

Experts agree that no short-term "diet" will keep weight off for the long haul. "Whatever you do to lose the weight you're going to have to do for the rest of your life," says Dr. Morton H. Shaevitz of the University of California, San Diego, School of Medicine.

A Winning Combination

There's no great mystery as to why people regain weight. In most cases they quit doing whatever it was that helped them trim down in the first place. When Dr. Wayne C. Miller of Indiana University surveyed 83 men and 273 women who had regained weight, he found that 83 percent had reverted to old eating habits and 82 percent had quit their exercise routines.

But even people who stick with healthy diets can have a hard time keeping pounds off. In a review of more than 60 weight-loss studies, researchers from the University of Pittsburgh School of Medicine found that healthy eating by itself didn't seem to guarantee success.

When healthy eating is combined with exercise, however, the success rate rises. "Losing the weight isn't the problem. It's maintaining it. And what the research shows is those

people who continue their exercise maintain their weight loss," says Dr. Miller.

Smart Moves

Exercise plays several key roles in weight loss. "Number one, it burns calories," says Dr. Paul Saltman of the University of California, San Diego. "Number two, it increases your metabolic rate. And number three, it actually depresses appetite."

If your goal is to lose a potbelly in particular, exercise still is your best hope. Two studies of older men found that those who cut back on calories without exercising had to lose four times as much weight overall as exercisers in order to shed the same amount of belly fat.

"People who maintain their exercise programs have a greater tendency to maintain their diets," Dr. Miller adds. When exercise falls off, good eating habits usually take a tumble.

Just Do It

Experts say you need to exercise at least 30 minutes a day, a minimum of three days a week, to gain maximum health benefits. But with only 10 to 15 percent of adults meeting that minimum exercise standard, clearly most Americans aren't heeding the call.

"For a lot of people, just getting more exercise will enable them to achieve a healthier weight," says Dr. Paul R. Thomas of the National Academy of Science's Food and Nutrition Board.

Think small. Little things add up. But if most of the little things are geared toward avoiding physical activity, what's being added are extra pounds.

You don't have to be a jock to get in shape. Activities as simple as walking up and down stairs instead of taking the elevator can make a difference in the long run, says Dr. Anderson. Climbing a flight of stairs, for ex-

ample, burns about 10 calories, he notes. Do that every day for a year, and you've burned off more than 3,500 calories—or one pound.

Ten calories may not seem like much. In fact, it's not. It's one peanut or one piece of hard candy, Dr. Anderson says. But combine walking the stairs with passing up one peanut a day, and you could have a net loss of two pounds over the course of a year.

Do what you like. When it comes to actual exercise, the form you choose—walking, jogging, cycling, swimming, weight lifting, martial arts, whatever—is less important than making sure it's something you enjoy.

"What turns you on? What gives you pleasure?" asks Dr. Saltman. "Don't do exercises that don't give you pleasure, because then you won't do the exercises."

Combine strategies. There are two types of exercise: aerobic and anaerobic. Aerobic exercises push your body at a steady rate over a prolonged period of time. Examples are walking, jogging and bicycling.

Anaerobic exercises are short and intense, like weight lifting or sprinting. The word *anaerobic* means without oxygen. In other words, the muscles being used don't have the benefit of extra oxygen to do their thing. Anaerobic exercises build up muscles and make your body mass leaner, allowing you to burn more calories even when you're sitting still.

A combination of aerobic and anaerobic activity is the best strategy for losing weight and keeping it off.

If you can't fit both jogging and weight lifting into your busy lifestyle, Dr. Miller gives a slight nod to aerobic exercise. "To maintain a lower weight, I'd probably go with the aerobic."

Keeping Score

Have you ever wondered how many calories life really burns—not when you're on the basketball court or slaving over free weights but when you're just going about your daily tasks? Assuming you weigh between 149 and 159 pounds, here's the breakdown.

Activity	Calories per Minute
At Home	
Mixing ingredients with an electric mixer	1.83
Mixing ingredients by hand	2.75
Using the dishwasher	1.83
Washing dishes by hand	2.25
Doing nothing, standing	1.66
Light activity, standing	2.25
Cutting wood with a power saw	3.66
Cutting wood by hand	7.5
With Friends	
Dancing to contemporary music	4.16
Dancing the polka	9
Golf, 18 holes, driving a cart	3.66
Golf, 18 holes, carrying clubs	12.66
On the Job	
Giving a speech, sitting	1.66
Giving a speech, standing	2
Writing by hand	1.5
Typing	1.75
Commuting in heavy traffic, automatic shift	1.66
Commuting in heavy traffic, standard shift	2.25
In Private	
Sex, foreplay	1.66
Sex, intercourse	5

A Realistic Game Plan

Setting Goals You Can Reach

For a microcosmic view of why it's so damned hard to lose weight, consider the granola bar. When it first appeared on supermarket shelves in the 1980s, it was honey-sweetened and high in complex carbs.

"Now what you have are fudge-filled, chocolate-covered granola bars," says Dr. Morton H. Shaevitz of the University of California, San Diego, School of Medicine. "What we have is a health junk food industry."

To successfully fight fat, you must understand that you're behind enemy lines. It means turning a deaf ear and blind eye to the relentless propaganda campaign for high-fat eating and easy living.

"This is really hard work," Dr. Shaevitz says. "You have to make long-term, permanent changes."

Follow the Plan

You wouldn't drive cross-country without first mapping a route and figuring out how long it will take. Let's face it: If you just got in the car and started cruising blind, you'd never get there.

Losing weight is like that. To accomplish goals—any goals—you have to know what they are. Moreover, the goals have to be realistic. You aren't going to lose 30 pounds in a month. Or even in three months.

"Some people run into inevitable failure because their weight-loss goals were unreal-

istic and could not have been maintained, even if achieved," says Dr. Paul R. Thomas of the National Academy of Sciences' Food and Nutrition Board.

Here is a road map, provided by expert guides, to safe, sane and effective weight loss.

Keep your goal within reach. You don't have to burn large amounts of flab to get the benefits. Losing as little as 10 percent of your weight will make you look better and substantially reduce health risks.

"Even moderate weight losses are beneficial," says Dr. John Erdman of the University of Illinois at Urbana. "People don't have to have what seems to be an unattainable goal of losing 50 pounds. If you can lose 15 and keep it off, that's important."

Take one step at a time. The best way to lose weight is to do it slowly, says Dr. John P. Foreyt of the Nutrition Research Clinic at Baylor College of Medicine.

"Whatever you weigh today, you can lose about 10 percent without a whole lot of difficulty," Dr. Foreyt says. "A 200-pound man can drop to about 180 and then maintain that reasonably well. If you get much lower than that, it becomes harder."

According to C. Everett Koop, M.D., the former U.S. Surgeon General and senior scholar at Koop Institute at Dartmouth Medical School in Hanover, New Hampshire, whose Shape Up America campaign encourages people to lose weight and be more physically active, weight loss should be taken about ten pounds at a time.

"If you come down from 220 to 210 and you hold it there for about six months, then it's pretty easy to do the next 10," Dr. Koop says. "It's pretty difficult to lose 10 pounds and then start right over next week and say 'I'm going to lose 10 more.' "

Go slow. When you're trying to lose weight, shedding it slowly and consistently is the only way to make it happen. It's also the only way to be safe, since dropping more than two pounds a week can cause serious health problems.

"I think a realistic goal would be one pound per week," says Dr. Wayne C. Miller of Indiana University. "People don't like to hear that because they want to lose 30 pounds in a month. But on the average, that's what I see with the people who are successful in terms of maintaining weight loss. That's the difficult thing—to convince people that it takes time and that it's a lifestyle change, rather than something they're going to do only until they lose weight."

Start with the basics. By making moderate changes in diet, it's not difficult to lose a half-pound or one pound a week—"not by being real restrictive, but by cutting back on the fat and sugars," says Dr. Miller.

Health experts recommend limiting fat in your diet to no more than 25 to 30 percent of total calories. "So my suggestion is, if you know you're consuming high, shoot for the 30 percent mark," says Dr. Miller. "If you're kind of moderate now, without too much trouble you can probably get it to around 25 percent or so.

"If you have a tendency to overeat, watch that," he adds. "Don't get dramatic; don't go cutting calories too low and fool with your metabolism. And exercise three, maybe four, days a week for 30 minutes or so."

Above all, don't get hung up on the details. There's nothing wrong with splurging now and then. It can even be good if the satisfaction of a special meal helps you stick with your diet the rest of the time.

"What the government guidelines recommend is that over a period of time you want to stay within 30 percent of calories from fat," says Dr. Foreyt. "But that doesn't mean every time you put something in your mouth it has to be less than 30 percent calories from fat."

The Write Stuff

It's probably inaccurate to say that most men don't know what they eat. "The bottom line," says Dr. John P. Foreyt of the Nutrition Research Clinic at Baylor College of Medicine, "is they don't care."

They should, especially if they care about their expanding waistlines. That's where a food diary comes in handy. Experts say it is extremely helpful for anyone trying to lose weight to write down what he eats over the course of several days.

"People are more likely to succeed if they keep a food diary. That's a fact," says Dr. Foreyt. "I think it works because it sensitizes people to what they're eating. It keeps reminding them."

If you're not interested in keeping track of all the food you eat over several days, try this: Draw up a simple scorecard. Down the side of the page, set up the following categories:

- I didn't cook anything in oil or fry in grease.
- I didn't add butter or oil-based products to foods.
- All dairy products I consumed were low-fat.
- The meat I had was lean red meat, fish or poultry without the skin.

Across the top of the page, write the days of the week. Now, post the scorecard on your refrigerator. Each day, check off the statements that are true. Then, at the end of the week, count the checks. The more checks you have, the closer you are to living the low-fat life.

The Bottom Line

How to Achieve the Goals You Set

According to former U.S. Surgeon General Dr. C. Everett Koop, the worst enemy of weight loss in America is a household appliance. But it's not your refrigerator.

"I think probably television is going to turn out to be the number-one culprit," says Dr. Koop. "It makes couch potatoes out of people. In addition to that, I think most people who spend an inordinate amount of time in front of television eat while they watch."

It's not just eating and watching that makes us fat. Scientists agree that genetics and metabolism play at least supporting roles in what goes around our waists.

Help Yourself

But biology—and television—are hardly destiny. You decide, by the foods you eat and the level of physical activity you enjoy, whether you stay lean or go to fat. "The reality is we do have a lot of control over the outcome," says Dr. Morton H. Shaevitz of the University of California, San Diego, School of Medicine.

A study at Indiana University in Bloomington of 14 men and 21 women concluded that overweight people can shed pounds without Richard Simmons or some other weight-loss guru. The Indiana researchers concluded that people can independently change their own eating and exercise habits to reduce fat.

And this is a crucial point, says Dr. Paul Saltman of the University of California, San Diego. "It ain't the doctor's responsibility; it

ain't science's responsibility; it ain't my mother's and father's," he says. "It's mine."

Apportioning Blame

It's a big country. Maybe that's why our food comes in big portions, making us big.

"If you go to a good Parisian restaurant, you'll get a little 6-ounce steak. If you go to an American restaurant, they advertise one that hangs over both ends of the plate and weighs 16 ounces," says Dr. Koop. "And people tend to eat what's put before them."

Even if you already follow a healthy, low-fat diet, you still have to think about portion size. "Remember, elephants eat nothing but salad, and without dressing," says Dr. Shaevitz.

"The bottom line is that you'll put more fat on your body from ten SnackWell's than from five Oreos," says Dr. Phillip M. Sinaikin, a psychiatrist who specializes in the treatment of obesity. "Wake up to that. Calories do count."

Fat-Fighting Tips

Here are some ways experts recommend to help you lose weight and keep it off.

Give peace a chance. Switching to a low-fat diet can be like waging war. It's a tough fight, and absolute victories are rare. Indiana University's Dr. Wayne C. Miller recommends a compromise position—what he calls a negotiated peace.

"We've got this internal struggle going on," Dr. Miller says. "The intellectual side is saying 'Reduce the fat, cut out the sugar.' Then there's the emotional side saying 'Yeah, but I like this. It tastes good.' "

Since you can't conquer your cravings outright, you need to figure out an eating plan that you can live with for the rest of your life.

"Maybe there are some things that are traditionally high in fat that you can give up and won't miss," he says. "Maybe there's something else you are more emotionally attached to that you just can't give up. You can have a liberal negotiated peace with that food. For example, instead of having french fries five days a week, have a serving two times a week."

Plan ahead. "On a Saturday or Sunday, we will always make something in quantity, so we will have it for late evening meals when we are busy and can't get home at the regular dinner time," says Dr. Paul R. Thomas of the National Academy of Sciences' Food and Nutrition Board. "We can just pop it out of the refrigerator and into the microwave. We eat it along with some good bread, a steamed veggie and a glass of skim milk, juice or water."

Bring your own. It's hard to eat healthy meals when you're dependent on the company cafeteria or the fast-food joint down the road. To take control of your noontime meal, make lunch a B.Y.O. affair. Packing a sandwich, some fruit and maybe pretzels, low-fat yogurt or snacks can save you from putting on the pounds.

Tune out. We don't think of television as being part of a high-fat diet, but it can play a key role not only in what you eat—chips and other eat-with-your-hands fare—but also in how often you eat it, says Dr. Koop.

"There are a number of strategies, ranging from watching less television and getting more activity to cutting back on the amounts of the nonessential, low-nutrition foods you eat," says Dr. Thomas.

At the very least, you may want to stock up on lower-fat alternatives, so you can enjoy your tube time without packing on the weight.

Sign on for three months. There's no way you're going to lose weight by dieting alone. You have to get some exercise as well. It doesn't have to be rigorous as long as you do it regularly, says Dr. Miller. What is important is sticking with it.

"If people can hang in there past the third month, they've probably established some behaviors that might carry over," Dr. Miller says. "But usually the dropouts occur around the end of the second or third month. So give yourself at least three months."

Let's Go to the Videotape

The remote control has become a universal symbol for man's slothfulness. True, it is essential for the couch potato's favorite sport of channel surfing. But you're not going to burn off many calories flipping through the cable lineup, no matter how many channels they add.

If you own a VCR, however, the remote could become the key to getting off the couch long enough to exercise every day.

Most men, given a choice between exercising for a half-hour and watching their favorite TV shows, will remain glued to the tube. But if you ask them why they don't work out, they'll say they don't have time. That's where the remote comes in.

According to Dr. Paul R. Thomas of the National Academy of Sciences' Food and Nutrition Board, that little switch is the secret to having it both ways: You'll have time to work out and watch your favorite shows.

"Tape the program, then watch it later and zap the commercials," Dr. Thomas advises. By fast-forwarding past the ads, you can save almost a half-hour for every two hours of television. "There's your half-hour to get some activity in," he says.

Part Two

Food

Why We Love to Eat Fat

Flavor and Forebears Foster Our Infatuation

Mike Archer knows paradise: It is pink in the middle and weighs 20 ounces.

"Cloud nine? It's a New York strip steak," says Archer, president of Morton's of Chicago, one of the country's premier steak house chains. "It's got a great char on it. It's cooked medium-rare. Cut into the steak—you actually see the juice falling out of it. Big baked potato and a great glass of cabernet. Maybe a few sautéed mushrooms on the side, but nothing to muck up the steak. It stands alone."

There's something in the male psyche that seems harnessed to cattle cuisine. In one survey, researchers at the University of Michigan's School of Public Health in Ann Arbor found that 72 percent of seriously over-weight guys put steak or roast among their top-ten favorite foods. (A prime tenderloin, in-cidentally, gets nearly half of its calories from fat.) Nearly half of the men listed ice cream as a favorite, and nearly 40 percent smacked their lips over doughnuts, cookies and cake.

John Erdman, Ph.D., professor of food science and director of the Division of Nutritional Sci-ences at the University of Illinois at Urbana.

Where we were raised also influences our lust for fat—both the amount and the kind of fat we consume. Finns, for instance, have an affinity for dairy products. The French love olive oil; Americans appreciate foods such as ham, eggs and other staples of the American diet. So a taste for fat is clearly one that can be acquired as well.

Our hankering for fat also appears to be a by-product of evolution: Our voracious hunter-gatherer ancestors had to gobble up those dense animal nutrients in order to sur-vive and reproduce. "In our evolutionary his-tory, we didn't have a supermarket around the corner," says Anthony Sclafani, Ph.D., pro-fessor of psychology at Brooklyn College of the City University of New York. "So we're programmed to acquire preferences for sub-stances that have a lot of nutrient value." In terms of pure energy, one gram of fat contains nine calories, whereas protein and carbohy-drates have less than half that amount. Eating fat paid off.

But Archer suspects that our soft spots for steak and other fatty foods also have more recent origins. "I remember my family had beef on the table pretty much five, six nights a week," he says. "It was always a sign of ac-complishment, of doing well. It's as much a comfort food as anything we have."

Tracing Our Fixation

What is it that drives our infatuation with fat? Some food experts say it comes down to taste: Where there's fat there's flavor. "Most of the flavor compo-nents that we find in foods are fat-soluble. They come along with the fat portion of the food," says

Learning to Love Lean

But times have changed, and the high-fat diets that once kept us in fighting trim are now bloating us to Jurassic size. Which is just one reason—some of the others being stroke, high blood pressure and heart dis-ease—experts say we should get no more than 25 to 30 percent of total calories from fat.

Even if your primeval caveman fat cravings are roaring at full throttle, there are ways to tame the beast. We are not permanently "hardwired" to love lipids, says Richard D. Mattes, R.D., Ph.D., member of the Monell Chemical Senses Center in Philadelphia.

To help your taste buds to make the change, here's what experts recommend.

Make it a family affair. Decisions made while shopping and cooking can make or break your low-fat eating plan, so it's critical to rally your family's support. Remember, the goal is not to give up fat entirely but to eat less of it. After a few weeks, no one's going to notice the difference anyway.

Try skim milk. Compared with the whole-fat kind, which has 8.9 grams of fat per serving, skim milk has less than 1 gram. But the difference shows: Skim milk looks pale and watery, and it lacks the creaminess of whole milk. That's why experts don't recommend switching from whole milk to skim all at once. Instead, start drinking 2 percent milk. Once you're used to that, switch to 1 percent, and only then move on to skim.

Don't go overboard. There are many products on the market that have virtually no fat, some of which are about as appetizing as a rice cake without the crunch. It's possible in the short run to force yourself to eat foods you don't enjoy. But it's unlikely you'll do it for the long haul. That's why it makes more sense to compromise—to find foods that are lower in fat that are still appetizing enough for you to enjoy.

Distract your taste buds. There's no question that switching to a low-fat diet after a lifetime of chowing on butter, sour cream and other delectable fare can give you a sense that something is, well, missing. It's like breaking

---

Living Off the Fat of the Tundra

If you think you're a meat-lover, consider the Inuit. In a climate too hostile for farming, Canada's Eskimos consume a diet that's 95 percent meat and extremely high in fat.

Sound appetizing? Don't pack your dogsled just yet. For one thing, the Inuit usually eat their meat raw—lack of firewood, you know. In addition, they get much of their vitamin intake from animal parts you won't find in your local steak house—like seal blood, caribou hearts and eyeballs. And for fiber, there are the contents of a caribou's stomach, consisting of partially digested tundra plants such as lichen and moss.

What's the payoff from this toothsome smorgasbord? The Inuit have a 40 percent lower mortality rate from heart disease than their fellow Canadians—presumably because their diet is rich in polyunsaturated omega-3 fatty acids from fish and monounsaturated fat from heart-healthy whale and seal blubber.

Seal intestines, anyone?

---

up—it helps when you can replace one love with another.

Adding a jolt of spices to your food can help make the transition easier. Instead of sour cream, for example, slather Mexican salsa on your baked potato or drop a few chili pods into a low-fat stew.

Beware of backsliding. Although it's not too hard for most guys to retrain their appetites, your taste buds have a long memory. They can go a long time without missing fat—until they get another taste. Then you might have to go through the whole process again. So keep temptation in check. Stock the fridge and pantry with foods you choose to eat—not the ones you can't resist.

Fat Substitute Strategies

Tools to Fool Your Taste Buds

You win your tennis matches one stroke at a time—whop, crosscourt with topspin. You win the showdown with fat the same way, making one fat-busting play after another. Vinegar instead of blue cheese dressing. (Thirty, love.) Chili sauce instead of butter. (Forty, love.) Steamed veggies instead of sautéed. (Game, set and match.)

The overall strategy in the fat-fighting game is to forgo fat calories and replace them (because your body won't run on thin air) with carbohydrate calories.

When you consume fat, your metabolic processes burn off only about 3 percent of those calories before they start adding an extra layer of tread to the spare tire around your waist. But when you consume carbohydrates—from grains, fruits and vegetables—your metabolism flames 23 percent of the calories before they're available for conversion to fat. With luck, any excess calories you consume will be burned up by your daily activities before they become long-term blubber.

Making Sense out of Meals

It's a familiar pattern. There was no time to prepare oatmeal and orange juice for breakfast, so you grabbed a Danish at the office. You had a craving for grilled chicken breast at lunch, but time ran out, so you had a Twinkie at your desk. After going hungry all day, you had the appetite of a crocodile when you got home. So you raided the refrigerator and half the pantry, plus the carton of ice cream in the freezer.

That's a meal pattern out of control. "The object is to curb your appetite before it gets to be too much, overwhelming, that famished feeling," says Pat Harper, R.D., a Pittsburgh nutritionist and spokesperson for the American Dietetic Association. "Then you lose control and you eat too much. So plan ahead—that's the big message. Be prepared."

Eat a solid breakfast. A morning meal as simple as juice and a high-fiber cereal with low-fat or skim milk will help protect you from fat as the day wears on. It's filling, so you'll be less tempted to graze on vending machine junk or overeat at lunch. It can also cause you to burn calories faster. Researchers at George Washington University in Washington, D.C., found that people who skipped breakfast burned 5 percent fewer calories than folks who ate three or more meals a day.

Munch often. "The guideline—the ideal—is not to go more than four or five hours without either a meal or a snack," Harper says. This will prevent you from becoming famished and gobbling down an entire sausage pizza as a mid-afternoon snack.

Load up early. Rather than having your big meal at night, try having it at noon instead. "Sometimes all men need to do is eat more in the first half of the day and less in the second half," says Harper. "In the first half of the day, they're up and about and burning up those calories. In the evening they're sitting and watching television, and they're not burning so many calories."

Practice portion control. To keep serving sizes down, make like a farmer: Devote most of the real estate on your dinner plate to plants and reserve just a little for livestock. "The way to deal with portions is to fill up your plate with vegetables and starches and go easy on the meat," says Harper.

Have It Fast and Lean

When you're starved for time—as well as just starved—snack cakes, burgers and candy bars are so available they seem to leap into your hands. But fast food doesn't have to be junk food. Here are a few healthy ideas for when you're on the run.

Make it mobile. Dried fruits such as raisins, dates and apricots are perfect for the man on the move. "They're concentrated in calories, and they're loaded with vitamins and minerals," says Chris Rosenbloom, R.D., Ph.D., associate professor in the Department of Nutrition and Dietetics at Georgia State University and nutrition consultant for the Georgia Tech Athletic Association, both in Atlanta. "I always encourage people to keep some in their desk drawers or, for students, in their backpacks."

Grab a bagel to go. If there's no time for breakfast, grab a bagel as you head for the door. It is compact and neat and doesn't require toasting. Bagels also come in a variety of flavors, so you'll never get bored. "Bagels are virtually fat-free," Harper adds. "They give you nutritional value, plus they fill you up and stay with you."

Slow-cook your supper. Slow-cooking Crock-Pots, stoked in the morning with things such as chicken, potatoes and onions, can have dinner ready for you the minute you walk in the door. In addition, they can keep food moist with virtually no added oil. Current models will not get you a beer or clear the table, however.

Grab a salad on the fly. Many fast-food restaurants and groceries now offer salad bars, so it's easy to make a salad raid part of your routine. Load up on the veggies and darker salad greens, which have more nutrients. Add the low-fat dressing. Skip the croutons. In the fat-fighting game, you'll be miles ahead of the guys who snapped up double cheeseburgers.

Spread the Risk

Here's a pat answer to the butter-versus-margarine debate: They're both losers.

Butter contains saturated fat, the kind found in meat and dairy products. Saturated fat increases blood cholesterol levels and contributes to coronary artery disease. Some prestigious health organizations, including the American Heart Association, say this is the worst stuff.

Margarine, on the other hand, contains trans-fatty acids—the stuff that's created when hydrogen is added to liquid vegetable oil to make it firm and spreadable. Scientists at Harvard School of Public Health say that trans-fatty acids may be the worst offender.

A study at George Washington University Medical Center in Washington, D.C., found that people given high amounts of either saturated fat or trans-fatty acids had similar increases in the heart-unhealthy LDL (low-density lipoprotein) levels. Those given trans-fatty acids also had a decline in "good" HDL (high-density lipoprotein) cholesterol. Those in the saturated fat group, however, saw their HDL levels rise.

So which bread-spread is worse for the heart? Research is continuing. But one thing is clear: Both butter and margarine have about 11 grams of fat per tablespoon. The bottom line for now is that too much of either fat will clog your arteries and pad your waist.

Switchin' in the Kitchen

A lean lifestyle depends heavily on swapping one food for a lower-fat substitute.

Sometimes the choices are clear, as when you swap the bacon and eggs for a bagel with jelly. More often, however, what's involved is an incremental rollback of the fat content—small changes that add up, like switching 1 or 2 percent milk for whole milk.

"In the past few years, the food industry has really tried to change its products to accommodate the low-fat recommendations," says Lisa Litin, R.D., a research dietitian at Harvard School of Public Health. "Many of these products actually do provide a lower-fat alternative—not necessarily low-fat, but definitely lower-fat."

A good general rule is always to reach for "natural" foods as opposed to their highly processed counterparts.

You'll also want to rethink the preparation and presentation of food. What's the point in giving vegetables a lean steaming, for instance, if you're just going to smother them in butter once they get to the table? "You need to watch the total fat that's added to the food, either before it gets to the table or at the table," says Litin.

To get into the swing of swapping away fat, try these tips from the food pros.

Know beans. Rather than stuffing yourself with red meat five days a week, make a move toward a healthier source of protein. Three-quarters of a cup of lima beans, for example, has seven grams of protein. The same amount of peas has more protein than an egg—with virtually no fat.

While you can use beans as a stand-alone dish, they can also be combined with traditional favorites. Instead of using ground beef in lasagna, for example, try substituting cooked and mashed garbanzo beans (chick-peas) or pintos, suggests Michele Tuttle, R.D., director of consumer affairs for the Food Marketing Institute in Washington, D.C.

Swear off the oils. While cake and pancake recipes typically call for lots of butter or oil, you can usually substitute nonfat sour cream in equal portions without substantially altering the flavor or texture of the food.

Hit the sauce. Who says white sauces have to clog your arteries? In lieu of a cream-based sauce, toss some low-fat or nonfat cottage cheese into the food processor and thin it with skim milk. Then stir in sautéed onions, garlic and basil.

Dress with less. When you're making salad dressing, toss out a third of the oil and substitute water. The taste and texture will barely change, and you'll be saving yourself 33 percent pure fat.

Try it on the side. Making a switch in presentation styles can shave off fat. Instead of sopping down salads with fatty dressing, serve the dressing in a small container at the side of the plate. "You dip the fork into the dressing and then pick up a forkful of salad," says Dr. Rosenbloom. "You use so little dressing that way, but you get a little flavor with each bite."

Use your noodle. Egg noodles are delicious. They're also loaded with fat. So switch to spaghetti instead. You probably won't notice the difference—it's under a sauce, right?—and you'll save one gram of fat and 16 calories per cup.

Catch a lean tuna. Fish belong in water, right, so why buy tuna that's packed in oil? Using the kind packed in H_2O will save you six grams of fat and 70 calories per three-ounce can.

Spice your java. Although those elegant little tins of instant gourmet coffee are convenient and delicious, they are decidedly high in fat. To get the flavor without the fat, try spicing up your regular brew with a pinch of cinnamon or nutmeg. "I put cinnamon in the grounds, and that gives it a nice flavor and aroma, and it doesn't add any calories," says Dr. Rosenbloom.

Do some reading. The food industry knows you're cruising for ideas, and many companies print recipes—both traditional and low-fat versions—on the backs of their packages. A pancake mix, for example, might recommend substituting two egg whites for each whole egg and using skim milk instead of whole.

Olive Oil: King of Hearts

Who'da thunk a lunk like Popeye would be such a visionary? Not only did he gobble nutrient-rich spinach, he also was fond of Olive Oyl.

These days, olive oil—the foodstuff, not the cartoon character—is a dietary darling. While it's still pure fat and loaded with calories, studies show that it may help lower levels of harmful low-density lipoprotein (LDL) cholesterol while leaving the "good" high-density lipoprotein (HDL) cholesterol unchanged.

In one study, researchers tested lipid levels of 12 people who consumed 30 percent of total calories derived from fat. Some got their fat from milk fats, while others got it in the form of sunflower, rapeseed or olive oil. With the olive oil diet, researchers not only saw the greatest drop in LDL levels, but they also saw HDL become smaller and more fluid, which may help it remove cholesterol from cells more effectively.

"This finding helps explain how higher HDL levels may protect against heart disease and how monounsaturated fat might play a helpful role; however, more research is needed," says lipid expert Margo Denke, M.D., assistant professor of medicine at the University of Texas Health Science Center at Dallas Southwestern Medical School Center for Human Nutrition.

You can use olive oil as a substitute for every oil in the kitchen—not only for frying and sautéing but for baking as well.

Incidentally, of the three grades of olive oil commonly available—virgin, extra-virgin and pure—only the pure oil should be used for frying. The virgin and extra-virgin are higher-grade oils. Their delicate nature—and considerably higher price—means they're best used for light sautés or just for drizzling on pasta, vegetables or bread.

Fat Substitutes: Texture without the Taint

In the world of processed foods, "low-fat" has often been synonymous with "low-taste." But new developments have enabled food manufacturers to produce low-fat or nonfat foods with taste and texture that are remarkably like those of their fat-rich predecessors.

The trick is fat substitutes—laboratory-altered ingredients that can imitate the "mouthfeel" of fat but that contain only about one to four calories per gram, as opposed to the nine calories per gram in natural fat.

"One fat replacement, Simplesse, is made from proteins that are microparticulated, or beaten into tiny spheres," says Rudolph Harris, Ph.D., consumer safety officer for the Food and Drug Administration (FDA) in Washington, D.C. "These particles are so small that when they are put into a food in place of fat, the product actually has the feel of a fat to the mouth."

A product called Olestra, by contrast, is totally synthetic. It would supply zero calories for the simple reason that it can't be digested. But don't look for Olestra on grocery store shelves just yet. It continues to undergo a lengthy approval process by the FDA.

In theory, fat substitutes are a great way for Americans to enjoy foods they love without the flab that invariably comes along. But skeptics argue that fat substitutes may not be any more successful at helping us lose weight than artificial sweeteners were. We may simply feel free to eat more junk.

Food Labels

Always Look before You Eat

For years, food companies could pretty much decide on their own what nutrition information to put on a package and how to present it. If you were lucky, you might find a smattering of numbers that would leave you wondering where that danged calculator had gotten to.

Today, federal regulations have made it easier to know exactly what you're getting. Information and language on the label are standardized. No more standing in the aisles wondering "What's in this stuff?"

"One of the nice things about the new food label is that right next to the listing of calories in the food is the listing of calories from fat," says Martin Yadrick, R.D., a Los Angeles dietitian and spokesman for the American Dietetic Association.

Zeroing In

But while today's food labels are accurate and accessible, they contain more information than you'll probably need. If your goal is losing weight, focus on the information that pertains to that—the serving size, for example, and the amounts of fat and calories that are in the product. "That gives a fairly good guide," says Mary C. Winston, R.D., Ed.D., senior science consultant for the American Heart Association.

Suppose you're looking for an eminently tasty spreadable that's not too bad for the waistline. The label on a package of margarine tells you that it contains 11 grams of fat in one tablespoon. Compare that with a soft spread, which may have only 5 grams of fat per

tablespoon. Clearly, going soft has its virtues.

You're not going to study, down to the last milligram, all the minutiae on every product that lands in your cart. But once you know what to look for, you can separate the wheat from the chaff—or the high-fat from the nonfat—with just a glance. Here's how.

Note the Daily Values. Along the right side of each food label is a column of percentages labeled "% Daily Value" (DV). These numbers are based on a 2,000-calorie diet (men typically eat more—about 2,200 to 2,400 calories a day). They provide an easy way to tell how far the different parts of the food—the total fat, cholesterol, carbohydrates and so on—go toward meeting your daily limits or needs.

Suppose, for example, one serving of cookies contains one gram of dietary fiber, or 3 percent of your DV (based on a 2,500-calorie-a-day diet). Obviously, not much of a fiber source.

Suppose the same serving had 6.5 grams of fat. That would be about 8 percent of your DV—a decent-size chunk of your daily budget. Based on this, you might decide to pass it by.

Size up the servings. You see that your favorite chocolate frozen yogurt has four grams of fat per serving. Sounds good. But look closely at the "serving size" figure at the top of the chart. The Food and Drug Administration—which presumably makes its decisions after a large lunch—has determined that a single serving of this product is a half-cup.

For most guys, a half-cup of something can seem like what they lick off their fingers before spooning it into a bowl. If your normal serving is a cup and a half, you're really getting 12 grams of fat. So before you buy, mentally multiply the serving size. If the calories or grams of fat come up high, say good-bye.

Beware of fat. High on each label is a line that reads "Total Fat." Since dietary fat, especially saturated fat, is a key contributor to obesity and heart

disease, you want this number to be as low as possible.

Many experts believe you should get no more than 25 to 30 percent of calories from fat. (For a guy who weighs 170 pounds, that would be about 69 grams a day.) So before buying any packaged food, check the total fat to see if that item sensibly fits into your eating plan.

On a carton of whole milk, for example, the label reveals that an eight-ounce glass has eight grams of fat—about one-eighth of the maximum allowed for that day. Do you want to use up that much of your "budget" just for a glass of milk? If not, then buying skim milk (which has only a trace of fat) will be a better choice.

Walk away from saturated fat. Right below the "Total Fat" line is "Saturated Fat." Again, you want this number to be low, low, low, since saturated fat—which has been linked to obesity and heart disease—is truly nasty.

Overall, no more than 10 percent of calories should come from saturated fat, experts say. (For most guys, this adds up to about 20 grams a day.) If that toothsome dessert you're eyeing comes in high—say at 10 percent of your daily limit—you may want to pass it by.

Focus on fiber. Move on down the label, and you'll come to "Dietary Fiber." High-fiber foods keep your digestive system healthy and, um, productive. They can also help you lose weight by making you feel full longer.

The experts recommend that you get 20 to 35 grams of fiber a day. So in this category, whether you're buying pasta, whole-wheat bread or breakfast cereal, higher is always better.

Health Claims: Coming to Terms

In the dark ages of food labeling, there were more disguises on supermarket shelves than at a Halloween ball. Consider terms such as *lite, reduced* or *all-natural.* What exactly did they mean? Light in nutrients? Reduced taste? All-natural—but inedible?

Thanks to federal regulations, food companies are speaking the same language on standardized labels. Here's what some of the terms mean.

-Free. As in fat-free or sugar-free. This means one serving has so little of the stuff in question that it won't make a blip on your dietary screen.

Low-. As in low-calorie or low-fat. This means the product doesn't have a lot of a particular substance, but it still has enough that it could make a difference in your diet. Specifically, low-calorie means 40 calories or less per serving; low-fat means three grams or less of total fat; low saturated fat means one gram or less; and low-cholesterol means less than 20 milligrams.

Lean, extra-lean. These terms refer to meat. Lean means one serving has less than ten grams of total fat, four grams of saturated fat and 95 milligrams of cholesterol. Extra-lean means one serving has less than five grams of total fat, two grams of saturated fat and 95 milligrams of cholesterol.

Reduced-, less. This means there's 25 percent less of a certain ingredient or nutrient as compared with a similar product. Reduced means the product was nutritionally altered to meet the claim. The term *less,* by contrast, is often used for comparisons, as in: "Our pretzels have 25 percent *less* sodium than potato chips."

The "Fight Fat" Eating Strategy

You Can Lose Weight and Still Dine Well

You've read the diet books. You know it's time to cut back on fat. You even know (or at least have been told) that some low-fat foods have gone from tasting like vinyl siding to being bona fide chow.

So how come you have this sudden urge for a 16-ounce porterhouse?

If you've ever been on a diet that went beyond New Year's Day, you know the sinking feeling that comes as you watch your favorite foods swirling down the flavor drain. In the real world, man does not live on bread—or carrots, tofu or celery sticks—alone. Which is why most diets ultimately fail.

It doesn't have to be this way. "There are ways of eating that are healthy yet also retain their integrity," says Chris Schlesinger, chef and co-owner of the restaurants East Coast Grill, Blue Room and Jake and Earl's Dixie BBQ, all in Cambridge, Massachusetts, and co-author of *The Thrill of the Grill* and *Big Flavors of the Hot Sun.* "Otherwise, you end up like the Jetsons, eating nutrition as a pill."

Whether you're popping into your favorite bistro or smokin' up the kitchen yourself, you can trim fat from your diet and still eat like a king. The trick, Schlesinger says, is fine-tuning your approach to food. Always eat well—but pick your foods wisely.

"Food plays a major quality-of-life role," says

Schlesinger. "I never go on a diet. If I feel like I'm eating too much, I try to eat just good things. I try to eat more fish entrées, cut down on the meat portions and eat more good stuff. I eat six pieces of fruit a day, and I try to eat a lot of rice and beans."

You say you'd rather eat like a linebacker? Go ahead. A survey of NFL trainers showed that pro football players average six servings a day of fruits and veggies—twice what the average American eats. The typical pregame meal includes fruits, fruit juices, pasta with low-fat sauce, pancakes, toast, scrambled eggs and bagels. When you eat like that, your padding goes under the jersey, not under the skin.

Customize Cravings

The only way you'll ever stick with a low-fat lifestyle is by enjoying yourself in the meantime. Go ahead: Indulge yourself. What counts is fat consumption over the long haul, not what you had for dinner last night. Rather than compromise by having tough little steaks more often, "I'd rather eat one steak a month and have it be the 16-ouncer," Schlesinger says. The occasional feast won't bust your budget. Plus, it will help keep you satisfied, so you're less tempted to stray.

"Moderation is the key—not to totally eliminate fat in the diet," says dietitian Lisa Litin of the Harvard School of Public Health. "If you're going to have something high-fat during the day, then you should plan ahead and control your fat intake during the other times of the day."

Besides, extreme deprivation plays strange tricks on the mind. When you deny yourself eating pleasure, you may instinctively want a reward—call it an eating binge—later on.

Satisfying Swaps

There are a lot of good-tasting, satisfying foods that can help you bridge the chasm between low-fat and high living. On the left is the traditional, high-fat fare; on the right, some lean alternatives that are still honest-to-goodness chow.

Fat City	Lean and Luscious	Fat City	Lean and Luscious
Seafood		**French**	
Breaded and fried clams (6 oz.) 342 calories 19 g. fat	Steamed clams (20 small) 155 calories 1 g. fat	Crème brûlée (4 oz.) 325 calories 25 g. fat	Orange soufflé (4 oz.) 155 calories 8 g. fat
Breaded and fried shrimp (6 oz.) 412 calories 20 g. fat	Seasoned shrimp (6 oz.) 154 calories 2 g. fat	Duck á l'orange (¼ duck) 835 calories 69 g. fat	Orange-glazed cornish hen with wild rice stuffing (1 hen) 560 calories 26 g. fat
Broiled swordfish steak, in olive oil (8 oz.) 600 calories 45 g. fat	Poached salmon (8 oz.) 368 calories 14 g. fat	Veal cordon bleu (4 oz.) 440 calories 27 g. fat	Chicken divan (6 oz.) 385 calories 18 g. fat
American*		**Italian**	
Chef's salad, before dressing (1½ cups) 260 calories 15 g. fat	Garden salad, before dressing (1½ cups) 50 calories 2 g. fat	Pasta with cream sauce and prosciutto (12 oz.) 906 calories 18 g. fat	Pasta with fresh tomato, basil and garlic (12 oz.) 520 calories 11 g. fat
Sirloin steak (8 oz.) 523 calories 27 g. fat	New York strip steak, lean (8 oz.) 478 calories 22 g. fat	**Mexican**	
		Beef burrito with sour cream 431 calories 21 g. fat	Chicken burrito 334 calories 12 g. fat
Chinese*			
Kung pao chicken 490 calories 25 g. fat	Chicken and vegetable stir-fry 245 calories 14 g. fat	Chicken chimichanga 605 calories 35 g. fat	Chicken fajita 190 calories 8 g. fat
Moo shu pork 630 calories 38 g. fat	Beef and green pepper stir-fry 290 calories 11 g. fat	Red beans with pork (3 oz.) 320 calories 19 g. fat	Refried beans (½ cup) 130 calories 2 g. fat
Pan-fried soft noodles 680 calories 36 g. fat	Shrimp chow mein 240 calories 5 g. fat	*All sizes are typical entrée servings.	

Fast-Food Strategies

Eating Sensibly When You're on the Go

For fat fighters, a shopping mall food court is the demilitarized zone. Only the danger isn't friendly fire. It's friendly fries. When you find yourself hungry, short on time and surrounded by fast-food joints, the temptation to wave the white flag and chow down is nearly irresistible.

Before you wolf down the super-deluxe-mega-triple-cheeseburger-with-bacon, ask yourself: How will I feel afterward, mentally and physically?

"It changes your food choices," says Phillip M. Sinaikin, M.D., a psychiatrist in Longwood, Florida, who specializes in the treatment of obesity and author of *Fat Madness: How to Stop the Diet Cycle and Achieve Permanent Well-Being*. "If it's going to sit like a lump in your stomach and not give you the pleasant sense of energy that carbohydrates do, then that probably makes it a bad choice."

Penny Wise, Pound Foolish

One national survey found that 58 percent of men eat in fast-food restaurants at least once a week.

Sure, you can go low-fat and buy a regular hamburger, salad and diet soda at most places. But it will probably cost you more than if you bought a combination meal with a huge burger, large fries and big drink. Yes, you can buy a small order of fries—but the large order often doesn't cost a hell of a lot more.

"It's ridiculous. You've got to be out of your mind to get small fries," says Bonnie Liebman, a licensed nutritionist and director of nutrition for the Center for Science in the Public Interest in Washington, D.C.

What you're gaining in quantity, however, you're paying for in fat. "We can't make the world stop advertising fast food," Dr. Sinaikin notes. "But we can step back from the world and look at it a bit and say 'Hey, what about the quality of my life—my single individual life? What can I do to enhance the quality of my life?'"

Fast and Good

The world isn't going to slow down any time soon, and until it does, we're always going to appreciate fast food. But it's still possible to get good food fast. Here's what you can do.

Start the day right. Most fast-food restaurants offer healthy breakfasts. Pancakes are almost always a good choice, assuming you hold the butter or margarine and go easy on the syrup. English muffins, toast, bagels or cereal with low-fat or skim milk can also get your engine humming in the morning. But avoid croissants, pastries and Danish. The high levels of sugar and fat can turn your idle way down—and push your waist out, says Megan Cordova, R.D., an outpatient dietitian at Johnston-Willis Hospital in Richmond, Virginia.

Don't be biased against burgers. You want one, get one—but use common sense. A single-patty burger at most fast-food restaurants has over ten grams of fat. That's no problem, says Dale L. Anderson, M.D., head of the complementary medicine department at Park Nicollet Medical Center in Minneapolis. But what happens when you pile burger on top of burger and cover both with cheese, mayonnaise or "special sauces"?

Dr. Anderson has a term

for this: Rather than calling them double or triple burgers, he jokes, we should call them double or triple bypasses.

Consider: A Double Whopper with Cheese at Burger King packs 63 grams of fat. For a lot of guys, that's more than a day's worth in one sitting.

Lean toward roast beef. Beef doesn't have to mean hamburger. A Roy Rogers roast beef sandwich has four grams of fat, while a hamburger carries nine grams. So if you like beef, make the leaner choice and go with the roasted kind, says Liebman.

Go ahead, chicken. Grilled, baked or broiled chicken sandwiches are a good bet most of the time. Again, watch the toppings and be sure to order it without mayo.

Flee fries. A burger and fries. They go together like Abbott and Costello. But for your health's sake, it would be better if they were more like Dean Martin and Jerry Lewis—ex-partners.

"A large order of fries is almost like having two sandwiches," Liebman says. "We think of it as a side dish, but it's really as fatty and caloric as a main dish. Large fries have 450 calories, compared with 420 in a Quarter Pounder at McDonald's. And the fries have 22 grams of fat, compared with 20 in the Quarter Pounder."

Pizza delivers. Great news, guys. Pizza can actually be part of a healthy, balanced meal.

Order the thin crust; it has less fat. And go for the veggie toppings like green pepper and onion, not the pepperoni and sausage.

Go convenient. It used to be that hitting the 7-Eleven or other convenience stores meant having a hot dog or—shudder—a microwave burrito. These days, a number of quick-stop stores carry items such as low-fat yogurt, turkey sandwiches, fresh fruits and salad fixings. Pick the one nearest you and shop around. You may be pleasantly surprised.

Fast Food: The Next Generation

Daily's Fit & Fresh, a health-conscious restaurant chain based in San Diego, hopes to follow the trail blazed by McDonald's 40 years ago.

Daily's, which opened its doors in 1992, offers speed and convenience but goes a step further: Nothing on the menu contains more than ten grams of fat or 20 percent of calories from fat.

Daily's is the dream-come-true of cardiac surgeon Pat Daily, M.D. "The vision for this concept is the wave of the future," says dietitian Patti Tveit Milligan, R.D., director of nutrition for Daily's. "We do hope it can be a national chain."

Among entrées, pasta, potatoes and rice receive star billing along with poultry and fish. Selections include grilled chicken breast in a pita pocket with salad greens and ginger-and-sesame dressing, and a chili-stuffed baked potato. But don't order a burger. Milligan says that Daily's decided not to mimic high-fat offerings from other fast-food restaurants. Instead, Daily's offers a veggie burger with brown rice and vegetables served on a whole-wheat bun.

Milligan admits she was skeptical when Dr. Daily first approached her in 1989 with the idea of starting a healthy fast-food restaurant. "People talk about how they want to eat healthy, but do they put their money where their mouth is?" She now believes that if you offer people tasty low-fat food at a reasonable price with fast service, they will buy it—again and again.

Fast-Food Comparisons

We Rate the Best of the Biggest

Most fast-food restaurants will gladly provide brochures that tell you what, nutrition-wise, is in their food. What the brochures don't include is the one thing health-conscious guys want to know: How does it taste?

Glad you asked. In our never-ending quest for truth and a free meal, the gang at *Men's Health* sampled ten of the relatively lower-fat—which is not necessarily the same as low-fat—offerings of five national fast-food chains. These are the kinds of sandwiches nutrition experts tell us we should eat, instead of the Big Macs and Whoppers we usually gobble down.

The reviews are based on items as they were served to us by local franchises. They may or may not strictly adhere to national franchise policies. And you may find differences in the way menu items are served at your local franchise.

To make sure you get exactly what you want—and avoid toppings you don't want, such as full-fat mayonnaise—make Burger King's ad slogan your fast-food mantra: Have it your way. No matter where you go, always tell them exactly what you want on your sandwich.

Now, here's a look at some of the sandwiches you've probably been missing. Or not. Taste ratings are on a scale of 1 to 10, with 1 representing "barely edible" and 10, "delicious."

The envelope, please (sorry about the ketchup stain).

Chicken

Burger King BK Broiler. This was the clear favorite among discerning poultry palates. The sandwich comes on a fresh sesame seed bun with lettuce and tomato. The hearty portion of flame-broiled chicken has a distinctive, smoky flavor. This sandwich fills you up and satisfies.

Be warned: You have to specifically order it without mayo; otherwise, the fat content skyrockets from 6 grams to a whopping 29 grams. (297 calories; 18% calories from fat)

Taste rating: 8

Wendy's Grilled Chicken. A fairly large and juicy piece of chicken, though not quite as big as Burger King's. The sesame seed bun is tasty and fresh.

The sandwich proves, however, that you can't fit a square chicken cutlet on a round bun unless you're willing to first eat several mouthfuls of bread. The toppings are generous: A tomato slice, a large hunk of fresh lettuce and honey-mustard sauce set this one apart. (290 calories; 20% calories from fat)

Taste rating: 6

McDonald's McGrilled Chicken Classic. From the flat, tasteless sesame seed bun to the meager lettuce, tomato and onion toppings, this is an unimpressive sandwich. The thin, somewhat rubbery chicken patty leaves you feeling like you're not getting very much. A heavy hand with the pepper adds spice but not life. (250 calories; 12% calories from fat)

Taste rating: 3

Hamburgers

Burger King. Adorned simply with ketchup and pickles, this one lives up to its regal name. A poofy sesame seed bun and a thicker and wider hamburger patty set it apart from

other burgers we tried. What makes it a standout is the flame-broiled taste—a wee bit of fire-scorching goes a long way. The flavors blend well, giving this burger the right balance of beefiness and other tastes. (330 calories; 42% calories from fat)

Taste rating: 8

Wendy's Junior. With an ultra-thin square beef patty on a bland, dry bun, the only thing that saves this burger is the condiments. It's the only burger to have sliced rings of raw onions. It also comes with equal parts of mustard and ketchup and two pickles. (270 calories; 29% calories from fat)

Taste rating: 4

McDonald's. The granddaddy of fast food, McDonald's offers the plainest bun and the smallest beef patty. To overcome these apparently intentional shortcomings, they load the burger with condiments—lots of ketchup, a small dab of mustard, two pickles and chopped onions. Together, they make for a sandwich that tastes mostly of ketchup and leaves you wondering: Where's the beef? (270 calories; 29% calories from fat)

Taste rating: 3.5

Roast Beef

Subway. For a variety of toppings, fresher taste and leaner mix, Subway is a clear winner. But if you like a lot of roast beef on your roast beef sandwich, this may not be for you.

Don't get us wrong: It's a big sandwich. But most of its heft—and flavor—stem from its thick roll and delicious mix of toppings, including lettuce, pickles, peppers, onions, tomatoes and olives. Though somewhat thin, the roast beef tastes like something you'd slice off a succulent leftover roast in the fridge. And the toppings are enough to put this one over the top. (326 calories; 6% calories from fat)

Taste rating: 7

Roy Rogers. Like its hamburger cousin, Roy's roast beef sandwich comes unadorned with toppings or condiments. But there's plenty of beef. Roy piles it on, and its lean-ness holds the fat content down. But the beef was a bit dry. And without toppings or condiments, any shortcoming in the roast beef is greatly magnified. (280 calories; 35% calories from fat)

Taste rating: 5

Subs

Subway Veggies and Cheese Sub. Cheese may get billing as a co-star in this one, but it's actually more like a cameo appearance. Nevertheless, the sub has a hearty crunch to it, thanks to the mixture of lettuce, onions, peppers, pickles, tomatoes and olives. As for the roll, the wheat bun is a gustatory gain over the serviceable white bun that you get with the Turkey Sub (below), so pick wheat if you can. It's not only healthier, it tastes better. This sub is quite satisfying, probably because the veggies provide the feeling of substance and volume you'd expect from a meat-filled sub. (258 calories; 21% calories from fat)

Taste rating: 7

Subway Turkey Sub. Overflowing with crunchy fresh veggie toppings on a fresh-tasting roll, this sub has a hefty feel and palate-pleasing texture. It should be noted, however, that the white-bread roll is a bit bland compared with the wheat bread on which the Veggies and Cheese Sub was served. The toppings—lettuce, tomato, peppers, black olives and onions—are generous and add zest.

There is only one thing missing on this turkey sub: the turkey. A few slices does not a turkey sub make. The paucity of turkey left it tasting like a house salad between two buns. So save yourself more than a buck by just ordering the Veggies and Cheese Sub. You won't miss the turkey much more than you would in the turkey sub. (312 calories; 22% calories from fat)

Taste rating: 5

Shopping Strategies

*How to Make a Lean Sweep
at the Grocery Store*

You drag yourself out of bed, slice a bagel and open the fridge. There sits a luscious brick of ten-grams-of-fat-per-ounce cream cheese. Yes, it will shellac the insides of your arteries and add flab to your middle, but you peel back the foil and slather it on anyway.

Who can blame you? At home, you can eat only what's available. All the major low-fat decisions are made at the grocery store. That's where you decide what's going to be available to eat at home. That's where you select the nonfat cream cheese.

But making command decisions in a grocery store is no easy task. Supermarkets are a chaotic midway. Signs and product labels scream from every direction. Coupons reach out to you from beeping automatic dispensers. Smiling ladies hand you a cracker spread with an unidentifiable cheese product. An overhead sound system murmurs seductive buying suggestions.

The range of irresistible foods is enormous, the arrangements bewildering. We reconnoitered with food experts to draw up the following plan of attack.

Scope Out the Territory

On your way home from work you approach the grocery store. Stomach growling, you grab a cart and start cruising the

aisles. You'll know what you need when you see it, right?

Mmmm, haven't had potato chips in a while. Two bags, in the cart. The kids will be surprised if you pick up snack cakes. Jumbo package, in the cart. Bacon for breakfast! A pound of pig, in the cart. And on you go, following your famished gut through the supermarket until you push your personal Fort Knox of fatty foods up to the checkout counter.

Sound familiar? To stop yourself from buying a lot of stuff you don't really need, you have to plan.

"I try to plan out meals for a week or two weeks," says Dr. Chris Rosenbloom of Georgia State University and the Georgia Tech Athletic Association. "It takes a lot less time to do that than run to the grocery store three times a week, which is what a lot of people do."

Here are pointers to help keep you focused on your low-fat mission.

Make a list. Check the pantry and refrigerator for ingredients you already have, then make a list of what you need. Sticking to the list will save you from impromptu (translation: gut-expanding) choices.

Eat, then shop. "Never, ever, ever shop on an empty stomach," says dietitian Michele Tuttle of the Food Marketing Institute. "You will always buy things you didn't intend to if you're hungry, and everything will always look more appealing."

Go wide and outside. As you cruise through the supermarket, stick to the outside walls of the room as much as you can. "The outside aisles are where you find the fresh produce cases, the dairy cases and the fresh meat case," says Tuttle. "Fresh items not only taste great, but depending on how you prepare them, they can also be lower in fat and salt and higher in fiber."

Make sure you dip into the interior aisles for low-fat

items such as pasta, beans and pretzels. Just don't get hornswoggled by a bag of potato chips along the way.

Beware the impulse buys. Ever walk up to the cash register and wonder how that chocolate bar—with its nine grams of fat per ounce—leapt into your hands? "That's where a lot of people get in trouble—all those impulse items right at the checkout," says Dr. Rosenbloom. "Stores put them there for a reason."

Produce: A Fresh Start

Maybe your idea of having fruits and vegetables at dinner is a sliver of lime in your cocktail and ketchup on your french fries. Well, wheel your cart over to the corner of the grocery store. The American Dietetic Association recommends three to five full servings of honest-to-goodness fruits and three to five servings of real live vegetables every day—a regimen that will guarantee you loads of nutrients and fiber and very little fat.

Only 10 percent of Americans meet this goal. So you have some heavy lifting to do in this department.

Snare some snacks. The fresh produce department is the best place to stock up on between-meal munchies. "Get in the habit of trying to keep fruit around and eat that in between," says Dr. Mary C. Winston of the American Heart Association. "Bulky things like that help keep you from getting hungry."

Snag something ripe, something green. Don't always reach for the perfect fruit. By stocking up on fruits that aren't quite ripe, you'll have something to nosh on a few days later.

Round up sauté suspects. Vegetables often play a minor role on the dinner plate, but there are easy ways to give them star

---

Cutting Fat Makes Cents

Reducing fat in your diet does a lot more than just trim your middle. Research suggests it can trim your grocery bills as well.

When 291 people were put on a cholesterol-lowering diet for nine months, those who stuck to the program best were rewarded with lower grocery bills—down by $.75 to $1.10 a day. For a family of four, scientists concluded, the savings would amount to $3 a day. By year's end, that would total about $1,000 for the Christmas fund.

Many people think that low-fat cooking means unusual, expensive ingredients, says study leader Thomas A. Pearson, M.D., Ph.D., professor of epidemiology at Columbia University in New York City. But if you think about the cost of oatmeal and chicken versus that of omelets and beef, the idea of cutting fat and cutting costs at the same time is pretty logical—and pretty easy.

---

billing. To stock up for a novel meal, scan the produce stands for a handful of your favorite fresh vegetables. At home you can slice 'em up to sauté in a little olive oil, then spread them over pasta instead of using spaghetti sauce.

Belly up to the bar. Most supermarkets these days maintain a salad bar where you can build your own salad-to-go. It's a great way to have a fast, nutritious meal—but only if you're smart.

"One strategy I like with the salad bars is to use only things you can pick up with tongs," says Dr. Rosenbloom. "If you have to use a spoon, there's usually a lot of oil in it."

Go dark. Color counts—in television, comic pages, sports cars and vegetables. "Any of the foods that are dark orange, dark red or dark green have a lot more beta-carotene than the others," says Dr. Rosenbloom. Beta-

Cross These off Your List

Forget traffic accidents, soaring radon levels or the cross fire of warring drug lords. Some of the gravest threats to your well-being are in the supermarket. Here are some of the worst foods money can buy.

Food	Serving Size (oz.)	Calories	Fat (g.)	Calories from Fat (%)	Cholesterol (mg.)	Sodium (mg.)
Egg, cheese and bacon biscuit	5	477	31.4	59	261	1,260
Beef potpie	7.5	517	30.5	53	44	596
French toast sticks (5)	5	478	29.1	55	75	499
Spareribs	3	337	25.8	69	103	79
Pepperoni stick (10 slices)	2	273	24.2	80	44	1,122
Pecan pie (1 slice)	3.75	431	23.6	49	65	228
Beef and cheese chimichanga	6.5	443	23.4	48	51	957
Smoked pork sausage links (2)	2.5	265	21.6	74	46	1,020
Breaded clams, fried (20)	6.75	380	21	50	115	684
Ground lamb, broiled	3	241	16.7	62	82	69
Canned cheese soup	8	156	10.5	61	30	958
Cream cheese	1	98	9.8	90	31	83

carotene is an antioxidant that is thought to lower the risk of conditions such as heart attack, certain cancers and cataracts.

The Dairy Case: Where Calcium Is King

Remember those simpler times when Mom would send you scampering to the corner store for a dozen eggs and a few sticks of butter? What would that little barefoot bubba have thought of nonfat cheese, tub margarine and egg substitute?

Today, there are luscious, nutritious, low-fat versions of just about every dairy product you can name. And they still do what dairy foods are famous for: rack up calcium and vitamin D points for your body, which you need for growth and strong bones.

Go low with yogurt. Low-fat yogurt can serve triple-duty in your refrigerator: It's a great substitute for sour cream; it supplies great taste and texture to a baked potato; and it's a fine snack unto itself.

Cut the fat with sharp. When you have a taste for cheese, pick out a stronger-flavored sharp variety, such as Cheddar. It's not that it will be lower in fat than other cheeses, but because the flavors go further, it's easier to get by with less.

Skim the profits. While kids up to age two may need the fat that's in whole milk, you don't. So go as low as you can. While whole milk gets about 45 percent of its calories from fat, the 1 percent variety gets only about 23 percent. Skim milk is the clear winner with just 4 percent of calories from fat.

Beat back the fat. An omelet without eggs is nothing but a plate of milky vegetables. Every egg, however, pumps five grams of fat and 213 milligrams of cholesterol into your system. The secret: Use twice as many eggs—but toss the yolks. Egg whites by themselves are fat- and cholesterol-free and can be used in place of whole eggs.

Take care with creamers. If you're considering a nondairy creamer to cut back on fat grams, look closely. Many are high in saturated oils such as coconut or palm, which can boost your cholesterol more than using natural milk would. Try using nonfat dry milk powder instead.

Meat: The Kindest Cuts

For a lot of guys, a slab of steak is the darling of the dinner plate. Others hanker for delights such as hamburger, sausage and bacon. In one survey, 71 percent of shoppers reported eating those meats one to six times per week. Problem is, no other food in the American diet has a higher concentration of fat than meat.

Fat-fighting experts recommend demoting red meat to a supporting role in your meal. This means limiting yourself to a serving about the size of a deck of cards, not the size of a roulette wheel. Try to eat more fish and poultry instead.

Here are more pointers on navigating the meat counter.

Choose your cuts. To choose the leanest beef, you gotta know the code. Meat marked "select" has the least fat. The "choice" grade has more fat, and "prime" is the fattiest.

Remember the ground rules. When selecting ground beef, look for varieties with "round" or "loin" in the name—they're going to be the leanest. The color is also a clue. "If it's really dark red, then there's a lot less fat than with the pinker or the gray meat," says Dr. Rosenbloom.

Know your birds. A general rule for buying poultry: Reach for the skinless white meat. The skin has loads of fat, and dark meat has more fat than light. Also, if you're buying whole birds, pass on the self-basting poultry—it usually has added fat.

Talk turkey. Ground turkey can be a lean substitute for ground beef. You know you're on safe ground if it carries a label like "Per 3½-ounce cooked serving: 2 grams of fat."

Strip out the bacon. You already know the dangers of sausage and bacon. Turkey bacon has been promoted as a leaner alternative, but it's still not great, says Dr. Rosenbloom. If a soup or stew calls for bacon, pick up some lean ham and use that instead.

The Deli: A Slice of Life

At the deli counter, think of yourself as a customs agent. Your mission is to identify any excess fat attempting to sneak into your body and send it packing.

The more heavily processed cold cuts like bologna and pastrami are likely to be high in fat. That's not to say that every processed meat is a heart stopper. Healthy Choice makes lean pressed turkey and chicken, for example. But you should read the label or, if there isn't one, ask an attendant about the food's fat content before buying.

Here are some other healthy deli possibilities.

Study the salads. The macaroni and potato salads you see behind the glass are often made with oil or mayonnaise, which means added fat. Better choices include coleslaw (it still has mayo, but not as much), carrot-raisin salad or macaroni or potato salad that's specifically labeled as low-fat.

Trick your taste buds. If you're pining for some of your old high-fat deli favorites—say, pastrami or corned beef—keep an eye on some of the new products hitting the counter. "One company is making a turkey breast that has the pastrami seasoning on the outside," says Dr. Rosenbloom. "So when you slice it up thin, it really has the flavor that you like with the pastrami."

Speak up. You know the egg rolls and chicken wings are fried, and that means higher fat. But what about the ziti in red sauce? First, look for an ingredients label. If you don't see one, ask the attendant what went in the recipe.

The Fish Counter: Safe Sailing

Stepping up to the seafood counter is almost a no-brainer. The fat that occurs naturally in seafood is generally the less harmful unsaturated kind. Unless you fry your catch or drown it in tartar sauce or butter, it's hard to go wrong in this department.

To catch a plateful of flavor while keeping the fat down, here's what experts suggest.

Try swordplay. If you want to satisfy your red meat craving, try swordfish, monkfish, shark or fresh tuna, all of which have a meaty taste and texture. By contrast, with more delicate creatures like orange roughy, flounder, cod and catfish, you're gonna know you're eating fish.

Go by smell. Ironically, a fish that smells like a fish is not one you should buy. It has probably been away from home too long. "For freshness, the best thing to do is to ask them to let you smell the fish before you buy it," says Dr. Rosenbloom.

Pass on processing. Skip seafoods that have been processed, such as fish sticks and crab cakes. It's likely that they contain added fat and salt.

Dry and Canned Goods: Pantry Provisions

Sounds like something out of science fiction: nutrient-rich, low-fat foods in suspended animation. They store indefinitely, just waiting for you to add water or pop open the container.

Come down to earth, spaceman, and explore that grocery aisle lined with boxes of spaghetti, jars of sauce and canned vegetables. They're pantry-perfect; great stockables.

Here's how to put canned and dried goods to your best low-fat advantage.

Put veggies in reserve. Pick up a few cans of vegetables. They make a low-fat, nutritious addition to any impromptu meal and cost zilch in preparation time. "If you're really in a pinch, a great meal is to take a can of vegetable soup and add a can of corn to it," says Dr. Rosenbloom. "With bread, that makes a pretty hearty meal."

Break the rules. While a lot of packaged foods contain almost no fat—that spice-and-rice combo, for example—the recipe on the back of the package sometimes calls for butter or oil. Try cutting the added fat in half or cutting it out altogether, Tuttle suggests. You'll get the same great taste with less grease.

Make beans a basic. Yes, rhymesters: Beans, beans are good for the heart—by virtue of being low in fat. They're also high in fiber and nutrients. When selecting beans, consider what you're willing to deal with in the kitchen. Dried beans require a longer soaking and cooking process, but you're getting pure beans. Canned beans are more convenient, but they carry more sodium (some of which you can rinse away in a colander). If the canned beans have added pork, they'll be higher in fat as well.

Savor soup. To enjoy the good taste of soup while keeping the fat quotient down, go for broth-based soups, such as chicken and rice, and avoid cream-based varieties. Soups containing pasta and beans will give you a nutritious boost and are particularly filling. For fiber, lentil soup's a winner, offering seven or eight grams per serving.

Cereal: Off to a Good Start

What could be simpler? Shake some flakes or squares or circles out of a box. Eat. Grab your hat. For convenience and fat savings, it sure beats bacon and eggs.

"I think cereal with milk and juice is the best way to start the day," says Dr. Rosenbloom. "It's quick and easy, and it gives you a good start on nutrients."

Some cereals have a nutritional edge over others. Check the labels for those that offer less sugar and at least two grams of fiber per serving.

Mix them up. With a little creativity you can have the best of both worlds in your cereal: low-fat plus taste. But you might have to pull two boxes down from the shelf to do it. "Let's face it, those high-fiber cereals don't taste that great," says Dr. Rosenbloom. "So I use a cereal that I like and then add a high-fiber cereal to it."

Think small. Buy a jumbo package containing those micro-boxes of cereal. You can toss one in your briefcase and have it ready for an at-your-desk meal just by adding skim milk, Dr. Winston says.

Put them on the snack track. Go ahead and buy a box of your favorite sweetened cereal. But don't use it to start the day. Save it for snack time. Such cereals may have little fiber, but they're generally lower in fat than candy bars or ice cream.

Be wary of granolas. The box may be brown and depict a pastoral scene, but that doesn't mean the cereal is throbbing with natural goodness. Granola cereals, even the lower-fat varieties, are higher in fat than flake cereals. "Still, the granolas are a nice condiment to other cereal if you sprinkle them on," says Tuttle. "That makes it more interesting."

Baked Goods: Rise and Shine

In the bakery section, simple is safe.

"Many breads are going to be low- to no-fat," says Tuttle. "If you get into a cinnamon swirl loaf with extra walnuts, that isn't going to work. But when you're talking about a straight loaf-bread, most are going to be low-fat."

Here's how to get the best out of the bakery.

Go for the grains. Reach for whole-grain products. You'll get more fiber, naturally occurring B and E vitamins and trace minerals that rarely get added back to processed breads. And remember that fancy items such as banana or zucchini bread are likely to be high in fat.

Get the "whole" story. When buying bread, make sure you see 'whole wheat' on the label. "Don't be fooled by 'wheat bread,' " Dr. Rosenbloom says. "Wheat bread is white bread. Flour is made from wheat, so that is a legitimate claim. But 'wheat bread' is just white bread with maybe a little caramel coloring and a brown wrapper."

Investigate those muffins. Muffins are often thought of as healthy, but check the label for fat before you buy. "You know those super giant–size muffins? They can have as much fat as two or three doughnuts," says Tuttle.

Look for an angel. Because angel food cake is made predominantly from egg whites, it's very low in fat—not nearly as sinful as pound cake. "You know that 'pound' word? It comes from 'a pound of flour, a pound of butter, a pound of eggs, a pound of sugar,' " Tuttle says.

Say au revoir to croissants. They're tasty. They're flaky. They have that exotic air. But just a two-ounce, 4½-inch croissant contains 12 grams of fat. That's because the dough is repeatedly rolled out and flecked with butter. "If something is incredibly flaky and buttery—you know how a croissant is—it's for a reason," Tuttle says. "That's fat. It isn't low."

Frozen Food Strategies

Your Entrée into the World of Meals on Ice

They used to be called TV dinners, and they were manly meals. Meat loaf, mashed potatoes, gravy, peas and—if you were lucky—even some applesauce for dessert. All in one convenient container. In the 1950s and 1960s, they were what men cooked—or burned—when their wives weren't home for dinner.

Those were simpler times, and your choices in the freezer section of the local grocery store were uncomplicated by matters such as calories, fat content or sodium. TV dinners were quick, easy and filling, and that was sufficient.

No more. In the health-conscious 1990s, we demand more from frozen foods. And mainly, we do it by demanding less—less calories, less fat and less sodium.

For harried men who want to fight fat, learning to choose the right frozen dinners can make a big difference, because we tend to eat higher-fat foods when we're short for time. Nearly half of the shoppers who eat high-fat foods do so when they're in a hurry, according to a survey.

TV dinners now go by the more upscale moniker of *frozen entrées*, and manufacturers have responded with an array of offerings that are labeled "healthy" or "low-fat."

But beware: You can't always judge a frozen entrée by its cover. At least not solely from the sumptuous photograph and catchy name on it.

"The definition of low-fat for dinners and entrées is more liberal than it is for individual foods," says Bonnie Liebman of the Center for Science in the Public Interest. "So you can often get up to nine or ten grams of fat in a dinner that's labeled 'low-fat.' Don't look at just the word 'low-fat' and assume that it's the lowest possible you can get."

The Lowdown on Calories

With frozen foods, it pays to read the label. First, check total calories. Today, you may have more of a problem with low-fat entrées having too few calories than too many.

Portion sizes probably are smaller than you're accustomed to. This is one of the ways packagers keep fat levels down. Most low-fat frozen dinners come with some type of sauce, which actually makes them more filling than they look, but side dishes like a salad and a piece of fruit are needed to satisfy a realistic appetite.

Concentrate on percentage of calories from fat, not on number of calories. Often, fewer calories means less food, not necessarily less fat.

"Interestingly for men, who tend to want more calories, we don't tell people to just get the fewest calories possible, because frankly, that isn't much of a dinner," Liebman says.

A frozen dinner with only 250 calories is about the same as what you'd get in a plain bagel or a cup of fruit yogurt. Now be honest: Would you ever consider a bagel or a cup of yogurt to be a complete dinner?

"We actually recommend that people look for dinners that supply a larger amount of food but are still low in fat," Liebman says.

Once again, percentage of calories from fat is what really counts. As a quick rule of thumb, look for frozen dinners that have seven grams of fat or less. And in the key category of saturated fat—what Liebman calls "the kind that clogs the arteries"—dinners should generally check in at about three or four grams or less.

Avoid Freezer Burn

To keep from getting burned by frozen foods, here are some important things to keep in mind.

Investigate ingredients. Not all meat is really all-meat—some is mixed with soy or wheat products to make it lower in fat. This doesn't always make a big difference in taste, however, and in some cases it allows for heartier portions.

Check the order of ingredients on the package. If it's supposed to be a cheese dish and you see cheese way down on the list, after things like xanthan gum, you know somebody's skimping. It's a good idea to look for products with generous amounts of low-fat cheese.

Stay off the sauce. Pass on the frozen vegetables with butter or cream sauces. "That's where the fat content really goes up," says Dr. Chris Rosenbloom of Georgia State University and the Georgia Tech Athletic Association.

Keep it simple. For example, frozen chicken potpies are almost always higher in everything you don't want than one-ingredient meals, like roasted chicken entrées.

Be wary of the all-in-one meals. The four-course dinner may look appetizing, but looks can be deceiving. Better to get just a nice pasta or rice dish. You can throw together a quick salad on the side.

Veg out. An analysis by the Center for Science in the Public Interest found that most frozen dinners shortchange you on vegetables.

"While the industry has made great strides in cutting fat and sodium, one thing it hasn't done is provide a decent amount of vegetables, which is not inconsequential considering that the National Cancer Institute recommends five to nine servings of fruits and vegetables a day," Liebman says. "Most people figure if you're eating a frozen dinner, it should at least have a serving or two. Many have less than a single half-cup serving, and very few of them have two servings, which is only a cup of vegetables."

Your best bet: Supplement your frozen dinner with either frozen or steamed vegetables, which are quick and convenient.

Chill out with desserts. Among the frozen desserts, grab up the nonfat yogurt, fruit bars, sorbets and pops. Don't forget: They are still sweetened with sugar and can be high in calories.

Consider the serving size. When you're checking a frozen food item's label for fat content, don't forget to factor in the serving size that's being used. For instance, your favorite frozen yogurt may boast only three grams of fat per serving. The serving size listed is ½ cup, however, and you usually spoon down 1½ cups of frozen yogurt in one sitting. That adds up to nine grams of fat per actual serving. Frozen pizzas often list the serving size as two slices. Be honest: When was the last time you ate two slices of a frozen pizza and put the rest in the fridge for another day?

Make your own. Great frozen meals aren't found only in the freezer section of the grocery store; you can make your own at home. During the weekend, whip up a good-sized batch of some stew or soup and stick it in the freezer. Then, on that night you get home from work too late—and too tired—to cook, pop some in the oven or microwave, says Paul R. Thomas, R.D., Ed.D., staff scientist with the National Academy of Sciences' Food and Nutrition Board in Washington, D.C. Add some good bread, some skim or 1 percent milk and a salad. You have an instant, healthy meal.

Dish it out. Unless you have to eat it right from the tray (some are pretty much wedged into plastic cartons), have a separate dish handy to spoon the ingredients into. A nice presentation will make a big difference in how you perceive your meal.

Frozen Food Comparisons

Finding Flavor in the Freezer

Sure, a lot of frozen entrées now have less fat. But if they taste like the cardboard boxes they come in, it doesn't much matter.

A panel of judges from *Men's Health* magazine found that many of the low-fat dinners in the frozen foods section of the grocery store are just as tasty as their higher-fat varieties.

Taste ratings are on a scale of 1 to 10, with 1 representing "barely edible" and 10, "delicious."

Tyson Healthy Portion Italian Style Chicken. This product got raves, looking and tasting as if it came right off a grill, thanks to being seared before packaging. The skinless breasts are presented on a bed of pasta primavera, which the manufacturers kept low-fat by using Parmesan cheese (a moderately low fat type) and nonfat milk. The vegetables (carrots, broccoli and zucchini) also deliver good amounts of thiamin (a B vitamin) and vitamins A and C. (13.75-ounce serving size; 310 calories; 12% calories from fat)

Taste rating: 10

Stouffer's Lean Cuisine Swedish Meatballs with Pasta. While the meatballs may not be 100 percent beef (soy protein is listed as an ingredient), they taste as good as or better than most of your cocktail-party varieties. The sauce and noodles are very good, although this meal is lacking in vegetables, so make sure you have some greens on hand. (9.13-ounce serving size; 290 calories; 25% calories from fat)

Taste rating: 9

Weight Watchers Smart Ones Roast Turkey Medallions and Mushrooms. This meal gives you lean, flavorful and moist turkey in respectable portions, with a really strong mushroom sauce. It comes in boiling bags that are also microwaveable—the packaging format is a little bit messy to work with, but it allows you to arrange your own plate, so you're not eating off a plastic tray. That may also be why no one groused about the 8.5-ounce serving size: It looks bigger when it's served. (8.5-ounce serving size; 200 calories; 4.5% calories from fat)

Taste rating: 9

Healthy Choice Beef Pepper Steak Oriental. There was enough meat to satisfy the judges and a good balance of peppers, broccoli and rice. It was also lower in sodium than you might expect—overall, a healthy alternative to Chinese food, which tends to be high in salt and fat. (9.5-ounce serving size; 250 calories; 14% calories from fat)

Taste rating: 8

Tyson Chicken Marsala. Reviewers griped about the tiny portion of meat; a man ought to expect more than four or five mouthfuls. This one could have been a winner, since the sauce was excellent, and the baby carrots and red potatoes that accompany the entrée made for a good combination. But at just 15 percent calories from fat, this meal could afford to be a little meatier. (9-ounce serving size; 180 calories; 15% calories from fat)

Taste rating: 8

Healthy Choice Seasoned Boneless Beef Ribs with Barbecue Sauce. The idea of low-fat ribs raised many an eyebrow in this office. Yet this is real meat—trimmed of all the fat and doused in a chili-and-brown-sugar sauce. It's accompanied by corn (no butter) and mashed potatoes (which are treated with a suspicious-sounding "potato enhancer–type flavor"). They have a taste that's vaguely buttery. (11-ounce serving size; 330 calories; 16% calories from fat)

　　Taste rating: 7.5

Banquet Healthy Balance Chicken Mesquite Meal.

If you like Chicken Mc-Nuggets, you'll like these pieces of breaded chicken. They didn't emerge from the microwave very crispy, though. We found that cooking the meal in a conventional oven was a better choice. We also liked the barbecue sauce, the green beans, the potatoes and the peach/pineapple dessert. (10.5-ounce serving size; 260 calories; 21% calories from fat)

　　Taste rating: 7

Budget Gourmet Light and Healthy Rigatoni in Cream Sauce with Broccoli and Chicken.

A straightforward pasta and cream sauce tossed with bits of chicken and broccoli, this dinner received the highest compliment for a low-fat food: "Tastes like it's bad for you." Unfortunately, if you're on a low-sodium diet, it might be. This product delivers 710 milligrams of the stuff, just shy of a third of the Daily Value. (11-ounce serving size; 290 calories; 21% calories from fat)

　　Taste rating: 7

Budget Gourmet Light and Healthy Shrimp Mariner.

Cooked in its own cardboard package, the meal pops out of the microwave in a most unappealing manner—itty-bitty shrimp in one corner, rice piled in the middle, vegetables shoved to the far side. Spoon it out into a bowl and mix it up, however, and the taste is good. We also liked the combination of white and wild rice and the fact that the broccoli helped the dish deliver an impressive 90 percent of the Recommended Dietary Allowance (RDA) for vitamin C. (11-ounce serving size; 230 calories; 23% calories from fat)

　　Taste rating: 7

Weight Watchers Smart Ones Ravioli Florentine.

What should have been a can't-miss meal turned out to be a disappointment. It has plenty of vegetables (and 45 percent of your RDA of vitamin A) but also an overwhelmingly tangy tomato sauce that drowned out the flavor of the ravioli. Since this product also comes in boiling pouches, your best bet might be to spoon out the spinach-and-cheese ravioli—which were actually quite cheesy and good—and cut way back on the sauce. (8.5-ounce serving size; 130 calories; 7% calories from fat)

　　Taste rating: 6

Weight Watchers Nacho Grande Chicken Enchiladas.

Judges reported finding only one or two tiny chicken pieces in the two enchiladas combined. In fact, they reported finding very little of anything in the enchiladas, despite the fact that they're supposed to be "stuffed" with beans, corn and peppers in addition to the chicken. Plenty of cheese and spices, but as for the enchiladas themselves, there's not much there. (9-ounce serving size; 290 calories; 24% calories from fat)

　　Taste rating: 3

Banquet Healthy Balance Salisbury Steak.

This dish was not enjoyed at all: "Gristly" was the word used to describe its flavor—not surprising, since the ingredients list identifies both beef and pork as components of the steak (not to mention water and bread crumbs). It also comes with an unfortunate choice of macaroni and cheese, green beans and a "cherry dessert" (which the manufacturers did not even try to classify)—and 800 milligrams of sodium. (10.5-ounce serving size; 270 calories; 27% calories from fat)

　　Taste rating: 2

Healthy Choice Fettucini with Beef and Broccoli.

The question "Where's the beef?" has never been so justly applied. In addition, the sauce seems to be nothing more than starch and water—a big disappointment compared with the other Healthy Choice meals. (12-ounce serving size; 290 calories; 9% calories from fat)

　　Taste rating: 2

Cooking Strategies

For Low-Fat Fun, Conquer the Kitchen

Maybe you've dreamed of being a sculptor, a wilderness guide or coach of the Dallas Cowboys. If being creative and in control appeals to you, then you should also explore the kitchen.

Cooking is fun. You'll impress friends and turn out some delectable chow. And for fighting fat—both in your diet and around your waist—the kitchen is the best place for taking a stand. In a country awash in convenient but larded foods, taking spatula in hand can be your best defense.

Cooking is a guy thing, you know. An American Dietetic Association survey found that 49.8 percent of men say they do at least half the cooking at home. In addition, the U.S. Department of Labor says that 54 percent of professional cooks in the United States are men.

One of these chefs is Tuan Lam, owner and head chef of Thuy Hoa restaurant in Denver.

"We don't use many things like cheese or butter," Lam says. "We have lots of customers now who don't want lots of oil. So we're using lots of vegetables and we're using lots of broth, adding them together."

The fat-busting techniques used by Lam and other cooks nationwide are easily adapted to your kitchen. The principles are basic: Invest in good hardware; keep lots of versatile, low-fat ingredients in the kitchen; and most important, be inventive—and have fun.

Gearing Up

You gotta have the right tool for the right job. That was true in shop class, and it applies in the kitchen, too. To help yourself work efficiently in the kitchen and, while you're at it, whittle fat from your food, here's what food experts recommend.

Put blenders in the mix. Yes, a blender is good for more than making margaritas. You can use it to whip up low-fat sauces as well. For example, Susan Harville, a member of the collective that owns Moosewood Restaurant in Ithaca, New York, recommends using a blender to make this tasty, no-oil pesto:

Combine one cup of basil leaves (packed), a teaspoon of salt, a tablespoon of toasted pine nuts, one whole fresh tomato and a clove or two of fresh garlic. Blend until smooth, then serve over pasta, steamed fish or vegetables. You can also use it as a sandwich spread or put it on a baked potato.

Rack up fat savings. Oven roasting makes meat crisp and brown on the outside and tender and juicy inside. Cooking a roast or chicken without a rack means that the meat lolls around in its own fat, picking up surplus calories along the way. Putting a rack underneath will allow the fat to drain away, giving a crisper skin in the process.

Skim the risks. When making soup or stew, you'll see globules of fat rising to the surface. Fat is easy to remove using a specially designed slotted spoon or ladle. Or if you're working ahead of time, cool your masterpiece in the fridge overnight. The fat will rise and congeal into a waxy film on the surface. Gently spoon it off. Nobody will miss it.

Make waves. Microwaves are not only fast, they can also cook food with little or no added fat. At the same time, they help preserve many of the nutrients that are lost when you boil.

"You can cook vegetables in a microwave quite easily," says Dan Remark, executive chef of Mustard Seed Market and Cafe in Akron, Ohio. "Place the vegetables on a plate, add a slight amount of water to create steam, put plastic wrap over the top and then microwave to the desired consistency. Great method."

Get past the sticking point. No-stick cookware is a blessing for the working chef. Not only does it help reduce cleanup time, it also allows you to sauté or bake without adding oil. Kitchen stores stock a large variety of no-stick pots and pans. The more expensive kinds are more likely to hold up to the rigors of hard kitchen use. But regardless of the kind you buy, treat the slick surface gingerly—wood and plastic utensils only.

Cook under pressure. Because pressure cookers can substantially shave the preparation time needed for slow-cooking foods such as dried beans, brown rice, potatoes and stews, they're a must for any chef living in the fast lane.

"Garbanzo beans would take two to four hours to cook just boiling them, but a pressure cooker will cut the time down to an hour and a half," says Tom Flener, a cook at the Sunlight Cafe in Seattle. "They're pretty convenient for things that take a long time to cook."

Try steam power. Like the microwave, cooking with steam can cook food fast with no oil added. At the same time, it helps preserve the color, flavor and nutrients that can be lost to boiling.

To steam vegetables, first allow the water to boil. Then throw the vegetables into the steamer and put the lid on. Be sure the water isn't so high that it touches the veggies—contact with the boiling water will sap away nutrients.

"We combine carrots, broccoli, cauliflower and green peppers," says Roger Brown, co-owner and cook at Valley Restaurant in Corvallis, Oregon. "Then we steam them until they are cooked but still have a slight crunch. We add onions right toward the end of the cooking. Mushrooms take the least amount of time, so they go in last."

Don't neglect man's best disposal. Canine disposal units come in a variety of sizes and colors and are a handy way of getting rid of trimmed fat, unwanted egg yolks and other scraps. "I give all that to my dog, and he loves it," says Dr. Chris Rosenbloom of Georgia State University and the Georgia Tech Athletic Association. "Dogs don't get atherosclerosis. So my dog's happy."

Ingredients for Success

The foods you stock in the refrigerator and pantry are the building blocks of your diet—and of any recipes you dream up. On the most basic level, taking low-fat ingredients and cooking them with low-fat techniques guarantee you're going to have healthy chow to take to the table. But there are other things to consider before laying in inventory.

• Are the ingredients easy to use? If preparing a certain food is as complex as the Manhattan Project, it's going to bomb as a menu item.

• Is it versatile? You don't want to waste shelf space on something you'll use only when you make rattlesnake fritters.

• Is it quick? Can you open a container and dump it in a pan, or do you have to whittle, soak, pound or otherwise negotiate with it?

The bottom line is that low-fat ingredients that slide easily into active duty are much more likely to wind up in your belly than the exotics you bought on a whim—those dried mushrooms, for example, that you shoved behind the canned brussels sprouts five years ago and that by now are harder than the concrete in Hoover Dam.

Use the ol' bean. Canned beans, be they pintos, black beans, kidney beans, split peas or any other kind of bean, are great staples to have on the shelf. Not only are they used in a vast array of recipes, but they also cook a heck of lot faster than the dried kind.

Explore combinations. Loosen up, man. There's no kitchen cop telling you not to dump a can of corn into a stir-fry or add anchovies to a tomato paste. So the next time you're shopping or perusing the pantry, make some educated guesses about what combinations will taste good together. Then toss them together.

"I've been buying a lot of reduced-fat cream soups—the low-fat mushroom soups and potato soups," says Dr. Rosenbloom. "Those are a quick, good basis for a casserole. You can take a chicken breast and a can of vegetables and one of those soups, mix them together, heat and serve the casserole with bread—it's real fast and it tastes pretty good."

Grab a cold one. Bags of frozen vegetables deserve top marks both for saving time and for cooking versatility. The veggies taste almost as good as fresh and are ready to toss right in the pot with no cleaning or chopping necessary. "You can take out a single serving size and put the rest back in the freezer," says Dr. Rosenbloom. "But don't get the ones with the butter sauces or cream sauces. That's where the fat content really goes up."

Put on the spritz. It's a good idea to keep a can of no-stick spray handy. Shooshing your frying pan with this stuff will add just 2 calories and a trace of fat to your meal, as opposed to the 102 calories and 11 grams of fat that come with a tablespoon of butter.

Spice up your life. The addition of spices to food is a wonderful and tasty way to fill the void left when fat and salt are reduced or eliminated. You probably already have the basics: black pepper, cinnamon, basil, dill, paprika and oregano. For more exotic offerings, check out the spice chart included in many cookbooks.

Taking Stock

To truly master low-fat cuisine at home, you have to lay in supplies.

"I like to look at it from a standpoint of 'What do I have in my pantry or my refrigerator that when I get home and it's late and I'm hungry, I can throw together in ten minutes and still eat healthy?' " says Dr. Chris Rosenbloom of Georgia State University and the Georgia Tech Athletic Association.

Here are 20 ingredients that no man's kitchen should be without.

In the Refrigerator
- A variety of fruits and vegetables
- Dijon mustard
- Nonfat yogurt
- Nonfat buttermilk
- Tortillas

In the Freezer
- Boneless chicken breast
- Turkey cutlets
- Frozen vegetables

In the Pantry
- Dried and canned beans
- Canned tomatoes, tomato puree and tomato paste
- Canned corn
- Canned peas
- Canned chicken broth
- White and brown rice
- Quick-cooking grains, such as bulgur and millet
- Onions
- Garlic
- Fresh ginger
- Olive oil
- Pasta

"If you're not familiar with the flavor of a spice, we suggest you try it in something bland like rice or scrambled eggs," says Camille Appel, manager of consumer communications at McCormick and Company in Hunt Valley, Maryland, the world's largest spice company.

Grow your own. Many herbs lose flavor in the drying process, so nothing will add kick to your low-fat cooking like using the fresh stuff. The problem with fresh spices is that they're usually sold only in huge bunches, most of which will turn into a science experiment at the bottom of the vegetable bin before you get around to using it.

An alternative is to grow your own, says Dr. Rosenbloom. "Keep them on the window sill, and you can just snip off what you might want for cooking." Since fresh herbs begin losing flavor and color with long cooking, it's best to stir them in just before serving.

Put ginger on ice. When added to sauces, stir-fries and marinades, fresh ginger packs a punch you just don't get from the powdered stuff. Problem is, it's perishable, and after a few weeks in the refrigerator, it generally resembles an ugly root that a pig wouldn't eat.

To keep fresh ginger handy, try grating the entire root, then freezing it in a plastic bag or small container. The shavings will stay loose and separate, so it's easy to scoop out small amounts as needed. Or freeze it whole, then grate it only as needed.

Freeze a block o' stock. While bouillon cubes are a passable substitute, nothing can match the rich flavors and cooking versatility of a homemade vegetable stock. It makes a fantastic soup, stew or gravy and contains virtually no fat.

Basically, all you need to do is throw leftover veggies—including peelings and onion skins—into a large pot of water. Fruits are good to use, too, especially apples and pears. "Put them on to cook for an hour while you're doing other things," says Harville. "Then strain out the vegetables and freeze the liquid. That way, you're ahead."

Ready the radicchio. Experts agree that greens such as spinach and other dark green leafy vegetables should be a mainstay of your refrigerator. They're packed with vitamins and have zero fat. They also tend to turn to mush before you get around to eating them.

To keep greens fresh, wash them as soon as you get home. Then shake off the excess water, roll them in paper towels or kitchen towels, place them in a plastic bag and pop them in the fridge. That way, they'll stay fresh for at least three or four days, and often longer.

Mastering Meat

What man is not familiar with temptations of the flesh? We mean, of course, a sizzling slab of beef on the backyard grill, a thick puck of hamburger oozing juice into a seeded bun or those crisp brown strips that transform a mere plate of eggs into a bona fide breakfast.

While we're indulging, however, there's a relentless accountant tallying up the fat: 60 grams in the 12-ounce sirloin, 48 grams in the half-pound burger and 9 grams for three slices of bacon. With those kinds of numbers, it's not surprising that health experts typically view cows or pigs as obesity on the hoof.

But with a little moderation and advance planning, it is still possible to make peace with pork and say "Wow!" to cow chow. Here's what experts recommend.

Give it a trim. The next time you have a craving for a thick pork chop or juicy New York strip, trim away the outer rim of fat before slapping it on the grill. It's easier to trim the fat if you first pop the meat in the freezer for 20 minutes. Chilling also causes hidden fat to turn white, making it easier to spot and lop off.

Let the fat flow. Trimming away visible fat is just one way to keep your meat lean. Another is to cook it properly. There are different low-fat cooking styles for different cuts of meat. For example:

• Broiling. This involves putting meat in

the oven directly under the flame or electric element—preferably no more than three to five inches away—and is recommended for relatively thin cuts. Put the meat on a broiling rack with a drip pan underneath to catch the fat.

•Roasting. This is usually recommended for larger cuts of meat such as a roast. The meat is placed on a rack and cooked in a medium-temperature (350°) oven.

•Stove-top grilling. Using a ridged cast-iron pan or one of the newer stove-top grills, this is a fast technique for cooking meat that is an inch thick or less. The fat flows down into the ridges and away from the meat.

Baste wisely. Traditional basting calls for sopping the beast with buttery, oily concoctions. Forget that. To keep your meat moist and flavorful, baste with defatted stock, a low-fat marinade, flavored vinegar or even fruit juice.

Towel off those burgers. Once you've browned burgers on the grill or stove, move them to a plate lined with paper towels and pat them dry. Or if you're using ground beef for a spaghetti sauce or casserole, drain it in a colander first. Then remove the meat and put it on a paper towel–lined plate.

Wash it away. To remove even more fat from ground beef destined for a casserole or sauce, put it in a colander and drench it with hot (not boiling) water. Let the meat drain for five minutes, then add it to the recipe.

Skip the skin. About half the fat in chicken is found in the skin or directly beneath it, so always peel the bird before you eat. It's a good idea to cook chicken before removing the skin, however, since this helps lock in flavor and moisture and doesn't add too much fat to the meat.

Go fish. Fresh fish and shellfish are al-

Cooking over the Coals

That grill in the backyard means a hump of fatty pork ribs slathered in barbecue sauce, right? Well, the ol' Weber grill can turn out lean chow as well, adding a distinctive smoky flavor to boot.

"We have the perception that healthy food is boring. But we're able to throw a piece of fish on the grill, or even a vegetable, and have it take on a lot of flavors," says Chris Schlesinger of East Coast Grill, Blue Room and Jake and Earl's Dixie BBQ restaurants in Cambridge, Massachusetts.

To make your grill a lean machine, here's what chefs recommend.

• Rather than slathering oil onto your ingredients, brush the oil directly onto the hot bars of the grill. Then wipe it off with a rag or paper towel before cooking.

• When grilling chicken, remove the skin and rub the meat with a garlic-herb paste made by mixing a half-cup of chopped fresh basil, two tablespoons of minced garlic and a little salt and cracked black pepper.

---

ways good choices because they're delicious, easy to cook and low in fat. But it's better to bake or broil fish without added fat than to fry it, which adds extra fat and calories to the meal, says dietitian Lisa Litin of the Harvard School of Public Health.

And once you get your fish to the table, "watch the cream sauces, tartar sauce and additions of margarine or butter," Litin adds. One tablespoon of tartar sauce has 8 grams of fat—only slightly less heart-stopping than the 11 grams found in butter.

Exercise control. If you're eating humongous quantities, even the leanest meat is going to give you fat overload. Limit your meat serving to about six ounces, experts say. That's about the size of a deck of playing cards. Then

- **Eggplant, onions, summer squash and peppers all make good grilling candidates. Char, let them cool, then peel the black stuff off. Eat with minced garlic, olive oil and crusty bread.**

- **Corn on the cob needs gentle handling. Shuck the ears and soak in water for 20 minutes, then cook them over low coals.**

- **Roasting eggplant gives it a delectably smoky flavor. Wrap it in foil and put it on the grill for 12 to 15 minutes. Then let cool, peel away the skin and spread the innards on bread, crackers, sandwiches or a baked potato.**

- **Tuna, salmon, swordfish, shark and halibut steaks all grill well because they are compact and of one thickness and don't fall apart on the grill as fillets do. If they're the usual one-inch-thick steaks, grill four or five minutes to a side.**

- **The most flavorful beefsteaks also tend to be the fattiest. Rather than sacrificing flavor by using leaner cuts, Schlesinger prefers to reduce the portion size. He recommends grilling a six-ounce steak, then slicing it over salad greens and tomatoes and making a steak salad.**

round out the meal with the other good stuff you've put on the table.

Wok on the Wild Side

A stir-fry meal may look and taste exotic, but it's really an easy, anything-goes, fantastically quick style of cooking. It requires little if any oil. And unlike traditional menus that feature meat, wok cookery gives vegetables star billing—they come out crisp, intensely colored and packed with their original nutrients because the cooking process is so fast.

"The nice thing about stir-frying is you can be creative. You can add whatever is on hand, using different types of vegetables, meats and liquids, and they all give different flavors,"

says dietitian Pat Harper, spokesperson for the American Dietetic Association. "It's more like you're creating a meal rather than just cooking it." So if you, too, would like to be a da Vinci of da kitchen, here are some stir-fry basics.

Create a stir. The first thing you need to stir-fry is a wok, although a large frying pan will do in a pinch. "I use an electric wok. I find that's really handy to use," says Dr. Rosenbloom.

Begin with marinades. For extra flavor with no added fat, try soaking some of your ingredients in a marinade. An easy one to begin with is a mixture of garlic, ginger and soy sauce. This works great when cooking seafood, tofu, tempeh and eggplant.

Synchronize your stir-fry. You want all of your stir-fry ingredients to finish cooking at the same time, so it's a good idea to chop all the vegetables into pieces of roughly the same size. Meat takes the longest to cook, so toss that in first. Delicate items such as snow peas should go in last.

Get ready for spaghetti. Rice may be the traditional accompaniment for stir-fry, but switching to an alternative will give your meal a new look. "You can put stir-fry over noodles, you can put it over rice, you can put it over spaghetti or different shapes of pasta, so every time it's like a different meal," says Harper.

Let the oil slide. The great thing about wok cooking is that you can often prepare an entire meal without adding any fat beyond a spritz of no-stick spray. Contrast that to a recipe that calls for frying vegetables—broccoli, carrots or onions, for example—in three teaspoons of vegetable oil, which could add 15 grams of fat to the meal.

Tuan Lam often forgoes the fat entirely. "A lot of our customers now don't want us to use a lot of oil," he says. "So we're using broth when we're cooking with vegetables."

Breakfast Ideas

Toast the New Day with These Delicious Eye-Openers

Breakfast is the most important meal of the day, yet it gets minimum effort—a splash of OJ, a slice of bagel, a few flakes shaken from a box. No wonder your family yawns in the morning.

To be a sunrise hero and really open their eyes, try these easy, low-fat day-starters. The normally high-cal French toast and frittata trim fat by using egg substitute, while the melon and sauces score major fruit points on the healthy eating scoreboard.

That French toast, by the way, doesn't need butter to make it delicious. Neither do other breakfast stalwarts like pancakes and waffles. The fruit sauces are quick and easy to make, and you can prepare them ahead of time and store them in the refrigerator. Which means you'll have a royal breakfast—and maybe even catch the early train to work.

Cinnamon-Scented French Toast

Serves 4

- ¾   cup skim milk
- ¾   cup fat-free egg substitute
- 1   teaspoon canola oil
- ½   teaspoon vanilla
- ¼   teaspoon ground cinnamon
- 8   slices oat-bran bread

In a 9″ × 13″ baking dish, mix the milk, egg substitute, oil, vanilla and cinnamon. Add the bread in a single layer. Turn the pieces to coat both sides with the mixture.

Coat a griddle or large no-stick frying pan with no-stick spray. Place over medium heat until hot. Transfer the bread slices to the griddle, working in batches if necessary. Brown on both sides.

Per serving: 218 calories, 3.2 g. fat (13% of calories), 5.1 g. dietary fiber, 1 mg. cholesterol, 280 mg. sodium.

Breakfast Melon Bowl

Serves 4

- 1   cup nonfat ricotta cheese
- ¾   cup nonfat vanilla yogurt
- 1   small cantaloupe
- 2   peaches, pitted and thinly sliced
- ½   cup sliced strawberries
- ½   cup blueberries
- 2   tablespoons toasted sunflower seeds
    Mint sprigs

In a food processor or blender, process the ricotta until very smooth. Transfer to a small bowl. Mix in the yogurt.

Halve the cantaloupe and remove the seeds. Cut into wedges, remove the rind and cut the flesh into bite-size chunks. Place in a medium bowl. Mix in the peaches and strawberries. Add the ricotta mixture and gently fold together.

Divide among 4 cereal bowls. Sprinkle with the blueberries and sunflower seeds. Garnish with the mint sprigs.

Per serving: 190 calories, 2.8 g. fat (13% of calories), 3 g. dietary fiber, 1 mg. cholesterol, 110 mg. sodium.

Potato and Onion Frittata

Serves 4

2 baking potatoes, peeled, halved lengthwise and thinly sliced crosswise

1 onion, thinly sliced

1 tablespoon olive oil

1½ cups fat-free egg substitute

¼ teaspoon curry powder

¼ teaspoon ground ginger

Steam the potatoes for 5 minutes, or until tender.

In a large ovenproof frying pan over medium heat, sauté the onions in the oil for 5 minutes, or until transparent.

In a medium bowl, whisk together the egg substitute, curry powder and ginger.

Add the potatoes to the pan with the onions. Pour the egg mixture over all and cook for 5 minutes over medium heat.

Transfer to the oven and broil 6″ from the heat for 5 minutes, or until the frittata has puffy edges and is a golden color.

Per serving: 145 calories, 3.5 g. fat (22% of calories), 2.2 g. dietary fiber, 0 mg. cholesterol, 127 mg. sodium.

Fast Fruit Sauces

To add great taste to your morning meal, try one of these delicious sauces. They work as well on pancakes as on French toast—and they contain almost no fat.

Strawberry Sauce

Makes about 3 cups

3 cups chopped strawberries

½ cup water

2 tablespoons maple syrup

2 teaspoons lemon juice

Place 2 cups of the strawberries in a blender. Add the water, maple syrup and lemon juice. Blend until pureed. Transfer to a bowl and stir in the remaining 1 cup strawberries.

Per ½ cup: 39 calories, 0.3 g. fat (7% of calories), 1.9 g. dietary fiber, 0 mg. cholesterol, 2 mg. sodium.

Pineapple Sauce

Makes about 2½ cups

1 can (15.25 ounces) pineapple pieces packed in juice

¼ cup honey

2 tablespoons orange juice

1 teaspoon grated orange rind

½ cup water

1 tablespoon cornstarch

Drain the pineapple and place the juice in a 2-quart saucepan. Set the pineapple aside.

Add the honey, orange juice and orange rind to the pan. Bring to a boil over medium heat.

In a cup, mix the water and cornstarch. Pour into the pan. Cook, stirring, for 2 minutes, or until the sauce thickens. Stir in the pineapple.

Per ½ cup: 113 calories, 0.1 g. fat (1% of calories), 0.8 g. dietary fiber, 0 mg. cholesterol, 2 mg. sodium.

Lunch Ideas

Some Great Meals with Legs

Lunch is often a road show. Whether you're at your desk, in the company break room, taking over a park bench or spreading out on the tailgate to watch a football game, noon nutrition typically consists of stuff you threw into a bag before leaving home.

You get by with a banana and a ham sandwich? Won't get much applause for that road show. Lunch doesn't have to be a yawn. Without much time, effort or cost, you can eat like a superstar wherever you go.

With the help of a few common items like plastic containers, plastic bags and a lunch box, plus a Thermos for hot soup and an insulated sack to keep sandwiches cool, you can be a regular gastronaut. Ready? Let's do lunch.

Lunch for Work

Ever open your lunch box only to find that your sandwich has imitated a California mud slide? Forget the bread slices. A pita pocket is engineered for life on the road. It's all one piece, and with its single narrow opening, it keeps that squish factor under control. That, plus a belly-warming bowl of hot soup, will get you through the day in style.

Chicken in Pita Pockets

Serves 4

2 cups diced cooked chicken breast

1 cup diced green peppers

2 plum tomatoes, diced

1 small onion, diced

¼ teaspoon dried tarragon

½ cup nonfat mayonnaise

4 pita breads, halved

1 cup shredded lettuce

In a large bowl, toss together the chicken, peppers, tomatoes, onions and tarragon. Add the mayonnaise and mix well.

Open the pita halves and divide the lettuce among them. Stuff with the chicken mixture.

Per serving: 250 calories, 2.9 g. fat (11% of calories), 2.2 g. dietary fiber, 48 mg. cholesterol, 644 mg. sodium.

White Bean and Corn Soup

Serves 6

1 cup dried navy beans, soaked overnight (see note)

1 cup chopped onions

1 teaspoon oil

2 cloves garlic, minced

6 cups defatted chicken stock

½ cup minced carrots

1 bay leaf

1 cup corn (see note)

½ cup peeled, seeded and diced tomatoes (see note)

2 tablespoons chopped fresh basil or parsley

¼ teaspoon ground black pepper

Drain the beans and set aside.

In a 3-quart saucepan over low heat, sauté the onions in the oil, stirring often, until golden, about 10 minutes. Add the garlic; sauté for 1 minute.

Add the stock, carrots, bay leaf and beans. Bring to a boil. Reduce the heat and simmer for 2 to 2½ hours, or until the beans are tender.

Add the corn and tomatoes. Cook for 15 minutes.

Season with the basil or parsley and pepper. Remove and discard the bay leaf.

Chef's Note: To quick-soak dried beans: Place in a 1-quart casserole and cover with cold water. Microwave on high power for 15 minutes, or until the beans have swelled. Drain; proceed with the recipe.

You can also use 3 cups rinsed and drained canned beans, but because these beans are already cooked, you should add them to the soup along with the corn.

In season, fresh corn is best. But you may also use frozen or canned kernels. You may also use canned tomatoes.

Per serving: 203 calories, 3 g. fat (13% of calories), 5.4 g. dietary fiber, 0 mg. cholesterol, 94 mg. sodium.

Lunch on the Tailgate

Park the car, lower the tailgate, pop open the cooler and picnic basket. Voilà: Where once there was gravel you now have gourmet. If there's a fall nip in the air, a little curry or chili powder will warm you up. The following tailgate treats will do the trick.

Curried Potato Salad

Serves 4

1	*pound potatoes*
¼	*cup raisins*
2	*scallions, minced*
3	*tablespoons sliced almonds*
½	*cup nonfat yogurt*
2	*tablespoons chutney*
1	*teaspoon curry powder*

Cut the potatoes into 1" chunks. Steam until tender, about 12 minutes. Transfer to a large bowl. Stir in the raisins, scallions and almonds.

In a small bowl, whisk together the yogurt, chutney and curry powder. Pour over the potatoes and combine well. Serve warm.

Per serving: 180 calories, 3.1 g. fat (16% calories), 3.5 g. dietary fiber, 1 mg. cholesterol, 34 mg. sodium.

Vegetable Chili

Serves 4

2	*tablespoons olive oil*
2	*cups finely chopped onions*
2	*cups diced celery*
2	*cups diced carrots*
1	*sweet red pepper, diced*
4	*cloves garlic, minced*
2	*tablespoons whole-wheat flour*
1	*tablespoon chili powder*
4	*cups crushed tomatoes*
1½	*cups defatted stock*
1	*cup dried adzuki beans, soaked overnight*

In a 4-quart pot, heat the oil. Add the onions, celery, carrots, peppers, and garlic. Sauté for 5 to 10 minutes, or until the vegetables are tender. Stir in the flour and chili powder.

Add the tomatoes and stock. Drain the beans and add them to the pot.

Cover and simmer for 30 minutes. Remove the lid and simmer 30 minutes, or until the vegetables and beans are tender and the liquid has thickened.

Per serving: 367 calories, 8.4 g. fat (20% calories), 10.8 g. dietary fiber, 0 mg. cholesterol, 337 mg. sodium.

Dinner for Two

For Romance, Try This Pasta Presentation

Here's a lean and luscious lineup that will impress any date. You'll be particularly relaxed, too, because it goes together hassle-free: basic ingredients, simple and quick cooking techniques. It may look like you started cooking at dawn, but that's your secret.

Ta-ta to the snooty waiters and Indy 500–style parking valets. Au revoir to the high-ticket restaurant meals that guilt-trip you into eating every bite. On a night like this, who needs the swollen belly and drooping eyelids that come with overeating?

So don your special duds. Light a few candles. And remember, pasta means carbohydrates, and carbohydrates mean energy. Who knows? You may need all the energy you can get. Plus, each of the recipes serves at least four people, so you'll have plenty of leftovers for quick meals on hectic days.

■

Basil Cauliflower and Sweet Peppers

Serves 4

2   *cups small cauliflower florets*

1   *small sweet red pepper, cut into thin strips*

1   *tablespoon minced fresh basil or 1 teaspoon dried basil*

In a large saucepan with a tight-fitting lid, bring about 1″ of water to a boil. Place the cauliflower in a steamer basket. Arrange the peppers on top. Set the basket in the saucepan, mak-

ing sure the basket sits above the water. Cover the saucepan and steam for 10 to 15 minutes, or until the cauliflower is crisp-tender.

Transfer the cauliflower and peppers to a serving bowl. Sprinkle with the basil and gently toss until combined.

Per serving: 17 calories, 0.2 g. fat (8% of calories), 1.5 g. dietary fiber, 0 mg. cholesterol, 8 mg. sodium.

■

Greens and Tangerines

Serves 4

2   *cups torn red lettuce*

1½   *teaspoons olive oil*

2   *cups tangerine sections*

1   *cup red grapes, halved*

1   *tart apple, diced*

2   *tablespoons lemon juice*

1   *teaspoon minced fresh tarragon*

¼   *teaspoon dried mint*

Place the lettuce in a large serving bowl. Toss with the oil until coated.

Add the tangerines, grapes and apples. Sprinkle with the lemon juice, tarragon and mint. Toss to combine.

Per serving: 77 calories, 2.1 g. fat (25% of calories), 2.2 g. dietary fiber, 0 mg. cholesterol, 4 mg. sodium.

■

Mushroom and Lentil Soup

Serves 6

1   *large onion, chopped*

1   *tablespoon olive oil*

5   *cups defatted stock*

8   *ounces mushrooms, sliced*

1   *carrot, diced*

½   *cup dried lentils*

1   *teaspoon dried rosemary*

1   *bay leaf*

In a 3-quart saucepan over medium heat, sauté the onions in the oil until lightly browned, about 12 to 15 minutes.

Add the stock, mushrooms, carrots, lentils, rosemary and bay leaf. Bring to a boil. Reduce the heat, cover loosely and let simmer until the lentils are tender, about 30 minutes.

Remove and discard the bay leaf.

Per serving: 130 calories, 3.6 g. fat (25% calories), 3.1 g. dietary fiber, 0 m.g cholesterol, 75 mg. sodium.

Linguine with Clam Sauce

Serves 4

2   medium onions, diced

2   cloves garlic, minced

1   tablespoon olive oil

2   cans (8 ounces each) minced clams

½   cup apple cider or nonalcoholic white wine

3   tablespoons lemon juice

½   teaspoon ground black pepper

¼   cup chopped pimentos

8   ounces linguine

¼   cup chopped fresh parsley

¼   cup chopped fresh basil

In a large no-stick frying pan over medium heat, sauté the onions and garlic in the oil for 3 minutes, or until softened.

Drain the clams, saving the liquid. Set the clams aside. Add the liquid to the frying pan. Add the cider or wine. Bring to a boil and cook until the total volume is reduced by half, about 15 minutes. Stir in the lemon juice, pepper and clams.

Cover the pan, reduce the heat to medium-low and simmer for 5 minutes. Stir in the pimentos.

Meanwhile, cook the linguine in a large pot of boiling water for about 8 minutes, or until just tender. Drain. Return the linguine to the pot. Add the clam mixture, parsley and basil. Toss to coat. Cover and cook over medium-low heat for 5 minutes.

Per serving: 453 calories, 6.7 g. fat (12% of calories), 0.5 g. dietary fiber, 76 mg. cholesterol, 138 mg. sodium.

Raspberry-Peach Flutes

Serves 4

4   cups fresh or frozen unsweetened sliced peaches

2   cups fresh or frozen unsweetened red raspberries

¼   cup shredded coconut

1   cup nonfat vanilla frozen yogurt

1   cup sparkling apple cider

Fresh mint (optional)

If using frozen peaches and raspberries, thaw them. Heat a small no-stick frying pan over medium heat. Add the coconut. Cook and stir for 3 to 4 minutes, or until just toasted. Remove the coconut from the pan and set aside.

To serve, spoon the peaches and raspberries into champagne or wine glasses. Top each with small scoops of the frozen yogurt. Then pour some of the cider over each serving. Sprinkle with the coconut and garnish with the mint (if using).

Per serving: 123 calories, 1.9 g. fat (13% of calories), 3 g. dietary fiber, 0 mg. cholesterol, 36 mg. sodium.

The Business Dinner

Show Your Boss You Can Take the Heat

Silly you. You invited the boss to dinner and figured you'd get points just for asking. But he accepted. Now you have to come up with a spread that shows him you're charming, sophisticated and able to handle multimillion-dollar accounts.

Well, go fish: This perch preparation is lean but elegant. Because it's simple to make—even when you include a soup, sides of veggies and rice and a dessert—you'll have loads of time for schmoozing with the big guy and freshening his drink. To make conversation, tell him that the omega-3 fatty acids in the perch will help him fend off heart attack and stroke. Instant promotion! Remember to toss a salad and polish your cuff links.

Broccoli-Buttermilk Soup

Serves 4

1   pound broccoli florets
1   cup sliced onions
4   cloves garlic
2   cups buttermilk

Combine the broccoli, onions and garlic in a steamer basket. Steam over boiling water until the broccoli is tender, about 12 minutes.

Transfer the vegetables to a food processor or blender and process until pureed. Stir in the buttermilk.

Per serving: 100 calories, 1.6 g. fat (14% of calories), 3.8 g. dietary fiber, 5 mg. cholesterol, 162 mg. sodium.

Spiced Carrots

Serves 4

1   pound carrots, thinly sliced on the diagonal
3   cloves garlic
2   tablespoons lemon juice
2   teaspoons olive oil
½   teaspoon ground cumin
    Pinch of ground red pepper
2   tablespoons minced fresh parsley

Steam the carrots and garlic for 5 minutes, or until the carrots are just tender. Remove the garlic and set aside. Transfer the carrots to a large no-stick frying pan.

Mash the garlic and place in a cup. Whisk in the lemon juice, oil, cumin and pepper. Pour over the carrots. Toss over medium heat for 2 minutes. Sprinkle with the parsley.

Per serving: 75 calories, 2.6 g. fat (31% of calories), 3.7 g. dietary fiber, 0 mg. cholesterol, 42 mg. sodium.

Perch with Mustard and Thyme

Serves 4

½   cup oat bran
1   pound perch fillets
2   teaspoons olive oil
½   cup defatted chicken stock
1   teaspoon Dijon mustard
½   teaspoon dried thyme

Place the oat bran on a large sheet of wax paper. Dredge both sides of each fillet in the oat bran to coat.

Heat the oil in a no-stick frying pan. Add the fillets and sauté until cooked through, about 3½ minutes on each side.

Carefully remove the fish to a heated platter. Pour the stock into the frying pan. Whisk in the mustard and thyme. Bring to a boil and cook until reduced by half. Pour over the fish.

Per serving: 158 calories, 4.4 g. fat (25% of calories), 1.6 g. dietary fiber, 101 mg. cholesterol, 102 mg. sodium.

Basmati Tomato and Ginger Rice

Serves 8

1	large tomato, coarsely chopped
1	tablespoon canola oil
½	cup chopped onions
2	cloves garlic, minced
2	teaspoons coriander seeds
1¼	cups basmati or other long-grain aromatic white rice
1	teaspoon powdered ginger
⅛	teaspoon red-pepper flakes

In a food processor, puree the tomatoes. Pour into a 4-cup glass measure. Add enough water to bring the level up to 2½ cups; set aside.

In a 2-quart saucepan over medium heat, warm the oil. Add the onions, garlic and coriander seeds; cook, stirring frequently, for 2 to 3 minutes, or until the onions are tender. Stir in the rice to coat with the oil.

Add the tomatoes and water, ginger and pepper flakes; bring to a boil. Reduce the heat to low. Cover and simmer for 30 to 35 minutes, or until the rice is tender and the liquid has been absorbed.

Remove from the heat and let stand, covered, for 10 minutes. Fluff with a fork.

Per serving: 131 calories, 2.1 g. fat (14% of calories), 0.6 g. dietary fiber, 0 mg. cholesterol, 4 mg. sodium.

Baked Apples Stuffed with Currants

Makes 4 servings

4	small Granny Smith apples, cored
¼	cup dried currants
1	tablespoon coconut
1	tablespoon toasted chopped walnuts
½	teaspoon ground cinnamon
2	teaspoons honey

Place each apple in a custard cup, then place the cups in an 8″ × 8″ baking pan.

In a small bowl, combine the currants, coconut, walnuts and cinnamon. Stir in the honey until well-combined. Spoon evenly into the center of each apple.

Cover the pan with foil and bake at 350° for 20 to 25 minutes, or until the apples are just tender when pierced with a fork. Let cool for 10 minutes before serving.

Per serving: 114 calories, 2 g. fat (14% of calories), 3.2 g. dietary fiber, 0 mg. cholesterol, 2 mg. sodium.

Fast Fixin's

Delicious Meals When You're Tight for Time

Here are two recipes just the way you like them: low-fat and fast. The sloppy joes call for low-sodium tomato products. It's a good idea to watch your salt intake, since sodium prompts your body to retain water, which shows up as unwanted pounds. And who wants to be dragged down when you're in a hurry?

■

Turkey Sloppy Joes

Serves 4

- 1   pound ground turkey
- 1   small onion, thinly sliced and separated into rings
- ½   cup chopped green peppers
- ½   cup reduced-calorie and reduced-sodium ketchup
- ¼   cup salt-free tomato sauce
- 1½ teaspoons chili powder
- ½   teaspoon garlic powder
- ¼   teaspoon celery seeds
- 4   whole-wheat hamburger buns, split and toasted

In a large no-stick frying pan, cook the turkey, onions and peppers over medium heat for about 5 minutes, or until the turkey is no longer pink and the vegetables are tender.

Stir in the ketchup, tomato sauce, chili powder, garlic powder and celery seeds. Bring to a boil, then reduce the heat to low. Cover and simmer for 15 minutes.

To serve, spoon about ½ cup of the mixture on the bottom half of each bun, then replace the tops.

Chef's Note: If you have any leftover meat mixture, cover and refrigerate it for up to 2 days. Before serving, bring the mixture to a boil.

Per serving: 286 calories, 4.3 g. fat (14% of calories), 2.9 g. dietary fiber, 66 mg. cholesterol, 555 mg. sodium.

■

Chicken Curry in a Hurry

Serves 4

- ½   cup nonfat plain yogurt
- ½   cup nonfat mayonnaise
- 3   tablespoons finely chopped onions
- 1   teaspoon ground ginger
- 1   teaspoon curry powder
- 1   pound skinless, boneless chicken breasts, cut into ½"-wide strips
- 1   teaspoon paprika
- ½   teaspoon ground black pepper
- 2   cups hot cooked brown rice

In a small bowl, stir together the yogurt, mayonnaise, onions, ginger and curry powder. Set the mixture aside.

Place the chicken in a medium bowl. Combine the paprika and pepper and sprinkle over the chicken. Toss until coated.

Spray an unheated, large no-stick frying pan with no-stick spray. Heat the pan over medium-high heat. Add the chicken. Cook and stir for 3 to 4 minutes, or until the chicken is no longer pink.

Stir in the yogurt mixture. Cook and stir for 2 minutes. Serve over the rice.

Per serving: 281 calories, 2.5 g. fat (8% of calories), 2 g. dietary fiber, 66 mg. cholesterol, 481 mg. sodium.

Family Food

Cooking for Fun and Moppets

Some foods just have that kid cachet. Popcorn, and fajitas, for instance. But traditional renditions of these fun foods invariably set off the lard alarms. Here are two approaches that are so tasty the kids will never suspect they're eating low-fat. Your cooking will be so popular that the neighbors' kids will be begging to stay for dinner. And truth be known, you're going to enjoy this chow as much as the rug rats.

Now, say this five times: Peter Piper prepares pesto popcorn.

Sizzling Fajitas

Serves 6

 1 *pound top round, trimmed of all visible fat*

 ½ *cup lime juice*

 2 *tablespoons minced fresh coriander*

 2 *teaspoons olive oil*

 1 *clove garlic, minced*

 ¾ *teaspoon ground cumin*

 ¼ *teaspoon dried oregano*

 ¼ *teaspoon black pepper*

 1 *cup thinly sliced onions*

 3 *chili peppers, cut into thin strips*

 1 *cup diced tomatoes*

 6 *flour tortillas, warmed*

Freeze the beef until firm enough to slice easily, about 30 minutes. Cutting across the grain, slice the meat diagonally into ¼″ pieces.

In a large bowl, combine

¼ cup of the lime juice, coriander, oil, garlic, cumin, oregano and black pepper. Add the beef. Cover, refrigerate and allow to marinate for 2 hours, stirring occasionally.

Coat a broiler rack with no-stick spray. With tongs, remove the beef from the marinade (reserve the marinade) and arrange in a single layer on the rack. Broil about 5 inches from the heat for 4 minutes. Turn and broil another 4 minutes, or until lightly browned.

In a large no-stick frying pan over medium-high heat, combine the reserved marinade, onions and chili peppers. Simmer and cook for 3 to 4 minutes.

Add the tomatoes and the remaining ¼ cup lime juice. Cook, stirring occasionally, for 3 minutes, or until just heated. Add the beef and toss to combine.

Divide the mixture among the tortillas. Roll to enclose the filling.

Per serving: 282 calories, 7.3 g. fat (23% of calories), 1.6 g. dietary fiber, 68 mg. cholesterol, 38 mg. sodium.

Pesto Popcorn

Makes 8 cups

 1 *clove garlic, minced*

 1 *teaspoon olive oil*

 ½ *teaspoon dried basil*

 ½ *teaspoon dried parsley*

 8 *cups popped corn*

 1 *tablespoon grated Parmesan cheese*

In a 4-quart saucepan, cook the garlic in the oil for 1 minute (don't brown). Stir in the basil and parsley. Add the popcorn and mix well. Sprinkle with the Parmesan and mix well.

Per cup: 34 calories, 0.8 g. fat (21% of calories), 0.4 g. dietary fiber, <1 mg. cholesterol, 15 mg. sodium.

Part Three

Exercise

Fat-Melting Theory

How to Banish Your Blubber

By the time most of us have reached middle age, we find that paunch has replaced our punch. That a beer belly now conceals our "six-pack" of chiseled stomach muscles. That our once-proud pecs, buried under layers of fat and hidden behind baggy "athletic-cut" shirts, have become shadows of their former sinewy selves.

The ticket to fitness, experts say, is exercise. It's the one proven way to get trim and stay that way without resorting to liquid meals or the latest in fad diets.

Exercise Your Options

We often say that exercise melts fat, as if fat were cool butter and exercise a warm frying pan. But that analogy isn't quite accurate. What really happens is even better.

"When you exercise, fat is metabolized in the muscles as energy," explains L. Jerome Brandon, Ph.D., associate professor of kinesiology in the Department of Kinesiology and Health at Georgia State University in Atlanta. "There's no such thing as melting fat. You're burning fat as energy."

Yet fat doesn't go willingly into the fire. Like us, it fights for a sedentary life—which is why the pounds we accumulate are so hard to get rid of. To burn just one pound of fat, for example, "you're going to need to burn 3,500 calories," Dr. Brandon says.

You'd have to walk 30 miles in order to burn that much energy. "That's a lot of calories," says Dr. Brandon.

Although sustained exercise is a highly efficient way to drop the pounds, more moderate approaches also work. Consider, for example, that hypothetical 30-mile walk. You could do it all at once. Or you could spread it out, walking a mile a day for 30 days. This will ultimately burn the same pound of blubber as a more concentrated approach—assuming, of course, you're not porking out on spareribs and pecan pie in the meantime.

Done consistently, exercise will help keep fat off for the long haul, says Wayne C. Miller, Ph.D., assistant professor of kinesiology at Indiana University in Bloomington and director of the university's weight-loss clinic.

"I think the critical role for exercise is in weight maintenance," Dr. Miller says. "Almost anything can help you lose weight, even a quack diet. People who continue exercising are the ones who maintain their weight loss."

High-Intensity Workouts: Foibles to Fleshiness

By far the best exercise for burning blubber, experts say, is aerobic exercise. *Aerobic* means with oxygen, and aerobic activities are those that raise your heart and breathing rates for an extended time.

"All exercise is good, but you need to elevate your pulse to 70 or 80 percent of its resting rate to burn fat effectively. Aerobic exercise does this," says Art Mollen, D.O., director of the Southwest Health Institute in Phoenix and author of *Run for Your Life* and *The Mollen Method*.

In addition to burning more fat, strenuous aerobic exercise keeps weight off by boosting metabolism—upping your RPMs, as it were. When your motor idles faster you burn more fuel, even when you're not driving.

To begin combating corpulence with exercise, here's what experts recommend.

Do it 'til you're breathing hard. As we've seen, aerobics is a total-body fat burner that supercharges your metabolism and ignites calories faster than normal for up to two hours after exercising.

Some of the best aerobic activities are running, swimming and cycling. To be most effective, these and other aerobic workouts are most effective when done for a minimum of 30 minutes, three times a week.

Make a long-term investment. Unless your goal is to lose weight once and then never eat again—a strategy that weight-loss experts don't recommend—fighting fat is an enduring commitment.

In order to succeed, you have to view exercise realistically and plan your regimen accordingly. If you hate the loneliness of running, for example, don't jog. Join an aerobic dance class instead, or take up squash or tennis with a friend.

Score with realistic goals. Losing weight takes long-term commitment. Trying to do it all at once will only make you frustrated and fat. Instead, define a big goal, then achieve it by reaching smaller ones.

If in the big picture you want to lose 50 pounds, shoot first for more modest goals, like losing a pound or two a week. Every day, take it a little bit further and don't backslide. You'll lose weight a lot more efficiently—and ultimately, faster—than by jumping on a crash plan that's sure to fail.

Hang in for three. You wouldn't expect that big promotion overnight, would you? So why expect more when it comes to kicking corpulence? "I find the break-off point for exercise for most people is about three months," Dr. Miller says. "If you can hang in there past the third month, you've probably established some behavior that might carry on, so give yourself at least three months."

Mentally Fit

Exercise is only as good as you make it. Focusing on two power-workouts a week is a hell of a lot better than slipshodding your way through four sloppy ones. Taking the test below will help you decide if you have true staying power or if you have the tendency—let's be blunt about this—to wimp out.

Whatever your score, be ever-vigilant about wasting time and making excuses, and always stay focused on the goal.

Circle your answer below, using this scoring key.

A Extremely uncharacteristic of me
B Somewhat uncharacteristic of me
C Neither characteristic nor uncharacteristic of me
D Somewhat characteristic of me
E Extremely characteristic of me

A	B	C	D	E	
5	4	3	2	1	1. I get discouraged easily.
5	4	3	2	1	2. I work no harder than I have to.
1	2	3	4	5	3. I seldom if ever let myself down.
5	4	3	2	1	4. I'm not the goal-setting type.
1	2	3	4	5	5. I'm good at keeping promises, especially to myself.
5	4	3	2	1	6. I don't impose much structure on my activities.
1	2	3	4	5	7. I have a very hard-driving, aggressive personality.

To score: Add your answers to get the total. The lower your score, the more likely you are to lose motivation quickly and drop out of an exercise program. If your score is 24 or less, you'd better get a motivation fix—fast.

The Role of Sweat

It Cools, but It Doesn't Reduce Weight

Remember Superman? He could leap tall buildings in a single bound, fly faster than a speeding bullet and flex muscles more powerful than a locomotive—all with no sweat.

We're serious. Did you ever see Superman sweat? We never did.

Unlike the Man of Steel (or at least the actors who've portrayed him), you don't have someone standing by with a terry towel to blot you dry between scenes. Whether you're participating in a fast-track aerobics class or walking up five flights of stairs, you've probably been getting a little damp around the collar—as well as under the arms, on your chest and between the shoulder blades.

But don't let sweat dampen your mood. While perspiration may necessitate having a few extra shirts on hand, it's your body's built-in radiator. Sweating keeps you cool when things get hot.

"Plus, the nice thing about sweat is that you know you've worked out hard," adds Michael N. Sawka, Ph.D., chief of the Thermal Physiology and Medicine Division of the U.S. Army Research Institute of Environmental Medicine in Natick, Massachusetts.

The Mechanics of Moisture

Sweat is more than just a little surplus moisture. It's controlled by the hypothalamus, a tiny part of your brain that also governs sleep, food intake and the development of secondary sex characteristics, like chest hair.

Although some parts of your anatomy get wetter than others, just about every square centimeter of skin—a centimeter is an area about the width of a paper clip—contains an average of 100 sweat glands. (Guys with more sweat glands will get wetter than those with less.) Clearly, nature intended you to sweat.

The sweat itself comes from two types of glands. The apocrine sweat glands, which are the largest, are concentrated in the armpits and groin. The second type of sweat glands are the eccrine glands. These cover your entire body except the lips, the nipples and portions of the genitals. Numbering about three million, they produce up to a quart of sweat a day. This fluid is thinner than apocrine sweat and is mainly water, with small amounts of salt, potassium, urea and lactate. Its major role is to assist in thermoregulation—to prevent the body from overheating.

Keeping Cool

When you're active, capillaries close to the skin dilate. As blood flow increases, your skin temperature rises. While your body can dissipate some of this heat through convection and radiation, there's still a tendency to overheat. Sweat picks up the slack, particularly when you are exercising and need to blow off heat in a hurry.

When you sweat, the fluid evaporates from the skin's surface, carrying away excess body heat. But sometimes even heavy sweating won't keep you cool. "As you exercise, about 80 percent of your energy goes into heat," Dr. Sawka explains. In extremely hot situations—for example, running a marathon on a muggy day in July—the body may not be able to dissipate the heat effectively. If you don't give yourself a cool-off period, this can lead to heat exhaustion or even heatstroke, which can kill you.

Fluid Facts

Despite what the $750 million antiperspirant and deodorant lobby tells you, sweat is good. But if you find yourself exuding large amounts of moist machismo, there are a few things you should know.

Don't be fooled by fluids. A lot of men, equating sweat with melted fat, thrill to the sight of perspiration dripping from their tired brows.

Might as well grab a towel. "When you sweat, you lose water weight," explains Georgia State University's Dr. Jerome L. Brandon. In other words, although you might lose as much as five pounds during a workout, you'll gain it all back as soon as you take a few drinks of water.

Don't suit up to sweat out. While wearing a plastic exercise suit will make you sweat more, it will have no effect on your long-term weight. "People who exercise in these sweat suits are foolish," says Dr. Sawka. "The suits put you at risk for heat exhaustion or heatstroke—they're the worst thing you can wear."

Keep the tank filled. To prevent your body from overheating, it's critical to replace the fluids you lose during exercise. If you've sweated out two pounds in water weight after a workout, for example, you should replace it with its fluid equivalent—about 32 ounces of water, Dr. Sawka advises. Weighing yourself before and after exercising will tell you how much fluid you'll need to take in.

Don't bother with commercial sports drinks, he adds. Unless you're into some serious training, like long-distance running, high-impact aerobics or hours of cross-country skiing, plain cold water is all you need.

Watch for warning signs. During times of heavy exertion, it's critical to watch out for heat exhaustion or heatstroke—potentially dangerous conditions that can cause symptoms ranging from headache and dizziness to a weak, rapid heartbeat.

While heat exhaustion can be relieved by resting, cooling off and drinking fluids, heatstroke is a medical emergency. The two conditions can be similar, but with heatstroke, you get extremely hot plus you stop sweating. If this happens, get out of the heat and call the pros immediately. While awaiting treatment, lower your temperature with alcohol rubs or ice packs or by immersing yourself in cold water.

Don't do as the Romans did. Roman rulers thought that salt was vital for health, so they partially paid their soldiers in salt. (It's from this ancient practice that we get the word *salary* and the phrase "worth his salt.") Today, the dangers of getting too much salt—the risk of developing high blood pressure, for example—are well-known. This goes for increasing salt intake during exercise as well. "There's enough salt in the American diet as is," Dr. Sawka says. "People do not need to supplement."

Sweaty Situations

We men are most likely to sweat when it comes to affairs of the heart. According to the makers of Dial deodorant in their 1994 "Big Sweat" telephone poll of 1,000 American adults, emotional factors are the ones most likely to turn our pits into leaky pipes. Here are the top five sweat producers and the percentage of guys who were afflicted.

Public speaking	45 percent
Getting divorced	45 percent
Getting married	44 percent
Interviewing for a job	44 percent
Going on a first date	34 percent

When it comes to relieving this sweat-causing stress, according to the poll, 48 percent of us exercise, 39 percent have sex, and 30 percent drink.

Spot Reducing

Why It Doesn't Work

Niiiinety-seeeeeevvven, niiiinety-eight, ninety-niiiiine, ooonnnnne hundred.

There. One hundred sit-ups. It won't be long before you lose that gut now, right?

Wrong, wild man. What you're attempting is called spot reducing, and you're wasting your time.

"In reality, there's no such thing as spot reducing," says Dr. Art Mollen of the Southwest Health Institute. "You can do 300 sit-ups a day, and it won't give you a washboard stomach. You'll probably have a stronger stomach, but it won't necessarily look it."

Hitting the Trouble Spots

Spot reduction sounds good in theory: You work extra hard on specific body parts to cut fat in those areas pronto. For example, a guy might try squats to reduce his caboose or labor over leg lifts to slash heavy thighs.

But while it's possible to build muscle at these and other target sites, fat burning just isn't that precise.

In one study, for example, researchers measured the forearms of 20 tennis players who were on the courts at least six hours a week. They found that while the players' racket arms were more muscularly developed than the "inactive" arms, they didn't contain significantly smaller amounts of fat.

"Fat is a metabolic fuel the body uses to produce energy," explains Dr. L. Jerome Brandon of Georgia State University. But the fuel tank, as it were, isn't located in one place. Instead, it consists of millions of individual

fat cells spread throughout your body. So even when you're killing yourself with crunches, your body is drawing fuel from those myriad cells in more or less equal amounts. That's why spot reducing doesn't work.

Yet most guys do want to banish belly fat—or at least firm up what they already have. Here are some tips that, when combined with a good overall fat-fighting regimen, should get your middle under control.

Go for the gut. Although exercises that target the midsection won't necessarily take the fat off, they can help you get stronger and stand straighter, says Indiana University's Dr. Wayne C. Miller. "In that vein, you'll look fitter, like you've lost maybe five or ten pounds," he says.

Try bunches of crunches. Stomach crunches and sit-ups, where you lie on your back, knees bent, and slowly curl your upper torso until your shoulders leave the floor, are great for toughening the midriff and building a strong muscle base. "If you work on the abdominal muscles enough, you can reduce some of the hanging and sagging," Dr. Brandon says. "Your stomach doesn't have to hang out. You can firm it up."

Try doing three sets of 10 to 15 crunches per set. To give your muscles time to recover, be sure to allow a day of rest between workouts.

Of course, when you finally do lose the spare tire, you'll have a rippling set of abs just waiting to be admired.

Get the bends. Doing side-bends is another great way to firm up the abs. Start by holding a lightweight dumbbell, say 20 pounds,  in each hand. Then slowly bend sideways at the waist, first to the left, then to the right. Do three sets of ten. As your muscles strengthen, gradually increase the weight and/or the repetitions. To maximize toning (as opposed to adding muscle bulk), it's best to stick with light-to-medium weights and go for the maximum reps.

How Much Exercise?

If you're like most men, you've occasionally cast a covetous eye on some forbiddingly rich, triple-decked dessert and asked yourself "How far would I have to run to work off that one piece of cake?"

Wonder no more. Thanks to Bob Abelson, Ph.D., a health and fitness instructor certified by the American College of Sports Medicine, you can now see for yourself exactly how much exercise you'll need to burn off the calories in 16 common foods and drinks.

The chart is based on a 150-pound person, so actual calories burned may vary depending on your weight.

Food	Minutes of Exercise			
	Running (7.5 mph)	Aerobic Dance	Walking (3 mph)	Cycling (9 mph)
Breakfast				
Bacon (2 strips)	6	13	22	13
Egg muffin sandwich	22	44	77	46
Oatmeal (⅔ cup)	7	13	23	14
Lunch				
Cheeseburger (¼ lb.)	39	78	136	82
Cheese pizza (5 oz., 1 slice)	11	22	38	46
Hot dog on roll	22	44	77	23
Dinner				
Beefsteak (3 oz.)	25	50	87	73
Beef burrito	35	71	123	52
Macaroni and cheese (1 cup)	33	65	113	68
Beverages				
Beer (12 oz.)	11	23	39	24
Martini (dry, 2.5 oz.)	11	21	37	22
Soda (12 oz.)	11	22	38	23
Snacks				
Chocolate cake (2-oz. slice)	19	38	66	39
Doughnut (filled, 2.5 oz.)	21	41	71	43
Potato chips (1 oz.)	11	23	39	24
Pretzels (1 oz.)	8	17	29	17

Walking

The Peripatetic Payoff

Steven M. Newman is a true globe-trotter. A former newspaperman from Ripley, Ohio, he set out in 1983 on a journey that spanned 20 countries and five continents. Newman, now in his forties, walked around the world alone, setting a Guinness record and logging more than 22,000 foot-punishing miles.

But roaming did more than just secure the itinerant's name in history. Newman has discovered what many experts have been preaching: Walking is an easy, inexpensive and enjoyable way to battle the bulge.

A Small Step for Man, a Big Step for Fitness

If you think all this talk about fitness is just perambulating poppycock, then think again. Researchers have long been extolling—and proving—the virtues of walking.

"We used to believe that you had to walk briskly before you would gain any health benefits," says John Duncan, Ph.D., exercise physiologist at the Cooper Institute for Aerobics Research in Dallas. "But we now know that metabolic changes occur at very moderate exercise intensities and that those metabolic changes confer health benefits."

Health and fitness instructor Dr. Bob Abelson can vouch for that. A geophysicist who started out at a staggering 400 pounds, Abelson devoted his life to walking after it helped him lose more than 200 pounds, most of which he has kept off

since 1983. Like Newman, he's a true believer. "You'll have better endurance, sleep better at night, and you'll probably perform better in bed and have better overall personal health," he says.

On the Right Path

Once you decide it's time to put on your walking shoes, you'll want to make the most of the first—and future—steps. Here's what experts recommend.

Pick proper tools. Shoes can be your best friend—or your worst enemy. An ill-fitting pair of shoes can spell blister-city, while good sneakers or walking shoes can make you feel like you're striding on air. All-purpose athletic shoes will do in a pinch, but you'd be better off considering a good walking shoe, says Dr. Duncan. They have firmer heels that are beveled, which help keep your foot stable. They also have good arches for support and sturdy lacing to keep your foot from sliding forward and back.

Ban the rays. Unless you're doing all your walking at night, you're going to want sun protection. Wearing a cap and shades and sunscreen will help keep your skin from looking like a football when you're 70. If you avoid the sun altogether by walking at night, wear reflective clothing and carry a flashlight, suggests Dr. Abelson.

Time your trek. Walking is fun, sure, but you'll want to know it's working. To stay motivated, experts say, try keeping track of your progress. Many beginners start out walking a mile or two at a time and then work up from there. When one day you discover that you've gone five miles without struggle, congratulate yourself—and set your sights on the next goal. An easier strategy is just to wear a watch. For example, start walking for 20 minutes at a time. When that gets easy, gradually increase your workouts by 15-minute increments. Whenever the distance (or time) you're walking gets easy, bump to the next level, says Dr. Duncan.

And remember, the total number of miles walked is more important for fat burning than the distance walked during any one stretch, Dr. Abelson adds. Don't let the goal to walk farther each time overshadow the goal to walk regularly.

Set a schedule. If you always walk on the same days and at the same times—say, Monday, Wednesday and Friday from 6:00 to 6:45 P.M. and Saturday from 8:00 to 9:00 A.M.—you'll be less likely to think of it as an expendable activity, says Dr. Duncan. Otherwise, you may find yourself canceling walks due to more pressing concerns—like watching *Star Trek* reruns.

Take your time. While some guys do everything at a competitive pace, when it comes to walking, slow and steady is what burns pounds.

In one study, researchers asked three groups of people to walk three miles a day, five days a week. Those in one group walked at a heart-pumping 12-minute-per-mile pace. Those in the second group walked a 15-minute mile, while those in the third group ambled along at 20 minutes per mile.

"We were as surprised as anyone to find that it was the slowest group that lost the most body fat," says Dr. Duncan. "And they lost the most despite the fact that the 12-minute-per-mile walkers burned 53 percent more calories!"

Save it for lunch. Studies have shown that brief bouts of exercise can help give your appetite a time-out. So rather than filling up on bratwurst during your lunch break, first take a 15-minute walk. When you come back you'll feel more energized but probably less hungry

---

Track Facts

Here are some facts and findings to ponder the next time you're on the road.

- There must be something about walking that gets the brain stirred up. Great thinkers who loved to walk include Hippocrates, Aristotle, Bertrand Russell, Harry Truman, Charles Dickens and Walt Whitman.

- If you can't walk fast, walking longer has the same effect. If you weigh 150 pounds, for example, and cover 1 mile at 4 miles per hour, you'll burn about 110 calories. You can burn the same amount by walking 1.1 miles at 3 miles per hour.

- If you walked 45 minutes a day, four times a week for one year, you'd burn about 18 pounds. And that doesn't include weight you'd also lose through sensible eating.

---

than when you started, says Dr. Duncan.

Get an earful. A lot of walkers say that wearing a Walkman makes the time pass pleasantly. You can groove to your favorite tunes or catch up on the latest books on tape. Or just enjoy the silence. "Walking is a great time to work out a lot of your mental chores," Newman says. If you do play tunes, just be sure to keep the volume low, so you can hear traffic or passing cyclists coming from behind you.

Take a hike. Who says that walking has to be on flat ground? If you want a bigger challenge, turn your walking into hiking by heading for the nearest hills. "I guarantee you'll lose pounds real fast," Newman says.

Expand your horizons. "Take the time to stop while you're walking to talk to other people," Newman says. "If you take an interest in the people around, you won't be like the runners and joggers who pass right on by."

Or to get the maximum cardiovascular benefit, Dr. Duncan suggests you walk with people at a slow enough pace to carry on a conversation. This way, you don't have to stop to socialize.

Aerobics

Fast Steps to Fitness

When it comes to aerobics, getting a man to shake and shimmy to fast-paced dance riffs is a bit like asking a fish to fly. That's why Joan Price, a fitness instructor and owner of Unconventional Moves, a fitness consulting service in Sebastopol, California, has to be something of a psychologist as well.

It's not that the average man objects to getting a great workout while being surrounded by sweaty women wearing nothing but form-fitting spandex and determined looks. It's the rhythm thing. It's about stepping right-left-right when you're supposed to be stepping left-right-left. It's about exercising to a beat when you can barely identify one. Most of all, it's about doing all of the above in front of a roomful of people. Call it embarrassment. Call it shyness. Call it— let's be honest about this—performance anxiety.

"The truth is, nobody's born being able to do aerobics—everybody's got to learn it," says Price, author of *The Honest Truth about Losing Weight and Keeping It Off.* "And when the women in my classes see a man attending, they love it. They pray he stays."

Heavy Breathing, Tough Workouts

Experts agree that aerobic exercise is the number-one best strategy for dropping fat. Note that's *aerobic* without the "s." *Aerobic* simply means with oxygen. The term is used to describe exercises that strengthen the cardiovascular and respiratory systems. They're done at a moderate intensity, which allows the muscles to use oxygen efficiently.

One of the better-known aerobic exercises is aerobics—the fast-paced exercise we associate with small outfits and loud music. While women have been crowding aerobics rooms for years, men have been more likely to stay behind in the weight room—sneaking furtive looks, sure, but not joining in.

Their loss. Aerobics is among the best ways to burn calories and shed pounds, says Morris B. Mellion, M.D., clinical associate professor of family practice and orthopedic surgery at the University of Nebraska Medical Center in Omaha. "One of the wonderful benefits of becoming fit is our increased ability to convert fat into an easily used energy source," he says.

You don't have to be a six-times-a-week maniac to benefit from aerobics. Attending a 30- to 60-minute class three times a week will go a long way toward reducing weight and keeping you fit, inside and out. To get started, here's what experts recommend.

Shop around. There are a lot of different styles, and which aerobics class you ultimately choose is entirely a matter of personal choice. Some guys enjoy the hard-driving intensity of high-impact aerobics, while others prefer low-impact step-and-slide classes. There is even "funk" aerobics, which more closely resembles hip-hop dance than exercise.

Get outfitted. The instructor might look nice wearing a leotard, but you won't. So make comfort the name of the game. First-

timers generally wear sweatpants or shorts. Since they stretch when you do, they'll help keep you comfortable without blocking mobility.

Don't be intimidated. It's always tough to be the new kid on the block. Don't sweat it, Price says. "Nobody has time to look at you. All the others in class are looking at themselves or the instructor."

Start from the ground up.

Remember how easy riding a bicycle looked until you actually mounted your first two-wheeled monster? It took time, but you eventually mastered pedal power. It's the same with aerobics. Start simple—say, by moving just your legs. Don't even try to keep up with the various arm movements until you've mastered the footwork.

"The legs are the large muscles, so that's where most of the calorie-burning is going to happen anyway," Price adds.

Get up in arms.

Eventually, you'll have the basics down and be ready to move on to more advanced routines—like moving your arms. Here's a key piece of insight: While in most sports the arm-leg action is synchronized (when you take a free-throw, for example, you shoot with your right hand while stepping forward on your right foot), in aerobics it's reversed. "Aerobic dance uses opposite arm–opposite leg motions. This is what throws guys off," Price says.

Don't overdo it.

While experts agree that any aerobic activity, including aerobics, should be done for about 30 minutes at a shot, don't go at it too hard. Take a break before you get to the point where you're feeling dizzy, flushed or gasping for breath.

Pick a mentor.

There are more aerobics instructors out there than out-of-work actors. Once you find an instructor you like and are comfortable with, stick with that person, Price says. "Even though the instructor may change her choreography, there are certain basic moves and cue words this person is going to use, and you'll already be used to them."

Buddy up with your better half.

A lot more people start aerobics classes than fin-

Choosing Your Program

So you've decided to see for yourself what aerobics can do for you. Here's a list of some of the more popular programs.

High-impact. Lots of leaping and bounding with both feet off the floor at the same time. Considered advanced.

Low-impact. At least one foot is in contact with the floor during roughly half the routine. Sometimes taught in a particular style, such as jazz or country-western. Considered manageable for first-timers.

Aerobic boxing. A relatively new style for Joltin' Joe wanna-bes. Incorporates boxing-type moves, including punching, into an aerobic routine. Look for kick-boxing spin-offs that look more like Bruce Lee's workout than Jane Fonda's. Considered middle-of-the-road to advanced.

Step aerobics. This involves stepping on and off a plastic step. The step ranges from six to ten inches high, depending on your fitness level. Considered low-impact but high-intensity.

Slide. Also called lateral training. Uses a plastic slide up to six feet long that you "skate" back and forth on. High-intensity and a great leg workout, but it takes some coordination and stamina.

Jumping. Uses trampolines or mini-tramps. Lots of bouncing and difficult choreography. Not suggested for the faint-hearted or coordination-impaired.

---

ish them. To keep yourself energized, try signing up for classes with a friend, spouse or lover. This way, you'll always have someone to talk to. You'll improve your relationship. You'll also have extra motivation on those days when you'd rather be schlepping than stepping. It's tough to bug out on class when your partner's beeping the horn.

Weight Lifting

How to Pump Up and Still Trim Down

There's something refreshing about heavy metal. Not the music, even though that may be to your liking, too. We're talking lifting heavy metal.

When you're hot, it's as if you can hear Arnold Schwarzenegger shouting encouragement in your ear as you pump out your last press: "C'mahn, you slug! You cahn do eet. Whan moor. Whan moor!"

As any lifter can tell you, doing a few good sets—with or without visions of Arnold lapping at your brain—leaves you pumped, primed and ready for anything. And it's a great way to burn fat.

Lift It to Lose It

There's no question that aerobic workouts are a great way to burn flab. But they're not the only way.

"Resistance training builds muscle much more quickly than aerobic activity, which mainly improves the cardiovascular system," says Dr. Morris B. Mellion of the University of Nebraska Medical Center. "And muscles are a major source of metabolic activity. More muscle mass means more metabolic activity."

Put another way, the more muscle you have, the more efficient your body is at burning fat.

There can also be more intangible, but infinitely more satisfying, benefits. Like having beefier biceps. A bigger chest. Stronger thighs. In other words,

self-confidence and satisfaction—and with it the desire to keep coming back for more.

Weighty Beginnings

You don't have to be a star athlete to find your way around a weight room. You don't even have to talk with a heavy Austrian accent. But there are some strategies that can make your entry a little bit easier.

Pick your place. These days, it's possible to set up a tidy home gym in the garage or spare bedroom without spending more than a few hundred bucks for some free weights and perhaps a bench. It's convenient, parking is easy, and you don't have to wait for some monster with 32-inch arms to step aside and let you work in.

On the other hand, you probably don't have amenities such as a whirlpool or snack bar in the basement. It can be lonely and boring to work out alone. Plus, you don't have more experienced people milling around to answer your questions, give you a spot or just hang out with.

Choose your tool. There has been much debate about which type of lifting gives the better workout—the barbell-style free weights or the machines popularized in upscale clubs.

In fact, both can provide an excellent workout. Bodybuilders typically prefer the free weights because they can confer bigger improvements at a faster rate. The machines, however, are safer to use and easier to set up.

Plus, you can work out on your own without depending on a partner to spot for you. Try both to see which you're more comfortable with.

Get Fit Fast

Although lifting is good for cardiovascular fitness, stress relief and weight loss, what good are they if you don't also look better in a T-shirt and jeans? To get the most gain from your strain, here's what experts recommend.

Don't forget to breathe. When lifting, a lot of guys literally forget to breathe—a trick that can send blood pressure skyrocketing and starve your brain of oxygen. Proper breathing means exhaling when you push, thrust or lift. Then inhale when you release.

Set reasonable goals. Unless you're moving to Muscle Beach or trying for a role in the next Stallone flick, a standard lifting regimen is ten repetitions of each exercise—curls, bench presses, whatever. The goal is always to keep your muscles challenged but not overly stressed. Not only will you get stronger, you'll also have the muscle definition to prove it.

Start light. Men are competitive, which is why the most common sight in any gym is the weight room warrior—the guy who piles so much weight on the bar that he's woofing like a walrus and his head looks like it's going to explode.

When it comes to lifting, good form counts more than sheer weight. As a rule of thumb, limit the amount you lift to about 70 percent of your ability. In other words, if you're capable of lifting 100 pounds, put 70 pounds on the bar. You're going to be lifting it more than once, and that last lift will feel a heck of a lot heavier than the first.

Lift less—more often. If your goal is to get stronger rather than add muscle mass, consider lifting light weights at high repetitions. In one preliminary study, Australian researchers got good results by having people lift at only 20 percent of their maximal capacity and doing multiple sets with a high number of repetitions.

Add weight to bulk up. If you're less interested in getting strong than in building a mighty chest or massive thighs, forget the strat-

The Rap of Reps

Before you hit the gym, you gotta know the lingo. Here are the basics.

Rep. Short for repetition, this means one completed exercise.

Set. This refers to a completed number of reps. For example, doing three sets of 8 arm curls means you did 24 curls.

Overload principle. Muscles must be taxed beyond what they are accustomed to in order to achieve strength and endurance gains. If your workout seems too easy, it probably is.

Concentric phase. When you're lifting, your muscles contract—the concentric phase. When doing a bicep curl, for example, the concentric phase is when you lift the dumbell.

Eccentric phase. Also called the negative phase, this is when the muscle lengthens. With the bicep curl, the eccentric phase is when you slowly lower the weight.

egy of high reps, low weights. Go for higher weights and fewer reps.

For example, if you would normally do several sets of ten reps using about 70 percent of your maximum weight, try doing sets of only five reps using 85 percent of your max. Tool around a bit to find what works for you and don't overdo it.

Muscle in on the big guys. Worried about looking like Ichabod Crane at a Mr. Universe competition? Fear not. Most gym rats are nice guys, even the ones who look like Godzilla. In fact, sometimes you'll need help, especially when you want a spotter standing by. Most guys love to give beginners a hand when it comes to the finer points of pumping iron. Just observe commonsense etiquette—like saying "sir" to the big guys.

Martial Arts

A Powerful Tool for Kicking Fat

More than 3.6 million Americans ages seven and older have tried their hands—and feet—in martial arts. While some weekend warriors dream of combat, most participants have little interest in developing fists of fury. Most begin martial arts study to learn self-defense and stay for the meditative aspect and to build confidence.

Regardless of the impulse that initially takes you to the mats, martial arts are a superb strategy for increasing strength, building muscle and burning fat.

"Not everybody likes martial arts, but they really are great training. They can be very aerobic, depending on your style," says Richard Carrera, Ph.D., psychologist at the University of Miami. Aerobic exercise, as we've seen, is the number-one choice among experts for burning off the pounds.

Support the Arts

Martial arts are specialized training techniques and strategies originally used in war—hence the term *martial*. The original purpose of karate, kung fu, judo and other styles of fighting was to make the practitioners more formidable on the field of battle.

While some guys still gravitate to the dojo—the workout area where martial arts are practiced—to get in fighting trim, many others swear by the total-body workout provided by martial arts. An hour on the mats several times a week combines serious aerobics with strength training. You'll gain speed, power and flexibility—which in turn can help prepare

you for other fat-fighting activities such as running or aerobics.

"Particularly for older guys, a lack of flexibility can lead to injuries," says black belt Dan Millman, author of *The Way of the Peaceful Warrior* and founder of Peaceful Warrior Services in San Rafael, California. "There are some wonderful things that come with flexibility, and martial arts definitely are one way to gain them.

"There's a martial art form for anyone and everyone, no matter what level of fitness they're at," adds Millman.

For people who fear martial arts as a muscular macho sport that forces you to break boards and bricks with your head, you should know that there are also soft arts such as Tai Chi Chuan, which emphasizes coordination, relaxation and suppleness, more like dance, Millman says.

Go to the Mats

If you think martial arts would be a kick, here are some tips on getting started.

Find your form. Martial arts are like cars: All will get you where you're going, but they come in a wide variety of makes and models. In martial arts, these differences are called styles.

Two of the best-known styles—Tae Kwon Do and Shotokan karate—are Asian. There are also martial arts that are indigenous to India, France and Brazil.

"Some martial arts don't offer as much aerobic training, while others offer supplementary training, like weight training or meditation,"

Millman says. "In terms of someone wanting to lose weight, you're going to want a more active type of training." Any style of karate will provide a good aerobic burn. So will styles like Tae Kwon Do, kung fu and judo.

Keep in mind, however, that virtually any martial art, done vigorously, will help get your heart rate up and your weight down, Millman adds.

Pick your teacher wisely. "It takes more than skill and a black belt to be a compassionate teacher," says Millman. "As in many fields, quality of instruction varies, but most teachers are sincerely interested in the progress and development of their students."

Before signing up for a program, visit for a few hours. Many instructors encourage newcomers to attend a few classes for free to see if it's right for them. Being in a hurry and choosing the wrong instructor or school could turn you off to what could otherwise be a lifetime avocation.

Go for comfort. A gi (pronounced GEE) is the most common karate uniform: baggy white pants and a jacketlike white top cinched with a belt. Don't buy it yet. "Most beginners start with sweatpants and a T-shirt. Comfort and utility are the most important things," Millman says. That way, if martial arts aren't for you, you don't get stuck with an expensive pair of white pajamas.

Tame the beast within. Guys are raised to be competitive and to win at all costs. While this attitude may work on the basketball or tennis court, it has no place in martial arts training, where unchecked aggression can get you or someone else hurt.

Discover positive control. With martial arts, perhaps more than with any other physical activity, you can develop a strong sense of confidence and physical control. Dr. Carrera studied aggression in male karate students. He found that compared with other men, the martial artists were better able to turn their aggression on or off.

"Karate devalues impulsive violence," he explains. "Because of its emphasis on discipline, a martial art tends to increase one's self-control." And just as martial arts can channel your aggres-sion to resist wily opponents, they can also give you the control to resist everyday enemies—like second helpings or third beers!

Explore your options. Depending on where you live and where the local instructors trained, each martial art can be subdivided into potentially dozens of styles.

"I myself explored a number of different styles of martial arts," Millman says. "In my own view, especially for beginners, it's important to make a point of exploring different styles, so you find one that works best for you."

Fighting Words

Just as life on earth is classified by kingdom, class and species, the broad term *martial arts* can also be subdivided. In this country there are dozens of martial arts styles to choose from. Among the more popular are:

Aikido (aye-KEE-do). This stresses flips, throws and joint locks, yet at the same time is graceful and dancelike. Requires tremendous discipline and concentration.

Judo. More like wrestling, it stresses flips and throws, with some emphasis on low kicks.

Karate. Originating in Japan, karate is known for its hard punches, blocks and no-nonsense kicks. Shotokan karate is considered one of the most rugged and demanding of all the martial arts.

Tae Kwon Do (TIE-KWON-doe). Now an Olympic sport, Tae Kwon Do originated in Korea. Known for airborne, breathtaking kicks, it requires great flexibility to manage the fancy footwork.

Tai Chi Chuan (tie-CHEE-chew-on). This is a very slow and relaxed martial art stressing coordination and grace. It is probably the softest of the martial arts and emphasizes mental concentration instead of physically demanding moves.

Biking

A Speedy Approach to Weight Loss

Men typically shove their beloved bikes aside about the time they learn to drive, at which point they begin questing for new toys, like Range Rovers.

Time to revisit your youth. Not only is the two-wheeler the most popular mode of transportation worldwide, it's a mighty machine in the fight against fat. Consider: An average Tour de France cyclist burns 5,900 calories in a day, compared with the 4,654 calories a pro baseball player burns in a whole season or the 3,136 calories a distance runner burns on a training day.

A study at Tufts University in Medford, Massachusetts, for example, monitored a group of cyclists using stationary bikes. After 12 weeks, the riders lost 19 pounds of fat and gained 3 pounds of lean muscle—all without dieting.

Getting Started

Whether you decide to take to the road or do your riding indoors, here are a few suggestions for getting started.

Get the right wheels. If you're like most guys, you probably are already convinced that the only way to ride is on the latest aerodynamic, carbon fiber multi-tech wonder. But when you're biking to burn fat, all that really matters is riding, no matter what kind of machine you eventually buy.

Dress the part. Although sweats are fine when you're riding a bike with a sealed drive chain in the comfort of your living room, in the real world, baggy pants have a tendency to get stuck in the chain. Opt for cycling shorts instead. Shorts won't get sucked into mov-

ing parts, and they move when you do, which helps prevent chafing, chapping or pinching. You needn't buy skintight Lycra shorts, either. If the thought of wearing those in public terrifies you, looser touring shorts are available that provide similar padding and support (not to mention more pockets).

Ride light. Any interaction between a car and a bicycle—no matter who initiated contact—can have only one outcome. (Hint: You won't be the winner.) Make it a point to always be maximally visible, experts advise. This means wearing bright, reflective clothing and making sure your bike is well-equipped with reflectors.

Of course, riding with a headlight at dusk or after dark is just common sense. In some areas it's also the law.

Don't neglect the headgear. Unless you're trying to make the critical list at the county hospital, always wear a helmet to protect your brain box.

While you're thinking about protection, don cycling gloves as well. They'll protect your hands if you take a spill. Plus, they absorb sweat, dampen vibration and give you a better grip on the handlebars.

Get the connection with footwear. When you're getting ready to ride, forget your favorite sneaks. "Soft, flexible running shoes are the worst things to ride in," says Len Pettyjohn, former director of the Coors Lite professional cycling team. Make the investment in some stiff-soled biking shoes, he advises. These are designed to grip the pedal, giving you more power and helping to prevent your feet from flying off and into the front wheels or pavement.

Smart Riding Techniques

The sun is shining, the car's parked, and you're ready to go. To make the most of your ride—and your new bike—here are a few tips from experts.

Get connected. To get the

most mileage from the same amount of oomph, experts recommend using clip-less pedals. What they do is enable the up stroke on one pedal to deliver power while you're pressing down on the other. The added force can increase your cruising speed by one to two miles per hour, experts say.

Gear down. Beginning riders have a tendency to ride in high gears, which gets tiresome quickly to both legs and lungs. Smart riders stay in lower, easy-to-push gears and keep the pedals revolving quickly. Strive to al-ways keep your pedal speed (the ca-dence) at 80 revolutions per minute or higher (serious bikers often sustain over 100 revolutions per minute). Once you get your pedal speed established, use your gears to maintain that rate as grades or terrain change; if you do it right, your pedals will turn at roughly the same rate. A little slower going up-hill, a little faster on the descents.

Theoretically, it's possible to count, shift and ride. However, an eas-ier solution is to invest in a cyclometer that also measures cadence.

Plan ahead. As the costs of gas, insurance and new cars have shot into the stratosphere, more and more guys have begun biking to work. While this type of "service" (as opposed to recreational) riding doesn't require a great investment of time or money, it does create some special demands.

Clothes, for instance. Your span-dex suit may work on the trail or at the weekend club, but it's not going to im-press your boss. What you need to do is drive to work one day in the car and drop off a week's worth of socks, shirts, pants and so on. Assuming your office also has a shower, you'll also want to bring along soap, deodorant and other toiletries.

A Program for Pedaling

You don't have to brave the elements or traffic to get the benefits of biking. A stationary bike is a superb way to shed fat fast while building lean muscle.

Here's a 20-minute routine that offers all the chal-lenges of real-life riding.

Saddle up. Sit comfortably on the saddle and bend forward. Rest your hands on top of the handlebars and relax your shoulders. This position is the corner-stone for steady, calorie-burning cycling. Adjust the re-sistance so you can pedal smoothly at 90 revolutions per minute. Breathe steadily.

Jump for explosive speed. "Jumps" give you an intense cardiovascular workout and develop balance, co-ordination and leg strength. Lean forward and rise up out of the saddle an inch or two while maintaining speed. Use your leg muscles to elevate yourself. Then sit down and pedal slower. In another three seconds, rise up again and repeat. Don't stop pedaling between jumps; the transition should be smooth. Do 5 to 10 jumps, building up to 30, 60 and eventually 100.

Stand for power. This builds strength in the arms, shoulders, abdominals and calves, and it gives your legs a good stretch. Simulate a hill indoors by switching to maximum resistance. Place both hands shoulder-width apart on the handlebars, stand upright and lean from side to side, using your body weight to push down the pedals. As you step down, pull up on the handlebar on that side of the bike to exercise your arms. Do this for one to two minutes and return to the crouch.

Sit back for endurance. Build leg strength and endurance by putting your large hip and butt muscles to work. This simulates pedaling into a head wind or up a long grade. Start by increasing the resistance slightly, then move back on the saddle so that your rear is hang-ing off a bit. This forces you to push the pedals forward instead of down. Lean forward and keep your head low, and rest your hands shoulder-width apart on the handle-bars. Pedal like this for three to five minutes, then return to the crouch.

Rowing

Fight Fat Sitting Down

As a member of the U.S. rowing team at the 1984 Olympics—and one of the oldest athletes on the team—Bruce Beall knows the importance of staying trim. But even if you're built more like a cargo cruiser than a canoe, rowing makes an outstanding way to throw fat overboard.

"Your initial response to rowing may be that you feel tired, because it takes a lot out of you and your body has to adapt," says Beall, a former rowing coach and fitness trainer now in his early forties. "But after that initial break-in period, then all of a sudden you'll start feeling more alert and seeing better muscle definition. You'll start noticing the difference rowing makes as a fat-fighting exercise."

Row versus Weight

Although rowing has long had a reputation of being a sport for upper-crust collegians, the U.S. Rowing Association estimates that more than 100,000 Americans regularly ply the oars.

Rowing provides more than opportunities for weekend excursions. It's also an efficient fat burner, ranking with cross-country skiing as one of the best aerobic exercises you can do, says rowing expert Fredrick C. Hagerman, Ph.D., biological sciences professor at Ohio University in Athens.

"If you look at the energy cost for any given level of exercise, rowing is probably one of the highest calorie burners you can find," says Dr. Hagerman, a training counselor for several U.S. Olympic rowing teams. Once you get moving, you can burn up to 1,200 calories an hour. "Rowing is easy to perform," he adds. "Heck, you're sitting down."

Here's advice for getting started and doing it right.

Get your feet wet. While some land-locked communities are unable to take up oars, most major cities—Philadelphia, Seattle and Boston, to name a few—boast a number of rowing clubs that are open to the public. You'll probably pay a nominal entry fee to join, plus rental fees when you take a boat on the water.

"Every club's looking for new members—it makes the club more viable," says Beall, executive director of the George Pocock Rowing Foundation in Seattle, an organization that promotes the sport of rowing. "The problem is, rowing has this deceptive elitist image. Even though it has been popularized by all the Ivy League schools, anyone can row."

Get a mentor. While it's not impossible to take up rowing without knowing port from starboard, it's a little more complicated than, say, jogging around the high school track. "Trust me. I'm not sure rowing lends itself well to learning it by reading out of a manual," Beall says. "You're better off learning from an accomplished rower."

Start slowly. If you go out on the water your first day and try to pull a Lewis and Clark—who, you'll recall, canoed through a substantial part of the Northwest—your muscles will feel as though they were hit with the oars instead of pulling them. If you're already in pretty good shape, you should be able to row nonstop for about two minutes, Dr. Hagerman says.

"Then rest for about 30 seconds and do it again," he says. Your goal should eventually be to row nonstop for 20 minutes, doing about 20 strokes per minute.

Don't back out. A lot of rowing newcomers worry that the sport is bad for their backs. Not true, says Dr. Hagerman. "Rowing really works your back, so if you hopped in a boat for the first time and pulled as hard as you could, you might do something to yourself," Beall adds. "But otherwise, it's good exercise."

Staying High and Dry

For those who get queasy even in the bathtub, or who live in areas where water is in short supply, it's still possible to take up oars. The solution, of course, is to use an indoor rowing machine or ergometer—machines that are compact and relatively affordable and that provide hours of fat-torching workouts.

All too often, however, would-be scullers buy machines in the first flush of enthusiasm, then lose interest and use them thereafter as a catch for dirty laundry. To get the right machine and keep your interest high, here's what experts recommend.

Go high-tech. While a number of rowing machines rely on pneumatic pistons to provide resistance—which makes it hard to adjust to various fitness levels—more expensive models deliver their power via a weighted flywheel coupled to a drive chain and fins. When you pull on the "oars," the fins catch air, creating drag much like water does. "If you look at most rowing machines, they put too much resistance on you—they're not ergonomically sound," says Dr. Hagerman.

Watch your form. Since good form is critical, not only to get the most out of your workout but also to prevent injury, it's a good idea to set your machine in front of a mirror, so you can see what you're doing. "Rowing is like anything else you do quickly and repetitively," says Beall. "You can pick up bad habits, and it can take a lifetime to correct the mistakes."

The Right Strokes

Rowing is a lot like running in that technique—good or bad—spells the difference between beginners and experts. Even if you've been a landlubber all your life, you can learn the basics on your rowing machine with just a few quick lessons.

According to Bruce Beall, executive director of the George Pocock Rowing Foundation, here's what you need to do.

Phase 1: the catch. With your upper body leaning slightly forward, move forward on the rower, drawing your knees up to your chest. Your back should be firm, your muscles flexed, your head up and your arms straight. Don't worry, it sounds more complicated than it really is.

Phase 2: the power stroke. With your feet braced on the pedals, push back, exhaling as you go. With your legs fully extended, continue the stroke by leaning backward slightly and drawing your hands to your abdomen. This stroke, which should be fluid and graceful, works muscles in the legs, back and arms.

Phase 3: the recovery. Push forward with your palms and wrists. This movement, which also works muscles in the arms, back and legs, completes the cycle.

Confront the competition. If you think indoor rowing is strictly a solitary activity, think again. Every February, more than 1,000 competitors arrive in Boston for the Crash B Sprint World Indoor Rowing Championship. Just be warned that the world record for the 2,500-meter "course" is 7 minutes, 11 seconds. For many of us, covering the course in double that time would mean a week's worth of physical rehabilitation just to regain use of our arms. For serious rowers, however, it's all in a day's work.

Golf

Take a Swing at Fat

Looking for a way to lose weight, get fresh air and schmooze the boss all at once? Then take to the links. Golf is great exercise. You'll walk about two miles playing the average 9-hole course. An 18-holer will take you four miles. Remember, walking one mile at a normal pace, assuming you weigh 170 pounds, will burn roughly 365 calories. Moreover, the game can be a heck of a lot of fun.

"Golf is an excellent activity to promote health," says Dr. John Duncan of the Cooper Institute for Aerobics Research. "Call it a pleasurable pursuit where you get exercise by accident."

One study found that golfers who played three times a week showed dramatic improvement in their cholesterol levels. The game is also good for business health. In a survey of top executives, 80 percent considered golf an excellent way to make contacts. Gaining clout while losing weight and improving cardiovascular health—what could be better?

The Greens Machine

Although golf has a reputation as a game for businessmen and guys named Biff, the National Golf Foundation estimates that as many as one in ten Americans plays, and upward of two million take their first swings every year.

Can the cart. Some clubs put a lot of pressure on players to use the carts. "Golf cart rentals make money for golf courses," explains Edward Palank, M.D., spokesman for the Professional Golf Association (PGA). Don't give in. Your goal is to get some fresh air and exercise. "Insist on your right to walk," he says.

Keep the caddy in the shack. To maximize the physical burn—and save a few bucks in the bargain—always carry your own clubs. "The benefit to carrying your own clubs is that you'll expend more energy and burn more calories," says Dr. Palank.

Be a night owl. If getting in to play during peak weekend hours is a challenge, try going at night. Many courses are well-lit and open until late. Also, many unlit public courses offer discounted twilight rates: all the golf you can get in from 4:00 P.M. to sunset for a fraction of the full-course rate. So break out of work early and do a fast-paced nine holes.

Foreplay

Perhaps more than any other sport, golf requires a modicum of talent—not to dazzle colleagues, necessarily, but even to progress to the next hole. It's hard to keep your weight-loss plan under par when you're wrapping an iron around the nearest tree. Here's what experts advise to take the kinks out of the links.

Start with a stretch. You might think that a round of golf is about as stressful as raising a Tom Collins. But lack of flexibility is a leading cause of back injury on the PGA Tour, says Lewis A. Yocum, M.D., assistant medical director of the PGA Tour and PGA Senior Tour.

To prevent injuries, get in the habit of loosening up and stretching before you hit the first tee, says Ralph Simpson, physical therapist with the PGA Tour. He recommends stretching your upper body for several minutes, including your arms, shoulders, chest, neck and back. Finish up by stretching your calves, hamstrings and the rest of your lower body. Improving flexibility may not improve your swing, but it'll keep you from throwing something out of whack on the 18th hole.

Perk up with putt-putt. Statistics show that 47 percent of your score in an average golf game comes from putts and half-swings. This means you should spend at least half your time practicing these shots instead of just whacking away at the driving range. Many public courses have putting greens and chipping areas, so you can practice your short game for a modest fee. An hour of quiet practice is good for your soul and your game.

Size matters here, fella. When choosing which club to hit with, be realistic and choose one size lower than what you think you'll need. (The lower the number of the golf club, the farther it hits.)

"Nine times out of ten, people wind up hitting the ball short," says Brad Faxon, the eighth-ranked money winner on the 1992 PGA tour. Choosing a club that hits slightly longer than you think you'll need will help keep your swing smooth.

Practice some posturing. Many golfers bend over too far or stand too erect when swinging. The posture that most pros teach is a comfortable athletic one with knees slightly flexed, feet comfortably apart and arms hanging down freely from the shoulders. Your weight should be on the balls of your feet. Your swing itself should be a slow coiling motion in the backswing, followed by a forward release of energy carried through the ball with full follow-through.

Stay in alignment. The late Harvey Penick, a golf teaching pro who lived into his eighties, wrote a book of golf tips called *Harvey Penick's Little Red Book*. His number-one tip: "Take dead aim." It sounds simple, but most golfers don't pay heed. Getting properly aligned means making sure your feet, knees, hips and shoulders are pointed in the same direction, which is perpendicular to the ball's line of flight. Taking dead aim by keeping everything in line is a near-guaranteed way to improve your technique.

Drive Away Back Pain

Just the thought of taking a mean slice can make some guys wince—and stay at home clutching their backs instead of going outside on the links. To continue golfing without groaning, heed these tips.

Monitor your movements. Every wrong move can potentially contribute to a back crisis. So don't just worry about your swing. Think about all the bending, lifting and carrying you're doing on the course, and do it with your back's health in mind.

Watch that bag. To keep from throwing your back out, watch how you handle your golf bag. Place your bag as close as you can to the front of your car's trunk, so you don't have to reach in to get it out.

Pack light. If you're prone to back pain, try to get by with a minimum number of clubs—say, 6 or 7 clubs instead of the maximum 14.

Use your good side. Most painful backs hurt on one side or the other, so carry your golf bag over the shoulder of your good side. There's no use pushing your back to the edge if it's already protesting.

Stick to flatter ground. Walking and playing downhill stress your back, especially when you're lugging clubs. If you can't find a flat course, stick to level ground whenever you can, even if it means walking a little bit out of your way (which will give you more exercise anyway).

Give it some knees, please. Putt with bent knees and bend at the knees every time you pick up or put down a ball. It'll save your back some straining.

Ice up afterward. Applying ice to a sore back for 15 minutes after a game goes a long way in warding off swelling and reducing pain. It might even help you forget about a bad score, if you're unlucky enough to get one.

Running

Fitness for the Long Run

Humans have been running—for survival, transportation or just the sheer fun of it—ever since they came down from the trees. Even today, while nature's two-footed transit system isn't the fastest or most efficient way of getting around, running is one of the best ways for getting in shape fast.

"It burns fat, keeps your heart healthy and can be done without a lot of preparation or trouble," says Dr. Art Mollen of the Southwest Health Institute.

First Steps

You've probably known hard-core runners so enthusiastic about their sport that you weren't sure whether to join them or call the police. But you don't have to be a maniac (or marathoner—same thing) to burn pounds. You just need to do it.

"Simply running a minimum of ten minutes every day is a very good workout," says Dr. Mollen. "It can increase cardiovascular endurance, muscle strength and muscle tone as well as enhance the overall efficiency of your metabolism, particularly for someone just starting out."

If this is your first time on the track, here are a few things to do before heading out the door.

Know when to stretch. "You don't want to stretch muscles that haven't received an increased level of circulation and increased core temperature," says Budd Coates, a four-time Olympic Marathon Trials qualifier and consultant to *Runner's World* magazine. "The time to stretch is either five to ten minutes into your program or after you're done."

You don't have to spend 20 minutes stretching, either: For each major muscle group, about 30 seconds may be all you need, says Coates.

For the hamstrings, for example, he recommends sitting on the floor cross-legged and unfolding one leg in front of you. Slowly reach down that leg toward your ankle and hold for about 30 seconds. If you can grab onto only your knee, that's okay. Keep doing it, and your flexibility will improve.

Get the right shoes. If you're running regularly, experts say, don't rely on your all-purpose sneaks to protect your feet. Buy some running shoes instead.

Take the soft route. During a run, every time your foot hits pavement it lands with a force equal to three or four times your body weight, says James M. Rippe, M.D., director of the Center for Clinical and Lifestyle Research and associate professor of medicine at Tufts University School of Medicine in Boston. Concrete is hard and unforgiving; so, you'll discover, are injured feet, ankles and knees.

To get the joy of running without the jolts, try limiting your strides to a track, dirt trails or a nearby grassy park. Or at least run on blacktop instead of cement or concrete. It has some give and will absorb shocks better.

Hit the Road

There's something about running that brings out the poetry in people. Rather than focusing on hot feet, chafed thighs or homicidal cab drivers, they rhapsodize about wind in their hair... the echo of falling footsteps... the rush of "runner's high." Sounds great—until you hit the streets and realize there's a real world out there.

To get the joy of running without the mishaps, here's what experts advise.

Face the danger. To avoid becoming roadkill, always run facing oncoming traffic. It makes you more visible to drivers, plus it gives you an extra second or two to dive to safety if you need to. And always wear light-colored reflective clothing, particularly when running after work or at night.

Break in slowly. If you're new to running, don't even run—not at first, says Coates. For about a week, just walk, he advises. Walk about 20 minutes for four days in a row. On days five through eight, increase the time to 30 minutes. But you're still walking.

As your legs (and lungs) start feeling stronger, do about two minutes of running followed by four minutes of walking, says Coates. Again, do this for about a week, 30 minutes each time. After that you may feel comfortable going into a full run—30 minutes without stopping. But don't be discouraged if you continue to walk and run. Every step is burning weight and helping you get into shape. The running will follow.

Check your speed. "One of the biggest mistakes most beginning runners make is they try to run too fast," says Coates. To keep your pace comfortable, use the talk-sing rule, he suggests. Run slow enough that you can talk without gasping for breath, yet fast enough that you can't sing opera.

Warm up to a winter run. If you live just about anywhere north of Florida, you'll face Old Man Winter eventually. Don't let him keep you home. But you will want to prepare for him.

Wear socks made of polypropylene or acrylic. They're better than cotton or wool at keeping your feet warm and dry. And be sure to wear a hat. This will keep your whole body warm, since a significant amount of body heat escapes through the head.

Beat the heat. To prevent yourself from overheating, drink plenty of fluids, even

Take to the High Country

Once you are comfortable with your running regimen and are looking for new challenges, consider heading off-road for some trail running. Trail running—in which you leave the urban jungle and take to meadow, beach or mountain trails—is like hiking in fifth gear: It can add a substantial amount to your usual running effort, giving you a tougher workout in less time.

"People are realizing that the trails are so much fun," says Nancy Hobbs, race coordinator for the Pikes Peak Ascent and Marathon in Manitou Springs, Colorado. "The visual experience is breathtaking, and they don't get injured as much as road runners—as long as they watch their footing."

In trail running, the "course" can change at a moment's notice, so you have to stay alert. Watch out for tree roots, rocks, uneven ground or other surprises. It's also a good idea to bring water, as well as purification tablets if you think you'll need a refill. You can also load a fannypack with a light jacket, sunglasses and sunscreen, plus a sports bar for added energy.

when you're not thirsty. Direct sun can cause your temperature to rise, so wear light clothing instead of going shirtless. If it's particularly hot, soak your shirt in water before setting out. You'll be wearing portable air-conditioning.

Stop slowly. A lot of runners hurl around the track like racehorses—then stop. Studies show a more gradual cooldown can help remove excess lactic acid, a waste product that causes muscle fatigue, from stressed tissues, says David Costill, Ph.D., an exercise physiologist in the human performance lab at Ball State University in Muncie, Indiana. He recommends ending workouts by slowly jogging until your heart rate returns to normal.

Skiing

A Slippery Slope to Slimness

When your goal is fighting fat, strap on skis. Downhill or cross-country, it's an exhilarating strategy for strengthening muscles and burning calories—and having a great time in the bargain.

"Cross-country skiing rates highest in lab tests for burning the most calories per minute because you're using your legs, your upper body and even your torso," says Wayne Westcott, Ph.D., of Quincy, Massachusetts, national strength-training consultant for the YMCA.

You don't need fresh flurries to make skiing part of your fitness plan. With a combination of snow-making technology and indoor ski machines, it's possible to be on the slopes every day of the year.

Down or Across?

If you're just now thinking about taking up skiing (and buying equipment), there's one decision you have to make up front: whether to go downhill or cross-country. Downhill is typically the favored style for speed-meisters and adrenaline junkies—guys who crave quick thrills. Cross-country, on the other hand, is slower and more contemplative. It's for guys who are more into the journey than the destination.

Cross-country scorches up to 660 calories per hour. Downhill is no slouch, either, burning about 570 calories per hour.

The Great Outdoors

Whether you opt for downhill or cross-country, take time beforehand to get prepared. Here's what ski pros advise.

Start with warm-ups. Doing a pre-ski warm-up will prime your body for peak performance and at the same time help prevent injuries. Experts advise doing a few light toe touches, hamstring stretches and shoulder rolls before heading out.

Dress the part. When you're spending all day in the cold and wet, what you wear can determine whether you'll have the time of your life or a miserable experience never to be repeated. Here's what experts recommend.

• Dress warmer than you think is necessary. Try wearing insulated pants over long underwear or spandex tights. Above the waist, start with a zip turtleneck made of a moisture-wicking material such as Capilene or Thermax. Add a fleece pullover if it's below 40°F or a wool sweater if it's below 25°F. Over that you can wear a waterproof and windproof shell or a parka, but a versatile midweight jacket works best. Don't forget a thick hat or hood.

• Wear shades or goggles. Nothing's brighter than sun on snow.

• Don't wear jeans. They may embody the spirit of the West, but once they get wet and freeze, you'll look more like cardboard than a cowboy.

• Go easy on the socks. Some people put on multiple pairs of socks to keep their feet warm. Too much bulk, however, can cut off circulation, prevent sweat evaporation and reduce foot-to-ski sensitivity. One pair of polypropylene socks combined with your boot's insulated lining should be enough.

Indoor Slopes

Unless you happen to live in some frosty northern clime, or are rich enough to jet-set in search of virgin slopes, skiing is something you can do only a few months out of the year. In addition, while some guys thrill to nature's chill, others would just as soon stay indoors.

No problem. With today's technology, it's easy to get the workout without the cold. Here's how.

Hit your stride. To get the fat-burning power of cross-country skiing without leaving the neighborhood, try walking with a pair of Exerstriders. Essentially, these are aluminum ski poles with rubber bumpers on the bottoms. You mimic the moves of cross-country skiing, except you do it on dry land.

Man the machine. Indoor ski machines work all the major muscle groups, plus you can work out year-round.

There are two types of ski machines. The ones popularized by NordicTrack actually look like skis. The user puts his feet through stirrup-like attachments similar to those on cross-country skis and pushes the two long ski-like rails back and forth while the arms, also swinging back and forth, pull on cables straight out in front. On the other kind, the ski-size tracks remain stationary but have planted-in "platforms" for the feet that do the actual sliding. The hands, meanwhile, usually pull on poles at the sides rather than on cables. The first type gives you a greater range of motion but generally requires more coordination.

Look for distractions. Only true exercise diehards can ride a ski machine for any length of time without getting bored. To make your workouts more enjoyable, set up the machine in front of the TV. Or listen to music or books on tape. Once you get the rhythm going, the time passes quickly.

Snow Spots

Ski resorts are a lot of fun. Conviviality, fireplaces and hot tubs all add up to a great time. The crowds, however, can make staying at home seem like a better option.

For excitement without the hoards, try these lesser-known resorts.

The Big Mountain, Montana. It is the biggest ski area in Montana but still draws only a sixth of what Vail does. The funky railroad town of Whitefish offers plenty of nightlife activity. The nearby Glacier National Park does an uncanny Switzerland impression. (P.O. Box 1400, Whitefish, MT 59937)

Park City, Utah. Where the nineteenth century's miners and soldiers went to get away from the tee-totaling Mormons. Rowdy on the streets, mellow on the slopes. (P.O. Box 39, Park City, UT 84060)

Smugglers' Notch, Vermont. A big mountain with diverse terrain—so why doesn't anyone go there? Because this unassuming resort is in the northern part of Vermont instead of the more accessible south. (Route 108, Smugglers' Notch, VT 05464)

Sugarloaf, Maine. The eastern ski area farthest from the Boston and New York megalopolises, Sugarloaf retains its unspoiled Yankee character and raw skiing. Plus, it's the only area in the East boasting lifts to above-timberline turns. (R.R. 1, Box 5000, Carrabassett Valley, ME 04947-9799)

Taos, New Mexico. As isolated as isolated gets, Taos doesn't draw unseemly crowds even though its Indian pueblos and Spanish heritage make it one of the more exciting ski towns in the world. (P.O. Box 90, Taos Ski Valley, NM 87525)

Short-Term Strategies

How to Pound Portliness in a Year or Less

High school. It was awkward, it was an adventure, and it was 20 years and 25 pounds ago. Now it's time for your reunion.

"I've been planning reunions for nine years, and one of the most common things people say is that they have to lose weight," says Sunny McGinnis, president of the National Association of Reunion Managers and owner of Reunion Celebrations in Tampa, Florida. "It all boils down to people wanting to look the way they did."

There's no easy way to make the pounds disappear, to quickly regain the body you had decades earlier. What took you 20 years to put on won't come off overnight. Still, it is possible to shed pounds without waiting years for results.

In one study, researchers monitored 40 obese recruits who were undergoing basic training for the Singapore Armed Forces. After 20 weeks of rigorous training, the recruits who stayed with the program lost an average of 39 pounds. Average body fat plummeted from 34 percent to 24 percent.

But how many of you are willing to go into full-time basic training for the military?

Getting On the Fast Track

"For most people, the biggest problem with losing weight for the short term is that their goal isn't to lose the weight

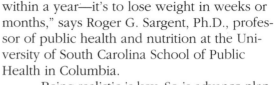

within a year—it's to lose weight in weeks or months," says Roger G. Sargent, Ph.D., professor of public health and nutrition at the University of South Carolina School of Public Health in Columbia.

Being realistic is key. So is advance planning. If you're going to lose weight for your reunion, you'll want to begin before it's two months away. And even before you begin lining up specific weight-loss strategies, here's what experts recommend.

Set a date. Yes, it would be fun to lose weight, buy a new suit and arrive at the reunion in a blue Mercedes—all in the same two weeks. It's not gonna happen.

"A person who weighed 150 pounds in high school and who weighs 225 now is not going to get back to 150 any time soon," says Georgia State University's Dr. L. Jerome Brandon.

The point is not to be discouraged but to plan ahead. "A person may lose somewhere between three and five pounds of fat reasonably and safely in a month's time," Dr. Brandon adds. Use that as a working number. If you hope to shed 20 pounds for the reunion in June, for example, get serious about losing weight sometime in January.

Make goals you can control. It's good to strive for long-range targets—in this case, that you'll lose 20 pounds by June—but don't make promises to yourself you're not sure you can keep. When you're trying to lose weight, nothing energizes like success or brings you down faster than failure.

"My advice is to set goals that you are completely in charge of," says fitness instructor Joan Price of Unconventional Moves in Sebastopol, California. "For example, that you will exercise five times a week as long as you're able is a goal that you're in charge of. That you will lose 20 pounds by your reunion is not, since you can't control how fast you lose weight."

Be a competitor. "Nothing inspires some men more than social conditions, like competition," says Bob Goldman, D.O., Ph.D., president of the National Academy of Sports Medicine and chairman of the Academy of Anti-Aging Medicine in Chicago.

So set goals for yourself. Promise yourself you'll lose at least two pounds by next month. Vow that you won't look like those other weeble-wobbles at the reunion. Or go in cahoots with another friend who's also trying to lose weight—and then do better.

"If the goal is to lose weight by a certain date, looking at it as a type of competition will work for some people," Dr. Goldman says.

Take affirmative action. One way to keep laserlike focus on your goal during a short-term fight against fat is to practice what are called affirmations. An affirmation is a positive statement you memorize and repeat, like a mantra. Doing this imprints your goal into your psyche, making you more likely to achieve your objective.

Make your affirmations short and specific, like "I will lose five pounds in the next two months." Write your goal on paper and post it somewhere you'll see it every day, like on the bathroom mirror. Spend a few minutes each day repeating your goal to yourself. Say it slowly, deliberately and with conviction.

"As you repeat affirmations, try to imagine each one is—or can be—true. Actually see yourself changing," says Dennis T. Jaffe, Ph.D., a consultant at HeartWork in San Francisco and co-author of *Self-Renewal and Rekindling Commitment*.

Look to the prize. You want to look good and impress your friends. You want to fit into your blue serge suit. Maybe you just want

---

Don't Get Creamed

You may have heard about the thigh-fat-reducing creams for women. Now there's a version for men. The idea is that rubbing the cream on your belly will cause fat to melt away. The manufacturer has trumpeted a study in which men who used the product daily lost an average of 2½ inches of waistline in six months.

Fat creams contain aminophylline, a caffeine derivative that manufacturers claim will cause fat cells to burn fat instead of storing it. As it turns out, however, the promise is anything but certain. "There is no scientific evidence that this is a safe or effective method for decreasing fat," says Susan Zelitch Yanovski, M.D., director of the obesity and eating disorders program at the National Institute of Diabetes and Digestive and Kidney Disease in Bethesda, Maryland.

According to the Food and Drug Administration, aminophylline has not been tested or approved as a fat reducer, which is why the fat creams are currently considered cosmetics, not drugs.

In other words, the one sure thing that will be lightened by a fat cream is your wallet. "The only way to trim body fat is to increase physical activity and decrease fat in your diet," Dr. Yanovski says. "You can't buy that in a store."

---

to sit on a bus without crowding the person next to you. All reasonable goals. But to keep yourself motivated throughout the year—and beyond—consider what you'll gain by losing weight.

• Physically fit men are 53 percent less likely to die a premature death than unfit men.

• Fit men are four times less likely to die from cancer than the unfit.

• Fit people are eight times less likely to die from cardiovascular disease than those who are unfit.

Be sane. Guys who are overambitious and mount a fat-fighting operation with the same ferocity they'd apply in a hostile corporate takeover may experience quick rewards, but they're almost guaranteed to have long-term setbacks as well.

As a rule, experts say, don't try to lose more than five pounds a month. Guys who try to lose more—say, 25 pounds in a month—will just become weak, or worse. "Once you lose body weight that soon, you're endangering your health," warns Dr. Brandon.

Back to Basics

Once you make the commitment and set a date for losing weight, you're going to use many of the same strategies you'd use for a long-term plan, like smart eating and exercise. "But you'll do more of it," Dr. Sargent adds.

"I think that if someone wants initially to start on a program for getting in shape in a small amount of time, he should focus on doing 20 to 30 minutes of exercise every day," says Dr. Art Mollen of the Southwest Health Institute. "If you really want to get into tremendous shape you'll need 45 minutes to an hour of good exercise every day."

Keep it fun. When you're trying to lose weight fast, don't get bogged down with a laundry list of activities that you loathe. Time's short, so stick with things you enjoy and know you'll do.

"Especially for the short term, people have to do the type of exercises they're comfortable with," Dr. Sargent says. "For some people this will be biking. For others it will be

running. You have to find something you're comfortable with in order to stick with it."

Duplicate your efforts. It takes discipline, but exercising twice a day enhances the probability that you'll burn fat fast.

"We also know that if you have limited time periods, two or three segments of exercise equals the benefit of a single bout of equal time. If I were serious about losing weight in the short term, I'd do my exercises twice a day," Dr. Sargent says. "Doubling your dose of exercise gives you a great metabolic kick. You'll put an enormous burden on your metabolism and get a great return."

Bring on the power. Serious weight loss requires serious effort—like combining aerobic exercise with strength training, says Dr. Sargent. Aerobic exercises such as running, cycling and walking mobilize fat throughout your body, while weight lifting builds lean muscle mass in those body parts

Getting Personal

When you're on tight deadlines, consider signing up with a personal trainer—an exercise expert who can help you get impressive results fast.

Personal trainers don't give away their time, but their rates aren't necessarily stratospheric, either. Most charge between $30 and $200 for a 50-minute session. The rate may include the use of a local gym or health club, or the trainer may work with you at home.

The advantage of working with a personal trainer is that you get personalized attention, plus you're able to work at your pace. Before making the hire, here's what experts suggest.

Cast a wide network. You can always peruse the Yellow Pages, but a better way to find a good trainer is to ask your friends and co-workers if they know anyone to recommend. Or ask around at the health club.

you work hardest. More muscle tissue means faster metabolism, which enables you to burn more calories even when you're driving home.

Try the walk-jog solution. It isn't necessary to kill yourself in order to shed pounds. If you are ready to burn flab but aren't already in good shape, Dr. Sargent recommends combining walking with jogging.

Once a day, hit the road for 20 to 30 minutes. Promise yourself you'll go the whole distance. Start out jogging until you're out of breath or your muscles start fatiguing. Walk until you're recovered, then jog some more. Do this daily, increasing the jogging time a few minutes every few days. Once you're jogging the distance, you know you're on the high road to slimming down.

Always be prepared. Promising yourself you'll never miss a workout is like saying you'll never be sick: Things happen.

Keeping a packed gym bag in the trunk, however, makes it easier to work out when the urge strikes. This is particularly helpful when you're trying to lose weight fast and every workout counts.

Maximize opportunity. Exercise doesn't happen only on the track or in the gym. Every day there are dozens of little opportunities—going shopping, walking to your car or just going from the basement to the fourth floor—that help us burn a little more flab, says Kelly Brownell, Ph.D., professor of psychology and a weight-loss expert at Yale University.

For starters, lose the remote control and actually walk to change channels. It's not a marathon, exactly, but it helps. So will getting out of the car and opening the garage door by hand; walking the shopping malls instead of ordering by mail; taking stairs instead of elevators; walking at lunch instead of having an hour-long meal. All these small efforts add up to decent workouts, and workouts subtract pounds. When you're in a race, every step you tale counts.

Eat smart. You can exercise five days a week, but if you're not alert to what goes into your mouth, you're going to lose, says Dr. Brownell. Consider this: One quarter-pound cheeseburger, a small order of fries and a shake has more than 1,000 calories—about the same amount you'd burn during an ten-mile run or a three-hour game of tennis.

You don't have to be fanatical about dieting to lose weight, says Dr. Sargent. In fact, you don't need to diet at all. Just cut back on fatty foods—things like burgers, fries and rich desserts—and eat more of the foods you know are good for you, like potatoes, beans, fruits, vegetables and bread.

Look for longevity. Ask prospective trainers how long they've been in business and what their experience is. You're looking for seasoned pros, not beginners trying to break into a new profession.

Ask about credentials. The oldest and most reputable programs that certify trainers are the American College of Sports Medicine, the National Academy of Sports Medicine and the National Strength and Conditioning Association. Other good programs include the Cooper Institute for Aerobics Research, the American Council on Exercise and the Aerobics and Fitness Association of America.

Request references. Good trainers have satisfied customers, and they won't hesitate to put you in touch. Ask to speak to three.

Take a trial run. Before signing up for a long-term program, arrange a one-month trial period. How well you get along with this person will really determine whether you stick with the program or drop out after two weeks. If it's not a good match, cut your losses and move on.

Long-Term Strategies

How To Lose Weight and Keep It Off

Which is harder, losing 20 pounds in six months or keeping it off the following year?

Lots of men would say the first is the hardest. You have the pressure of a deadline. Old habits to break. Being hungry all the time. No question, it's tough to get thin.

But the really hard part, experts say, is staying that way. Of those millions of overweight Americans who manage to lose weight, 40 to 60 percent regain it within a year. Others are luckier: They might have up to five years before all the pounds pile back on.

"Losing fat and keeping it off in the long term for many people is difficult, but it's by far one of the most important things you can do for your health," says Dr. Roger G. Sargent of the University of South Carolina School of Public Health.

Healing Moves

Despite the health benefits of staying trim, most guys tend to overlook exercise as their number-one weapon in the lifelong fight against fat. You know you should exercise. Often you even plan to exercise. But in the hectic crush of day-to-day commitments, it's easy to just skip it.

Don't overlook the obvious. While exercise may seem like just another obligation in an already complicated life, it's a critical part of any long-term strategy you take to lose weight, says Dr. Art Mollen of the Southwest Health Institute.

"If you want to fight fat long-term, you must exercise long-term," Dr. Mollen says. "Do you eat every day? Of course. If you're putting energy into your system, you need to take energy out of it to maintain your weight."

Indiana University's Dr. Wayne C. Miller agrees. "Anything can help you lose weight, but research shows that people who want to keep off the weight need to exercise."

Make Health Your Hobby

Don't you wish you could approach exercise and weight loss with the same zeal you bring to your hobbies? Imagine talking about weight lifting or aerobics with the same gleam in your eye you get when you talk about the NCAA finals, or your Hawaiian vacation, or a classic car you just saw.

Unlike hobbies, which are labors of love, we tend to view exercise as being a necessary, but dull, part of life, like eating brussels sprouts. But there are ways to bring to exercise and fitness the same vigor you bring to your play.

Follow your heart. The best exercise for long-term weight control isn't the one that makes you sweat the most. It's the one you'll actually do, be it golf, aerobics, rappelling or even gardening or chopping wood.

"You don't get people to change to a healthy lifestyle by boring them. You have to make exercise fun," says fitness instructor Joan Price of Unconventional Moves in Sebastopol, California.

Get involved. Serious hobbyists get nearly fanatical when it comes to pursuing the minutiae of their interests—which is why they stick with it year after year. To turn an exercise habit into a hobby, get involved. No matter what you like, somewhere there's a newspaper, magazine or newsletter that covers it. Check your local newsstand or magazine rack. If you can't find what you're looking for, ask your librarian for help.

Join your peers. Joining a club with like-minded fitness buffs is a great way to keep in long-term shape, says Price. Not only will you make new friends and have a regular group to hang out with, but you'll also have someone pushing you to work out on days you'd rather slump.

Get the record straight. If you love cars and just inherited a '57 Chevy—handyman special—you'd probably take pictures of the ol' clunker, then record each stage of the restoration. Treat your chassis with the same respect.

If you take up weight lifting, for example, measure your waist, biceps, chest and legs when you start. Take pictures of the body parts under construction. Three months later, update your records with new measurements and pics. Eventually, you'll have a paper trail documenting how your 13-inch arms were transformed into 15-inch pythons.

"We're goal-setting animals. By recording and monitoring our improvements, we give ourselves a pat on the back to continue," Price says.

Be a contender. For some guys, it's not victory but the thrill of competition that stokes their fires. Contact your local fitness club or check at the local sporting goods store for information on amateur competitions in your area.

Jim Schwartz, a pilot in Santa Cruz, California, first took up cycling to trim down his midsection. Then he branched into competition triathlons. He found that competing—and the training that precedes it—is a great strategy for staying fit and motivated.

"I think competing helps you set goals, and setting goals is important," says Schwartz, who has finished more than a half-dozen triathlons. "When you compete it's a real emo-

Buddy Up for Fitness

Scuba divers, mountaineers and even professional wrestlers depend on the buddy system. While these and other high-risk activities require buddies for safety reasons, some of the same benefits of working with friends apply to you, too.

"For some people, having a buddy gives them a buzz of energy on days when they don't feel like exercising," says Jonathan Robison, Ph.D., executive co-director of the Michigan Center for Preventative Medicine in Lansing and adjunct assistant professor in the Department of Physical Activity and Exercise Science at Michigan State University in East Lansing.

"Any physical activity may become much more enjoyable if you can add a social component to it," Dr. Robison says.

The buddy system can be as simple as playing basketball with the same group of friends at the office or as demanding as dividing up obligations for a caving expedition. Your buddy doesn't even have to stand upright: Tom McMillen, co-chair of the President's Council on Physical Fitness and Sports, gets his motivation from taking his canine crew—two Labrador retrievers—for daily runs.

"If you spend your life doing everything by yourself, I question how much fulfillment you're getting," Dr. Robison says. "I always suggest people try to do things with another person. It gives you a sense of being connected, and that's very important for good health."

tional charge. But you don't have to be an Olympic athlete. It's more about achieving personal victory."

Diversify. When you make exercise or sports your hobby, it's like being part of a family, says Price. That means sharing similarities and differences.

"For example, if you're both cyclists and your new friend likes to box, try it," says Price. "You might pick up another hobby, and at the very least, you'll be getting more exercise and broadening your horizons."

Creative Tricks for Staying in Shape

It's easy to talk about exercise as a way to stay in shape, but it's a lot harder to actually get around to doing it. Or is it?

Not necessarily. You don't even have to do sports, lift weights or sweat to music. "You need to work fat off any way you can, so the more creative your solution, the better," says Steven N. Blair, P.E.D., director of epidemiology and clinical applications at the Cooper Institute for Aerobics Research in Dallas.

"I suspect the traditional advice, like exercising three times a week for 30 minutes, is good for some people, but I'm not convinced that it's the best approach for everybody," says Dr. Blair.

In one study, researchers divided overweight kids into three groups. Kids in one group did a prescribed amount (and type) of exercise. Those in the second group were allowed to choose their activity, while kids in the third group did regular calisthenics and stretching. After eight weeks, children in all groups lost about the same amount of weight. But in a two-year follow-up, it was the

ones who had chosen their activities—like walking to and from school—who managed to keep the weight off.

"The bottom line is you need to increase your physical activity any way you can—do something rather than nothing," Dr. Blair says.

Here are some creative approaches to staying thin—year after year.

Control the remote. If you spend every night clicking away the channels with a remote control, don't be surprised when you start resembling sofa sediment with a paunch. "The technology revolution is such that it's engineered physical activity right out of our lifestyle," Dr. Blair says. "We can do so much nowadays without even moving."

Build Brawn Fast

With today's deadlines and commitments, the prospect of spending hours sweating in the gym—particularly as part of an ongoing, do-it-for-life plan—may be less than appealing. But there are ways to get a decent workout fast. A study by the YMCA found that people who worked out for 20 minutes three times a week with an intense weight-lifting program gained 6 pounds of muscle and lost up to 15 pounds of fat in just seven weeks.

But you don't need a grueling workout to get stronger and leaner. A 20-minute routine of "compound exercises," which involve working several muscle groups with each lift, will get you where you want to be fast.

Do two sets of each exercise, with weights that allow you to do ten repetitions per set easily. Do the exercises in order, resting 15 to 30 seconds between each exercise. Take a minute or two between sets to jog in place or do some other cardiovascular exercise. Then start the circuit again.

Bench press. This hits most of the major chest and arm muscles, which involve some of the body's largest

That's the trend, but it's easy to reverse. Just losing the remote control can help. Really. Rather than giving your thumb the workout, take those few extra steps across the living room and change the channels yourself. Doing this several times an hour will burn more calories than lying still, and every little bit helps.

Make use of tube time. The average 35- to 54-year-old guy watches 27 hours of television a week, or roughly 4 hours a day. If you spent even half that time watching and doing calisthenics, you'd burn about 825 calories—more than the burn you'd get in an hour of cross-country skiing at a moderate pace.

Take to the streets. You don't have to be a runner to put your legs in motion. If you live reasonably close to work, for instance, try leaving the car parked and hoof it instead. Walking an hour at a leisurely 3.5 miles an hour will burn about 300 calories.

Too far to walk? Try cycling. An increasing number of men are two-wheeling their ways to work every day, burning about 650 calories an hour while cruising along at 13 miles an hour.

Mark the years. Rather than just plunging another candle in your birthday cake, why not take a hint from Tom Monaghan, president and chairman of the board of Domino's Pizza in Ann Arbor, Michigan, and try your hand—and arms, shoulders and chest—at a few push-ups?

Monaghan vowed to do one push-up for each year of his life on every birthday. "When I promised myself to do this, I was in my early forties, and I really had to work at it," he recalls. Now Monaghan is in his late fifties—and instead of pumping out one push-up for every year, he does 125 straight.

Your goal is not to beat Monaghan but simply to give yourself a yearly marker, so you can see how well you're doing—and what you should strive for next year.

Make the most of vacations. It's hard to think of anything negative to say about spending a week on a sandy Mexican beach. Suffice it to say that it won't help your beer gut get any smaller. In fact, after a few days of margaritas and rich food, you can expect it to be *mucho grande* by the time you say adios.

A fun alternative to the usual lounge-about is to take an exercise vacation—a few days or weeks in which you put your muscles to work instead of to bed. Rather than tanning on the beach in Cancún, for example, you could be cycling through the country-

---

muscle groups. **Alternate exercise: dumbbell fly.**

Leg extension and leg curl. **Alternating one set of each will help build the bulkiest parts of your legs, the quadriceps and hamstring muscles.**

Seated pulley row. **This works nearly every upper-body muscle group, including your back, shoulders, biceps and neck. Alternate exercise: dumbbell bent-over row.**

Leg press. **This builds the quadriceps, calves and hamstrings and helps tighten the buttocks. Alternate exercise: lunge with dumbbells.**

Shoulder press. **This hits the deltoids, triceps and upper back muscles. Alternate exercise: dumbbell military press.**

Lat pulldown. **Works those big muscles on the sides of your back—the ones that give you a V shape. Alternate exercise: pull-up.**

Dumbbell biceps curl. **Pumps up your biceps while also working the shoulders and forearms. Alternate exercise: barbell curl.**

side in Mexico or here in the United States—take your pick. Even spinning at a moderate pace of ten miles an hour will burn about 400 calories an hour.

If you aren't sure where to go or what you want to do, here's a start.

• Backpacking through California's Yosemite National Park with Yosemite Mountaineering School, Yosemite Valley, CA 95389.

• Kayaking. Try Riversport, P.O. Box 95, Confluence, PA 15424; Otter Bar Lodge, Box 210, Forks of Salmon, CA 96031; or Kayak and Canoe Institute, University of Minnesota, Duluth Outdoor Program, 121 SpHC, 10 University Drive, Duluth, MN 55812.

• The Go Active Sports Sampler from Backroads, 1516 Fifth Street, Berkeley, CA 94710. Features a variety of activities, including rock climbing, swimming, sailboarding, running, weight lifting, mountain biking, aerobics and yoga.

Get Pumping

Any time the talk turns to losing weight and keeping it off, you're going to hear about the two cornerstones of exercise: aerobic activities and resistance training.

Aerobic exercises are those that make your body demand oxygen and burn calories, like walking, running, rowing, aerobic dancing or any other moderate-to-vigorous physical activity. Resistance training (weight lifting), on the other hand, is anaerobic exercise, which builds muscle mass through resistance.

Whichever workout you choose, here are a few steps to make it most efficient.

Don't lie to yourself. If you resemble Danny DeVito but want to look like Sylvester Stallone, it's time to conduct a reality check. "Understand that some goals are achievable and others are pipe dreams," Dr. Blair says. "We all come in different shapes and sizes. I've come to grips with the fact that I'll never look like a movie star. No matter how much I run,

I'll always be short, stocky and bald."

Lift for life. You probably haven't seen many 70-year-old men pumping iron at the local gym, but you might in the future. That's because experts are now realizing that weight lifting is the unsung hero of fat-fighting exercises, says Dr. Sargent.

"I feel that the only reason resistance training hasn't had the same glory attached to it as aerobics is that it hasn't had as much study," Dr. Sargent says. "You'll find in the past five or six years that the results of weight-loss studies on resistance training and aerobics have been fairly equivalent."

While advanced lifters can spend hours pumping iron, 20 to 30 minutes is enough for most guys. Begin by doing a few sets on the bench press. Then work your way through the major muscle groups, including curls for biceps, military presses for shoulders and leg extensions and leg curls for the lower body. Finish with some back extension and abdominal work for a complete program.

As you get stronger and more experienced, you may want to start experimenting with different lifting styles: lifting light weights using higher repetitions, or going for more weight with fewer reps. According to Dr. Sargent, evidence suggests lifting light weights more often yields greater muscle strength than using heavier weights. Regardless of the strategy you choose, lifting weights increases muscle mass, which ups your metabolism and helps you burn fat more efficiently.

Go aerobic. If experts could choose just one type of exercise to rout that Rubinesque look, they'd choose aerobic exercise—roughly defined as any exercise that increases your consumption of oxygen, causing your heart rate to increase.

These days there are more aerobic options than New York City has pizza joints: running, cycling, rowing, skiing, boxing, wrestling, basketball, walking—all of which can provide a fantastic aerobic workout.

The American College of Sports Medicine and the federal Centers for Disease Control and Prevention in Atlanta recommend doing 30 minutes of moderate-intensity activity, such as walking or running, every day. It doesn't have to be done all at once, however. Rather, it can be accumulated with small amounts of activity scattered throughout the day.

"For real results you're going to have to work at it," notes Dr. Mollen. While you may choose to start out doing 30 minutes of exercise seven times a week, eventually you'll want to bump your times to 45 to 60 minutes daily, he says.

Team up with team sports. Not every guy wants to be a lonely marathoner trodding for hours in self-imposed solitude. Some of us want to shoot the breeze while we're sweating away the pounds. For both the workout and the social fun, team sports are ideal.

Tom McMillen, co-chair of the President's Council on Physical Fitness and Sports and a former NBA player and U.S. congressman, still finds time to shoot occasional hoops with friends. "I'll get together with some friends once in a while for a game or two, but it's nowhere near as often as I used to," says McMillen, now chairman and chief executive officer of Complete Wellness Centers, a health care clinic management company in Washington, D.C.

If you don't already have a network of friends active on a variety of playing fields, check the newspaper for sports leagues near you. A spot on the community softball team or bowling league might be all you need to stick to a lifelong exercise regimen.

If you strike out finding an established community league, start a game yourself by re-

Hit the Target

Aerobic exercise is the cornerstone of any long-term fat-burning plan because it does the most to fire up the metabolism. Fat starts to melt away about 20 minutes into a workout, and the higher the heart rate, the more calories you'll burn. Aerobic exercise also makes your charged-up metabolism ignite calories even after you've quit your workout.

To get the most benefit from any aerobic workout, however, you need to hit your "target" heart range. Here's how.

- Determine your maximum heart rate by subtracting your age from 220.
- Multiply your maximum heart rate by 0.65 to find your minimum training rate.
- Multiply your maximum heart rate by 0.8 to get your maximum training rate.

Here's how it works. Suppose you're 35 years old. Subtracting your age from 220 says your maximum heart rate is 185 beats per minute. Multiplying that by 0.65 tells you your minimum training rate is 120. Multiplying it by 0.8 says your maximum training rate is 148.

Your goal, then, would be to get your heart pumping between 120 and 148 beats a minute.

How do you check your heart rate while you're exercising? Feel the pulse in your wrist and count the beats for 15 seconds. Multiplying by four will give you your pulse rate.

If you're below the minimum of your target range (in the above example, that's 120 beats a minute), pick up the pace. If you're above the maximum (148 beats), slow down.

cruiting in the office. Your co-workers might jump at the chance for some high-noon athletic antics.

Part Four

Lifestyle

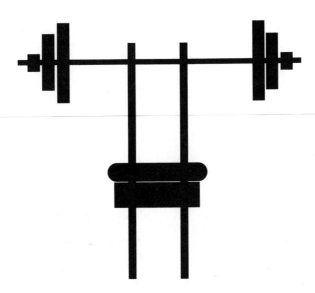

The Low-Fat Lifestyle

Practical Strategies for Staying Lean

Unless you've been in hibernation the past ten years, you've already heard a lot about fat: what it is, what foods have it and how to burn it off. How about incorporating that knowledge into your daily life? Fat chance.

We aren't doing ourselves any favors when it comes to ignoring fat. We work long hours, eat atrocious foods and let opportunities for regular exercise slip between the cracks of our daily lives. The result is a lot of 38-inch waists on 32-inch frames.

"Being thin or fat is not completely at the whim of genetics, or something incidental to the rest of your life; it can be a lifestyle choice," says Patti Tveit Milligan, R.D., a San Diego dietitian who writes a nutrition column for the business magazine *Selling*.

Harsh as it sounds, leading a life without fat does not require dramatic shifts in behavior. In most cases, all that's involved is minor retooling of a few key areas. You can live the lower-fat life without ever stretching yourself too thin.

Laying a Fit Foundation

When you hear the term *low-fat life*, you probably start thinking "diet"—and quickly take a dim view of it. But living lean isn't about dieting. It's about making the commitment to burn energy more efficiently: to work, play, eat, sleep and even dress in

such a way that you push fat further and further out of your life until one day, it's barely there. For example:

Lay in provisions. "If you have to take time each day to figure out what you're going to eat that's low in fat, pretty soon you won't bother," says Bob Arnot, M.D., medical and health correspondent for the *CBS Evening News* and author of *Dr. Bob Arnot's Guide to Turning Back the Clock*. To make decision-making easy, he recommends stocking up on healthful foods such as oatmeal, pasta, grains, skim milk and fresh fruits and vegetables.

"Look at this as some new project, like something you have to do at work," he says. "In this case, your job is to set up your support structure, to make your low-fat lifestyle automatic."

Set a fat budget. Fat is darned near unavoidable—and sometimes irresistible. There's no way you'll ever cut your fat intake to zero—even if it were possible it wouldn't be healthy—but you can keep the numbers down.

"One of the best ways to cut down on fat is to set yourself a daily fat budget," suggests Milligan. The American Heart Association recommends getting no more than 30 percent of daily calories from fat—that figures out to about 0.5 gram of fat per pound of body weight per day. So a 150-pound man would have a daily fat budget of a maximum of 75 grams, or about 2.5 ounces of fat.

"Use it however you want," Milligan says. "If you want to spend a good chunk of that budget on a glazed doughnut early in the

day, that's fine. Just remember, it's that much less fat you can eat later." Don't overspend and dip into the next day's budget, either: As the government can attest, deficit spending doesn't work.

Write it down. There's no way you're going to remember every item of food you eat in a day without a little bookkeeping. To track fat, try keeping a food journal. Write down everything you eat. Sometimes the act of writing alone will cause you to be conscious of your habits.

"Because eating is such an everyday activity, often we're not aware of what we consume. By writing down what we eat, we put ourselves more in control," says Cheryl C. Marco, R.D., a dietitian and manager of outpatient nutrition at Thomas Jefferson University Hospital in Philadelphia.

Name your PIG. Food cravings are tough to resist. Sometimes we all chow down—and then blame ourselves later. Don't: Blame the PIG instead.

"It's a lot easier to cope with a craving if you externalize it, give it a name. We call it the Problem with Immediate Gratification—the PIG," says G. Alan Marlatt, Ph.D., professor of psychology and director of the Addictive Behaviors Research Center at the University of Washington in Seattle and an expert on food cravings. "When you have a craving for something, stop and ask yourself: Is it me who's hungry, or is it my PIG? And if it's the PIG, you don't have to listen to it—you can distract it. Take your PIG for a walk, or try to feed it some low-fat food that might satisfy it. Because if you feed your PIG every time it oinks, pretty soon you'll end up with a bigger PIG."

And as any farmer can tell you, the bigger the PIG, the harder it is to fence in.

Take it slow. Once you've made up your mind to cut fat from your life, don't try to cut it all out the first day. This is a marathon, not a sprint. If you make changes slowly and gradually, you may not even notice the changes.

"The cold turkey approach is kind of brutal, really. You'll have more luck sticking to a low-fat diet if you gradually phase the fat out of your life," explains Marco. She recommends gradually cutting back on fattening snacks. Eat them less often and in smaller portions. Or use substitutes, she adds.

Taming the Hunger Within

Making a conscious effort to trim fat is hard enough, but research suggests you may have to mollify the subconscious as well. Here's a quick look at the scene behind the scenes.

Dine in the dark. Studies at Johns Hopkins University in Baltimore suggest that bright lights and bright colors make us want to eat more. So when you're trying to cut back, switch to candlelight. Or at least dim the lights.

Break the pattern. Researchers say patterned dishes stir us up and stimulate us to keep eating. Stick with plain dinnerware. And buy smaller plates; they make your portions look bigger.

Keep the music slow. Playing slow music causes us to take smaller bites and eat more slowly, say Johns Hopkins researchers.

"I'm working with a man right now who literally eats a whole pepperoni pizza every day. In his case, the simple change we made was going from a pepperoni pizza to a plain cheese or vegetable-and-cheese pizza. Because of that change, he actually lost six or seven pounds. He's still got a ways to go, but that's a good beginning, and for him, the change was relatively painless."

Weight Loss without Dieting

Now that you've busied your mind with strategies to defeat flab, it's time to draft your body to the cause.

"Raising your awareness of fat is only the first step. Once you've got the groundwork in place—the strategies that help you keep track of fat intake—there are things you can do every day to limit it," says Milligan.

Whether you're planning a dinner menu or ordering from one, here are some day-to-day tips for fighting fat.

Eat often. This might be tough advice to follow, but if you're going to maintain a trimmer way of living, you've got to eat—the more, the better.

It's no joke. "When men try to lose weight, the first thing they try to do is starve themselves. It's absolutely the wrong thing to do," says Peter M. Miller, Ph.D., executive director of the Hilton Head Health Institute in South Carolina and author of *The Hilton Head Executive Stamina Program*. "Your metabolism has to increase in order to digest food. The more often you eat, the higher you'll raise your metabolism. The higher your metabolism is, the faster you'll burn calories, even when you're sitting still," says Dr. Miller. Just make sure your meals are heavy on the carbohydrates, like grains, fruits and vegetables, and light on fat.

Don't be a sofa spud. You can't pursue a low-fat lifestyle from the comfort of your couch.

"You may be getting fat because you're eating too much, but chances are it's also because you're not the least bit active," says former U.S. Surgeon General C. Everett Koop, M.D., senior scholar at Koop Institute at Dartmouth Medical School in Hanover, New Hampshire.

. Next time you settle in to watch the game, watch it from your exercise cycle or treadmill, if you have one. Or view each commercial as a chance to move around. See how many push-ups you can do during the halftime show.

And don't stop at the sofa. Look around your life and see what other sedentary distractions you can liven up. Rather than spend a day lying immobile on the beach, for example, take a volleyball and strike up a game. On vacation, instead of that bus tour of European hamlets, make it a bike tour.

Exercise at every opportunity. Not everyone has time to hit the gym every day, but you can work a healthy dose of physical

Weighty Advice

Two of the things men hate most—asking for help and seeing a medical-type person—may be necessary when those rolls of fat won't melt away.

Get over it. You wouldn't hesitate to see a surgeon if you had a ruptured appendix or a cardiologist for heart problems. When the problem is food and diet, you can't do better than meeting with a nutrition expert.

"If you meet one-on-one with someone who can look at your situation exclusively, you can get a lot of useful and realistic information, and it's not going to take a lot of time or money," says dietitian Cheryl C. Marco of Thomas Jefferson University Hospital.

Nutritionists recommend that first-time patients fill out a food diary for a few days before coming in. That way they'll have some idea of what your typical eating habits are. "From there it's easy for you to discover, with the dietitian's guidance, some painless ways that you can

activity into your schedule no matter how busy you are.

"We're so busy during the day, we don't always have a consistent time to set aside for a workout," says Dr. Miller. But there are plenty of times during the day—a few minutes before a meeting, for example, or ten minutes after lunch—when you can probably sneak in whatever kind of workout you're able to manage. Check your daily schedule and look for the gaps, nooks and crannies of time that you can fill in with exercise.

"For example, I like to point out that just a little bit of walking right before or after every meal gives you an enormous benefit in terms of burning off calories from that meal," says Dr. Miller. "It accounts for maybe 10 or 15 minutes out of the day, but even that short span of time can do you some good if you spend it exercising."

decrease the fat in your diet," says Marco.

The payoff can be almost immediate, she adds. "Where we do the most good is in spotting hidden sources of fat in a person's life and helping him develop realistic strategies that are going to make a real difference."

It doesn't have to be an extended relationship. "For most men, it probably takes only two or three sessions at the most," she says. "We point them in the right direction, and off they go."

To find a registered dietitian in your area, call your doctor or the local hospital or medical center. Ask if they have an outpatient nutrition counseling service. Or ask to be referred to a dietitian who sees nonpatients. Also, you can call the American Dietetic Association's Consumer Nutrition Hotline at 1-800-366-1655 for the names of some registered dietitians in your area.

Speak up. Whether you're at a restaurant or helping your partner compose the shopping list, don't be afraid to make special requests.

"If you're at a restaurant and you're paying for that food, there's no reason why you shouldn't ask to have some fatty sauce served on the side or if a dish can be broiled instead of fried," Milligan says.

Play with your food. There's a lot you can do on the home front to keep dietary fat down to tolerable levels. Instead of crowning that baked potato with a dollop of sour cream, for example, try a spoonful of low-fat yogurt or low-fat sour cream. "They have very similar textures, colors, even flavors—only the low-fat toppings have much less fat," Milligan points out. And don't plunk that burger into a frying pan—fire up the grill or the broiler instead. That way, the fat drips away from the meat and into the fire.

Whatever you're eating, do some quick brainstorming about what you can do to make it lower-fat the next time around. "It stretches your creative muscles a little, and it can be fun," Milligan says.

Think like a kid. "Most of your healthier snacks—raisins, low-fat cookies and puddings—are packaged and designed for children in these great little snack-size containers," says Milligan. Anything's fair game, from colorful juice boxes (better than soda) to animal crackers (a good low-fat munchie). "Anything that will fit in a lunch box will fit nicely into a briefcase," she adds.

Drown your hunger. If your appetite feels strong, sometimes you can water it down.

"It's not uncommon at all for thirst to masquerade as hunger," says Barbara Whedon, R.D., dietitian and nutrition counselor at Thomas Jefferson University Hospital. "It's really essential to stay well-hydrated during the day."

She recommends drinking about eight glasses of water a day. "It'll prevent dehydration and thus keep your energy level up. When we have energy slumps we often reach for food, when in fact it's fluid we need."

Indulge yourself. Living the low-fat life would be completely intolerable if you didn't give in to temptation now and again.

"You should never forbid yourself from eating a certain kind of food, even if that food is high in fat or sugar," says Milligan.

There's a good reason for not being too strict: Whatever you refuse yourself is the one thing you're certain to crave. So relax. Have that chocolate fudge ripple ice cream. Just don't eat it every day, and don't inhale it in huge amounts.

"The trick is to indulge yourself in moderation," Dr. Marlatt says. "Yes, go ahead and have that fattening food, but always make a special occasion of it. You'll enjoy it that much more."

An All-Day Plan

24 Hours in the Life
of a Fat Fighter

Work, play, food, rest: These are the four poles on the compass of a man's life. Rather than partaking of each in a measured, deliberate way, sometimes it seems like we're spinning wildly, careening from one extreme to the next as we try to find balance and direction in another hectic day.

The report's due—cancel the workout. Can't sleep—have a snack. Kids need rides—forget the walk. It's no wonder that a lot of us wake up one day and discover we're frustrated, tired and overweight.

"It's all a balancing act," says Dr. Peter M. Miller of the Hilton Head Health Institute. "Men need to learn how to adopt a set of strategies that they can use every day, making their daily activities—meals, business, exercise, leisure and so on—work together. If they can do that, they'll go a long way toward being slimmer, healthier people with a lot more energy and a lot less stress to boot."

More Is Less

Despite what your stomach would have you believe, food is not your life—it's the fuel that powers your life. But a lot of us have been topping off our tanks the wrong way—and losing energy and gaining weight in the bargain.

Although men in our society are brought up to eat three squares a day—with breakfast being the smallest meal and dinner the largest—nutrition experts say this approach is all wrong.

"A calorie is not the same calorie at different times of the day," says Franz Halberg, M.D., professor of bioengineering, pathology, physiology, oral medicine and laboratory medicine at the University of Minnesota in Minneapolis. Studies of lean men suggest that calories consumed at dinner are more likely to be stored than those taken in at breakfast.

Another problem with the three-a-day scheme is that it requires us to go long periods without eating. By the time lunch or dinner rolls around, we're ravenous—and more than willing to grab the biggest, fattiest food we can find and stuff it down our gullets.

"Instead of eating three big meals a day, a lot of men make better choices by spreading their calorie intakes over four or five meals—the three basic meals, plus one or two snacks," says Dr. Miller. With all-day grazing, you may be eating more often, but you're less likely to put on weight, he adds.

Rather than alternating from feast to famine, a better strategy is to keep your metabolism running at a consistent high idle throughout the day. Here's a daylong look at how to do it.

Starting Right

When you exercise and what you eat in the morning can dictate how much energy you'll have—and how much more you'll eat—later on. "It's truly one of the most important times to eat," says dietitian Cheryl C. Marco of Thomas Jefferson University Hospital. "Your body has been without food for several hours, and your brain is going to need some carbohydrates soon to function effectively."

To make the most of your mornings, here's what experts recommend.

Break into a walk. After eight hours in the sack, your me-

tabolism is running slow. So even before you eat, experts say, prime your
food furnace. Get up and pull on
your sweats. Just taking a brisk walk
up the street and back—10 or 15
minutes—will get you revved.

Eat big—but eat right. "By
the time you wake up, it has been
hours since your last meal—your
body's literally starving for nutrients," says Marco. Since we tend to
burn food more efficiently in the
morning, it's also a good time to eat
well.

Traditional breakfast foods
that are high in fat—such as bacon,
eggs, doughnuts and hash browns—
can be your ticket back to dream-
land. "Heavy, fatty foods take longer
to digest. Your stomach draws more
blood away from the brain. You'll
have less energy and you're going to
get drowsy again," says Marco.

The best foods are those your
body can convert quickly to energy—carbohydrates and proteins
that keep you sharp. Good examples
include dry cereal with skim milk,
whole-grain toast with jelly (ease up
on the butter or peanut butter), oatmeal and any of your favorite fresh
fruits.

Take ten at 10. There's no
good reason to wait for lunch when
your stomach's growling. Feed the
beast—with a bagel and jelly, for
example, or a cup of yogurt. Mid-
morning snacks will help keep your
stomach satisfied and your brain
sharp for whatever you're dealing with before
lunch rolls around.

While you're taking a break, go ahead
and stretch your legs by walking around a bit.
This will help keep your engine running fast,
so you'll continue burning more calories even
after you go back to work.

Stoke Signals

When you're eating, it can take up to 20 minutes
for your brain to realize your stomach's full. In the meantime, you're still shoveling it in.

To get your stomach and brain working in synch,
here's what experts recommend.

Eat a multicourse meal. Having a few small
courses works better than having one huge portion,
says Steven Peikin, M.D., professor of medicine at
University of Medicine and Dentistry of New Jersey
Robert Wood Johnson Medical School and Cooper
Hospital/University Medical Center in Camden and
author of *The Feel Full Diet*. For instance, eating a bowl
of tomato soup 20 minutes before your main course has
been shown to reduce caloric intake in the main course.
By the time you reach the entrée, you're less likely to
pig out because the brain has already gotten word that
you're filling up.

Don't feel you have to eat it all. None of us is
so old we can't remember the childhood pride of being a
member of the Clean Plate Club. Now that we're adults,
however, it's time to let the membership lapse.

"Follow the 'taste everything, finish nothing'
rule," suggests Dr. Morton H. Shaevitz of the University
of California, San Diego, School of Medicine. By taking
time to savor everything, he says, you'll feel fuller and
take in fewer calories than if you wolf everything down.

Delay getting seconds. Waiting ten minutes
before helping yourself to seconds is a delaying tactic
that gives your brain more time to catch up with your
stomach. Then see if you really want more.

The Battle of Midday

Noon to quitting time—that long stretch
is when we're most likely to be bored, tired
and hungry.

"We've all been victims of that afternoon
slump in energy," says Dr. Miller. "A lot of that
has to do with the fact that we may have eaten

during a heavy meal at lunch. And sitting at a desk doesn't burn it off very quickly." Our energy levels dip, and so do our heads.

Here are a few ways to keep the metabolic momentum running high.

Lunch large. Even if you're eating five (or more) meals a day, most food experts say that lunch should be the biggest spread. You have a long afternoon of work ahead of you, so eat accordingly. But don't gorge—big doesn't mean huge.

A good example of a power lunch might be a hearty bowl of bean or minestrone soup and half a chicken breast sandwich with lettuce and tomato on whole-grain bread. You're getting enough protein and a lot of carbohydrates, but not a lot of fat. Throw in a handful of pretzels, a cup of yogurt and an apple or some other fruit.

Stay active. After lunch, instead of going back to your desk and dozing off, fire up your system by getting in a quick workout. If you can sneak away to the club for 15 minutes on the stair machine, so much the better. If not, at least walk around the parking lot or down the street. "This way, lunch isn't going to sit so heavily on you. You'll feel refreshed and better able to sail through the afternoon," says Dr. Miller.

Eat again. Usually around 3:00 P.M., our bodies' natural rhythms kick in, and we start feeling drowsy. Let your drooping eyelids serve as a signal to have another snack— something that's going to wake you up, not put you to sleep. Yogurt, pretzels or fruit will provide a quick, low-fat burst of energy—and help head off a ravenous appetite later on.

"That's important—at the end of the day you don't want to feel starved for dinner, or you'll make bad food choices," says Dr. Miller.

Hit the gym. To keep your metabolism running high, you should get at least 30 minutes of exercise three days a week. Do plenty of cardiovascular exercises—stair climbing, walking, running, cycling—to keep your heart rate up. That way you'll burn more

calories. It's also a good idea to lift—either on a circuit trainer or using free weights. As you build more muscle, you burn more calories— approximately 50 more calories a day for every pound of muscle you gain. Keep pumping.

Feed within 15. Maximizing muscle is key to keeping fat in the fire. Experts recommend enhancing muscle repair and replacing muscle energy stores by consuming a combination of carbohydrate and protein foods within 15 to 20 minutes after your workout.

"After a workout, you're going to need to replace the muscle's energy stores to assist with muscle repair," explains Becky Zimmerman, R.D., a dietitian at the National Institute for Fitness and Sport in Indianapolis.

She recommends eating about 0.5 gram of carbohydrates for each pound of body weight: In a 150-pound man, that means 75 grams of carbohydrates, or a little over two cups of pasta. You'll find protein in low-fat dairy products, in lean meats such as chicken or turkey and in whole-grain products, beans and rice.

Not only will eating soon after workouts help maximize muscle repair, but it will also fill you up, so you'll be less likely to stuff yourself later on.

Good Night

The traditional thing is to get home from work, kick off your shoes, loosen the tie and enjoy a big dinner. You work hard, you deserve it, right? Maybe not. Your just desserts might be your unwanted gains.

"If there's a time to drop eating, it's probably the time we eat the most, which is in the evening," says Marco. "There's some evidence that calories eaten in the evening are more likely to be stored as fat—they're not used as efficiently by the body as they would be at other times."

Evening is usually a time to relax, catch

up on some reading, do a little channel-surfing. But when you're winding down your day, you can still keep fat away—even after you've gone to bed. Here's how.

Have a dinky dinner. Some men consume 80 percent of their daily food intakes at the dinner table and at night. As a rule, dinner should account for no more than 40 to 50 percent of daily calories, says Morton H. Shaevitz, Ph.D., associate clinical professor of psychiatry at the University of California, San Diego, School of Medicine and author of *Lean and Mean: The No Hassle Life-Extending Weight Loss Program for Men.*

Regularly eating between three and five meals a day will help keep you from loading up in the evening.

But even when you are hungry at night, keep your dinners light. Focus on fish or fowl. Eat no more than four to six ounces of red meat no more than twice a week and load up on vegetables, legumes, pasta or rice instead.

Eat before 8:00 P.M. Research suggests that the later you eat, the more likely it is your body will store the food as flab. So whether you're eating a three-course meal or just a light snack, do it early in the evening, experts say.

Sleep with sweets. Some guys crave sweet bedtime snacks, possibly because sugary foods tend to elevate blood levels of tryptophan, an amino acid that is involved in sleep.

"The mistake you could make is satisfying that sweet craving with something huge, like a piece of pie or an ice cream sundae," says Martin B. Scharf, Ph.D., director of the Sleep Disorders Center at Mercy Hospital in Cincinnati. To get the sweet without the flab, go for

Mind over Meal

Food does more than just fill us up. We also eat to satisfy moods and emotions. "When we're depressed, we make ourselves feel better with some big, sugary treat," says Dr. Bob Arnot, medical and health correspondent for the *CBS Evening News.*

Dr. Arnot refers to this impulse as feedback eating—a primitive response to feelings and sensations. A better approach, he says, is to practice what he calls feedforward eating. This means looking ahead at tasks you'll be doing and then eating specific foods to help you perform them more efficiently. For example:

***Brain work.* Eating grains and high-protein foods such as skim milk, yogurt and lean meat helps keep mind and body alert, Dr. Arnot says.**

***Physical activity.* Eating protein provides needed material to build muscle, while slow-burning carbohydrates—such as grains, rice and legumes—aid in muscle repair.**

***Rest.* Cut back on mind-reviving protein and load up on carbohydrates instead.**

something low-fat: hard candies or licorice, for example, or a scoop of frozen yogurt.

Get busy. "Let's think about this. You've just eaten dinner, your biggest meal of the day. Are you really hungry just a few hours later, or are you just bored?" says Dr. G. Alan Marlatt of the University of Washington.

He recommends doing something—anything—that takes your mind off food. "Meditating works for me. Or get dressed and go for a walk. Play a game on the computer. Do anything to distract you until the urge passes."

Office Strategies

Churn Fat out of Your Daily Grind

In the context of work, the words "trimming the fat" probably make you wonder when the ax is going to fall—and whom it's going to hit.

Relax. We're not talking about layoffs here. The problem is corporate fat—and the need to do some serious downsizing. Let's face it: When you're pulling 12-hour days, work comes first and everything else—including a decent meal—comes a distant second. Daily workouts get postponed in the crunch of conference calls and strategy meetings. Meals come to you courtesy of the doughnut tray, the vending machine and the greasy spoon down the road. Your desk is transformed into a workaholic's table for one.

The battle of the bulge isn't fought only over office goodies and order-in lunches. No matter how far you've moved in your career, you probably haven't budged from behind your desk—with predictable results. If only there were some way to give your nose a break and press your gut to the grindstone instead.

Secrets of Executive Success

Staying on top of fitness can seem like a second career—another activity in an already jam-packed day. "The main enemy to most men's fitness is the fact that their jobs are very time-consuming things that involve sitting and not moving a lot," says Dr. Peter M. Miller of the Hilton Head Health Institute.

There's another obstacle as well: your mind-set. "A lot of men still don't see the advantage of making time during the day to

get a proper meal and to exercise," says Dr. Miller. "If more men scheduled them into their days—like any other important appointment—they'd find that they have more energy and are more physically fit, without cutting into their job performance."

Indeed, following a basic fitness program will make you feel better and work sharper, help you lose weight and look better in the eyes of the corporate bigwigs.

Between-Meeting Eating

You skipped breakfast so you could get an early start on the day—and get first crack at the glazed goodies in the cafeteria. Your lunchtime strategy meeting ran long, so you put your heads together, made a policy decision and ordered a bevy of salami torpedoes from the sub shop around the corner. At sunset, with a stack of paperwork still to file, you decided to postpone dinner—until you swung into a drive-thru on your way home and ordered the Belly Buster Bonus Meal.

"Work always gets in the way of eating a decent meal," observes Dr. Miller. "But if you wait to eat until you're starving, you make terrible food choices." What's more, you set yourself up for a ride on the energy roller coaster. "You go and go until you run out of fuel, then everything crashes down around you: your energy, your stamina and your mood," he says.

To keep your business day running at peak efficiency and with a minimum of fat, Dr. Miller recommends eating several small meals several times a day and packing those meals  with complex carbohydrates, the kind found in fruits, vegetables and grains. Not only will your energy be higher, you'll also be less likely to bite into a fattening quick fix. Here are some excellent food fixes.

Brown-bag it. For a real power lunch, pack your own. "If you take your own meals to work—even once or twice a week—you're more in control of your food choices, and you can eat a bit healthier," says dietitian Patti Tveit Milligan, who writes a nutrition column for the business magazine *Selling*. So pack a sack before you hit the sack—for example, a nice lean-meat sandwich with lettuce and tomato, some pretzels and a piece of fruit.

Make yourself a super hero. Whether you make your own lunch or order it from the deli, try to stock sandwiches with the leaner meats—turkey, chicken, even lean roast beef. "Stay away from the cured meats, like salami, pepperoni and corned beef," which have hidden fat, advises Milligan. Top your sandwich with some lettuce and tomato for filling fiber. And go easy on the mayonnaise—a single tablespoon holds 11 grams of fat. "Mustard, ketchup, even barbecue sauce are better choices," says Milligan.

Take up snack-packing. Foraging in the break room for an afternoon snack will almost guarantee you membership in the Lard-Butt Brigade. So anticipate trouble—and beat it by bringing your own grub.

"If you keep a stash of healthy snacks in your briefcase or your desk drawer, you're going to resist the temptation of fattier foods that are available at work," says Dr. Miller. Some of the best daylong noshables are fruits and vegetables. Not only will they help keep you full, but their stores of carbohydrates quickly translate into ready brain food. And fruits are ready-wrapped, so they're easy to pack.

It's also a good idea to pack your desk with snacks that keep, like graham crackers, animal crackers (your kids will never miss them), raisins, rice cakes, dried fruit or pretzels. And lay in a few dried soup packets for when you need a more substantial energy fix.

Working In Your Workout

The trouble with most of us busy drones is that we always put exercise at the outer fringes of the day—either late in the evening after work or at an ungodly early hour of the morning. The more marginal exercise becomes, the easier it is to blow it off.

"The point is not to treat fitness like some inferior part of our day," says Dr. Peter Miller of the Hilton Head Health Institute. "You really need to make time during the business day for some physical activity."

Scheduling an appointment for exercise? Well, why not? In *The Hilton Head Executive Stamina Program*, Dr. Miller outlines some simple steps for incorporating a workout into your corporate routine.

Jot it down. Since exercise is now an official part of your business day, pencil it into your calendar or planner. You'll be more likely to treat it like any other appointment—too important to miss.

Keep others in the loop. Tell friends, co-workers and family members about your exercise time. Once they understand that you're treating it like business—that is, something that can't be skipped—they'll be more supportive and less likely to interrupt.

Keep your eyes on the goal. Yes, exercise will help you lose weight and look better. More important from an office point of view, it will help you work harder and with more energy.

Ditch the doughnuts. Man does not live on carrots alone, but some office snacks will knock the bulb out of your personal fat meter. Doughnuts, for example, are veritable sponges of fat, containing 17 grams of fat in some cases. When the urge for a round, doughy object with a hole in the middle strikes, opt for a toasted bagel and jelly instead.

Snack early and often. "I suggest that

men have a snack at least twice during the workday—once around 10:00 in the morning, and again around 3:00 in the afternoon," says Dr. Miller. Those are the times our appetites tend to rear their insatiable heads. "A couple of pretzels or a piece of fruit can really take the edge off, so you won't be making bad food choices at a regular meal."

Same deal for evenings when you're forsaking dinner for work. "It's too easy to fall into the trap of eating a big meal late. Instead, make yourself a snack when you'd normally eat dinner," says Dr. Miller. "That should tide you over until you can get home and have something sensible."

Pour another drink. The average work environment is a dry one, and it's common for men to mistake thirst for hunger—and raid the vending machine when all they really wanted was a drink. "We should be drinking about eight glasses of water a day," says Milligan. "If you keep a bottle at your desk and just sip from it all day, you probably won't feel as hungry."

Working Late and Working Out

Everyone else has punched out for the day, but you're still slaving away on that year-end report. By the time you leave work, you barely have energy to flip a quarter into the toll basket, never mind hitting the gym for some much-needed exercise.

"Because most work schedules don't leave us time to work out at night, it's important for the working man to make sure he's moving and getting exercise during the day while he's at work," says Dr. Miller.

We're not talking here about a full-blown aerobics drill in front of the water cooler. Just going through your daily activities a bit more vigorously can get blood pumping and your metabolism kicking in more efficiently. A study at Tufts University in Medford, Massachusetts, showed that men who shifted frequently in their chairs, paced around the office or even got excited about a good idea burned up more calo-

ries over a 16-hour period than when they got a half-hour of solid exercise.

So while that report is printing or you're waiting for a ten-page fax—or even before you hit the front door—take a couple of minutes to try these at-work exercises recommended by experts.

Park and walk. Remember how hard you worked to get that parking space by the door? Well, give it up and promote yourself to the back parking lot. That will give you a chance to stretch your legs before you embark on the nine-to-five.

"I would try to park as far away from the building as possible and then walk or jog in," suggests Dr. Miller. The quick rush of physical activity will boost your metabolism, helping you stay lean and energized. If you take public transport, get off one stop before your office and hoof it the rest of the way.

Take the stairs. Elevators are great for hauling a tray of cappuccino up three floors or making an impromptu sales pitch to a captive audience. But for the quick transit from your desk to a meeting with the guys upstairs, skip the elevator. "If we're talking a distance of one or two floors, it's really kind of lazy to take an elevator," says Dr. Miller. "I always take the stairs—it's actually a lot quicker, too."

Adopt an open-door policy. When you have a few free minutes and want to rev the engine fast, find an open office door. Stand with your feet straddling the edge. Grab the inside knob with one hand, the outside knob with the other, and slowly lean back until you encounter resistance in your arms. Then bend your knees and let your body sink down until your arms are fully extended and your thighs are parallel to the floor. Now slowly pull yourself up with your arms and push slightly with your legs. Repeat 10 to 12 times. Just be sure the door you're using is strong enough to bear your weight.

Let it slide. To burn a few extra calories without leaving your desk, stand up straight, with your feet about three feet apart, and grab the edge of your desk. Keep your right foot

When Fat Holds You Back

Fat does more than slow you down on the basketball court. It can take you off the corporate fast track as well.

In one study, researchers at Harvard School of Public Health found that people who were overweight tended to complete fewer years of school and make less money (in some cases, more than $9,000 less) than their leaner peers. In addition, men who were overweight were 11 percent less likely to marry than those with thinner physiques.

Another study found that overweight workers had up to 40 percent more problems doing simple tasks quickly, like dialing the phone or working the computer. Heavy workers were 3.5 to 4.1 times more likely to develop abnormal nerve conduction in the wrist, a characteristic symptom of carpal tunnel syndrome.

planted and your right leg straight, point your left foot to the side and slowly bend your left knee until your left thigh is parallel to the floor (don't let your knee extend past your foot). Hold for a count of three, then push back to starting position and repeat for the right side. Repeat ten times.

Shove off from your desk. For a good desk-side push-up, place your hands shoulder-width apart on your desk and step back until your feet are four feet away. Lean forward until your body is at a 45-degree angle from the floor. Make sure your weight is resting on your hands and the balls of your feet. Bend your elbows until your chest almost touches the desk. Push back to the starting position. Repeat 10 to 12 times.

Throw the book at flab. Those heavy reference books are good for more than trapping dust. Grab two books. With your arms at your sides and your palms facing your thighs,

hold one book in each hand. Keeping your right arm straight, slowly raise the book in front of you until it's parallel to the floor, simultaneously rotating your wrist so your palm is now facing downward. Hold for a count of three. Then lower your arm to the starting position and repeat with the left arm. Repeat ten times.

Get a leg up. Nothing burns fat like a good one-legged squat. Stand facing the seat of a handy chair—the kind without wheels, please. Lean over and grip the armrests or the sides of the seat. Bend one leg and lift your foot off the floor behind you so it's suspended in midair, shin parallel to the floor. With your weight resting on the other leg, slowly bend that knee and squat about six to eight inches until you feel tension in the front of that thigh. Slowly raise back to the starting position. Repeat ten times, then do the other leg.

Never let it be said that you don't do squat at work.

Don't take it sitting down. Okay, sit-ups aren't much fun, but if you do them right, they're an incredibly effective way to boost your metabolism and rev your energy levels—and, while you're at it, give you some washboard abs to be proud of. Plus, you can do sit-ups anywhere there's room to lie down. (Just be sure to close your office door first.)

To get the most from your efforts, don't jerk yourself up and forward, experts advise. You want to lift just your shoulders and upper back off the floor, not your whole torso. It may seem like a less demanding exercise, but it's not; it just cuts out the wasted motion and the wasted time that's typical of the traditional sit-up. And when you're working out at work, every second counts.

Spend ten seconds curling upward and another ten seconds easing back down. The slower you go, the more muscle fibers you call into play, and the more defined you'll get.

Holiday Strategies

Watch Those Season's Eatings

Trying to get through the holidays without gaining weight is like crawling through a culinary mine field. From Halloween to Christmas to the Fourth of July, we're surrounded by potential bomb blasts of overindulgence, from lavish cocktail parties and sumptuous holiday feasts to boxes of cookies in the mail. We try to rein in our cravings, but all it takes is one misstep, an excessive meal or two—and we could blow up.

Caught in the Holiday Vortex

Keeping a steady weight can be tough at any time of year, but the holidays, experts agree, pose particular risks. Research has shown that we put on weight when we put on our party hats. In a study of Christmas revelers, for example, Swedish researchers found that people who were otherwise in good trim typically put on almost a pound over the yuletide season. Some gained as much as 2⅔ pounds.

"It's not just the sheer amount of rich food and treats that starts piling up around the holidays, it's the fact that you're also socializing with friends and relatives and paying less attention to what you're eating," says dietitian Barbara Whedon of Thomas Jefferson University Hospital. "It all starts to add up."

Nor are you likely to get much relief from overly hospitable hosts—living embodiments of Mom who beg you to eat, please eat, just a little smidge, just another bite, just one more helping.

"Even if you're not especially hungry at a big dinner,

there's always some social pressure to eat—this is your host's best recipe, and you wouldn't want to offend her," Whedon says. "It can be a complicated situation, and a lot of people give up and overeat."

Fit for Feasts

There's no reason you should become a holiday hermit, a sad soul consigned to watching the festive gorging from the culinary sidelines.

No one should have to forgo entirely the traditional holiday spread we get to enjoy only once or twice a year. Be it a Thanksgiving turkey with all the trimmings or a sizzling Independence Day barbecue, you have every right to eat your fill. But it's possible, Whedon says, to eat well without blowing your good intentions in the process. "Don't obsess about it—you won't enjoy the holiday if you're frantic about eating too much," she adds.

What you should do, however, is plot your moves before laying a napkin in your lap. That way you can enjoy the holidays—and the good food that goes with them—without carrying around the weighty consequences later.

Don't starve ahead. It's natural, when a major spread is pending, to think about skipping a few meals to leave room for the big event. Problem is, this makes about as much sense as giving up sex for three weeks to enjoy one good night. Your appetite may be stronger, but your enjoyment of the experience won't be much improved.

"By dinner you'll be starving, so you won't be making good decisions about what you eat," Whedon adds.

Get loaded before the party. Instead of eating light before a big holiday event, load up with some low-fat food beforehand. "This curbs your appetite, so you can make better choices," says Whedon.

Some good choices include soup and bread, pasta and vegetables or even a few pieces of fruit. Carbohydrates quickly convert to body fuel. Since your body can store only a limited amount of this fuel, your appetite is going to lose some of its insistence. In comparison, your body can store about 50 times more fat before your stomach says "Full."

The idea isn't to fill yourself so full you won't be able to cram in another mouthful later. But by taking in at least some calories before the big event, you'll take the edge off your appetite and help control yourself from going overboard.

Exert cocktail control. Studies have shown that alcohol makes people hungrier. At the same time, it lowers their inhibitions, so they're more likely to gorge. "The more you drink, the less you care about what you're eating—especially if you're drinking on an empty stomach," says Dr. Steven Peikin of the University of Medicine and Dentistry of New Jersey Robert Wood Johnson Medical School and Cooper Hospital/University Medical Center. To keep alcohol from crashing your party, he recommends drinking only water or some other low-cal, nonalcoholic beverage until after the dinner bell rings. Or at least stick with a low-cal alcoholic beverage like a wine spritzer.

Reward yourself later. There's nothing wrong with having a beer or a glass of wine with your dinner, Whedon adds. "By waiting for the meal, you're not drinking on an empty stomach, so you're controlling your appetite better," she says. So revel in the holiday spirit. Drink a toast to your host—and to your own good health.

Wet your appetite. "Drinking generous amounts of water is overwhelmingly the number-one way to reduce appetite," says George Blackburn, M.D., Ph.D., associate professor of surgery at Harvard Medical School.

Reinventing Your Holiday Routine

Eating, drinking, napping, channel-surfing—if these pastimes sum up your holiday routine, it's no wonder you're having a hard time keeping the weight off. But with a little creative retooling, you can curb fat and have fun at the same time. For example:

Last Year...	This Year...
Watched the game on TV with the guys	Organize a game in the backyard
Watched *A Christmas Carol*	Go out and sing Christmas carols
Cleaned out the buffet table	Help clean up the buffet table
Ate turkey smothered in gravy	Eat turkey smothered in cranberry sauce
Got up from the table and took a nap in the La-Z-Boy	Get up from the table, go for a 15-minute walk and then take a nap in the La-Z-Boy

---

"Many people think they're having a food craving when in fact they're thirsty," says Dr. Blackburn.

As a rule, experts say, you should drink at least eight glasses of water a day. And when you're planning a big feed, pouring in a few extra ounces will help keep your appetite under control.

Eat the chow, skim the fat. While not all holiday calories can be easily trimmed away, there are ways to limit the damage. If you're eating turkey, for example, a serving of white meat has less than half the fat of a comparable serving of dark meat. If you're having roast, trim away the visible fat, including the crispy bits—they're nothing more than burned fat.

Go easy on the salt. Guys concerned about their blood pressure already know enough to watch their salt intakes—but the possible evils of sodium aren't restricted to those with high blood pressure. Salt may make you want to eat more, perhaps by boosting levels of hormones that stimulate appetite. So if you want to spice up your food, try vinegar, lemon, dried herbs or other low-sodium alternatives instead.

Give up the skin. Much as you might love the crackly skin on the holiday bird, it can really cook your goose. One serving of light-meat turkey without skin, for example, contains a little more than three grams of fat; one serving with the skin has over eight grams. Whedon recommends discreetly peeling the skin off the bird and setting it to the side of your plate.

Be careful with add-ons. Don't cover your plate with a whopping serving of stuffing and a wash of gravy. Both gravy and stuffing are often made with organ meats, which are extremely high in artery-clogging fat and cholesterol.

Go for the greens. The cornucopia of vegetables at the holiday table will satisfy just about any taste. At the same time, vegetables fill you up, so you eat less fat. "They're a good choice as long as they're not dripping with a cheese or butter sauce," adds Dr. Peikin.

In fact, don't look on greens as being only a supporting player. By giving them star billing, you'll naturally eat less of the fattening foods you're trying to avoid.

Always keep something on your plate. During the holidays especially, an empty plate is to the host what red flags are to a bull. "No one believes you're full if your plate is empty. But if your plate still has a bit of food on it, that sends the signal you've had all you can possibly eat," says Whedon.

While you're at it, make sure that little something left behind is your least favorite dish. Otherwise, you're more likely to forget yourself and eat it, thus devouring your anti-fat shield.

Enjoy your just desserts. It's no easy task to forgo a delicious slice of apple pie or a heaping helping of baked Alaska. So don't even try. Enjoy yourself. "You don't want to overdo it, but you don't want to deny yourself completely, either," Whedon says.

What you can do is avoid those desserts that you can pig out on any time of the year. For this special day, focus on holiday treats. "If you can't resist having more than one dessert, limit yourself to just one or two bites of each treat. Or share it with someone—it's better than eating the whole thing by yourself," says Whedon.

Skip the sofa. Your war against weight doesn't end at the dining room table. Once the feast is over, the temptation to sink into the nearest chair can be almost overwhelming. By staying on your feet and getting a little exercise—a fast walk, for example—you'll fight off the stupefying urge to sleep, and you'll burn a few of the calories you just consumed. "It won't make up for all of the food you just ate, but it will help your body burn more calories," Whedon says.

Go easy on yourself. Don't despair if occasionally your appetite gets the best of you. It's a holiday, you're surrounded by great food, and all your friends and relatives are eating like kings. You'd have to be Superman to always keep your appetite under control. So cut yourself some slack if you slip a little in the discipline department.

"You can compensate for the calorie load by choosing lower-fat foods for the next day or so and being more physically active," Whedon advises.

On the other hand, don't let a momentary lapse lead you farther down the road to culinary temptation.

Going Light at a Hearty Party

Although meals make up the biggest fat threat around the holidays, parties and other social events can be pound-packing experiences, too.

"Parties are just as damaging to someone trying to watch his weight as big dinners are,"

Whedon says. "All that finger food looks small, but it's very big in fat."

What follows is a safer way to work the room—without lingering too long at the bar or over the hors d'oeuvres.

Begin with the buffet. While this is usually where a party's heartiest—and heaviest—fare resides, you should be able to scavenge at least a few good-tasting items that don't contain fat in the double digits.

"Some good choices are things like shrimp cocktail, fruit salad and any vegetable that's light on the dip," Whedon says. And don't forget the pretzels, which are also low in fat. "If there's a cold-cut platter, stick with turkey, ham or lean roast beef," she adds. By contrast, other meats, such as bologna, salami and pepperoni, and most cheeses are extremely high in fat.

Eat fruit, not fruitcake. Foods high in fiber are good choices when you're cruising the buffet line, for a couple of reasons. You have to thoroughly chew fibrous foods such as apples, pears, oranges and carrots, which means you'll eat them more slowly. The longer it takes you to eat, the fuller you can feel. Plus, the fiber in those foods take up more room in the stomach, leaving less room for fattier choices.

Turn up the heat. Adding a dash of spicy food to your meals increases metabolism, allowing you to burn some of those holiday foods a little faster. At the same time, spicy food decreases appetite. So when you're at that holiday cookout, ladle on a little extra barbecue sauce or add jalapeño peppers to your burger. And seek out buffet sauces such as hot mustard, cocktail sauce, salsa or horseradish.

Watch your hands. It feels awkward while mingling not to have a drink or snack in hand. "It's kind of a social security blanket,"

Winning the Drinking Game

When it comes to putting on weight, alcohol is a dangerous accessory. It inhibits your inhibitions. It makes you careless about what you eat. And it packs more than a few calories of its own.

It can be tough to say no when it's the boss who's buying the rounds or when your buddies are quaffing and want you to quaff along. But according to James Horan, longtime bar manager of Boston's Statler-Hilton Hotel, there are ways to resist the pressure without making a scene.

Make it last. "Get a big beer and sip it all night," Horan advises. "The guy you're with won't feel like he's drinking alone—he'll think you're keeping up."

Cede the victory. Don't even try to match a guy drink for drink. Admit right off the bat that you're no match for his prowess. "It should satisfy his honor," Horan says.

Befriend the barkeep. If you want to keep your drinking under control, don't hesitate to approach the bartender beforehand. Tell him that when you order a gin-and-tonic, for example, what you really want is sparkling water. Or ask him to reduce the alcohol in your mixed drinks. "Then slip him five bucks," says Horan. "He'll be your friend after that."

says Dr. Peikin. "The problem is, you're going to consume whatever you're holding." He recommends cruising the room with a glass of water or a nonalcoholic beverage in hand. Or if you're walking and noshing, make sure the chow's low-cal.

Keep moving. When you don't know many people at a party, it's tempting to hover where there's food—at least that's one place you feel at home! It's better to move on, Whedon says. "It's amazing how much less you eat when the food's not right in front of you."

Travel Strategies

Safe Passage through Fat Country

Unlike Willie Nelson, many of us probably can wait to get on the road again.

They say getting there is half the fun, but time spent traveling when you're trying to stay fit is really half the battle. It's tough to get your workout fix when you're cruising Route 66. Arrival and departure schedules turn meals into grab-anything affairs—and let's face it, airports, bus terminals and train stations aren't exactly famous for their salad bars. As for those roadside fast-food joints, take the *s* out of "fast," and you have a pretty good idea what you're getting.

The bottom line is that any kind of travel can turn lofty aspirations for a good diet and exercise into so much lost luggage.

How to Travel Light

Experts acknowledge that keeping trim while traveling can be as frustrating as trying to refold a road map, but it's not impossible.

"Being away from home is not a license to gain weight," insists Dr. Morton H. Shaevitz of the University of California, San Diego, School of Medicine. "It may be a bit more difficult to keep up a fitness routine, but you've got to convince yourself that whatever you do at home for your health and well-being you can do when you're not at home, too."

Whether you're stuck in some endless airport layover, trapped in a hotel with no gym, road-tripping down the interstate or even in the midst of a well-earned vacation, with a few sim-

ple methods, you can wring a fitness plan out of any trip.

Plane Talk

Being on the go might seem fun and glamorous to the desk-bound, but anyone who travels for a living will tell you it's about as exciting as a car crash—and only a little less damaging to your health in the long run.

"I travel several weeks out of the year, and it just throws off my eating and exercising habits," says Steve Brackett, a sales manager in Des Plaines, Illinois, who's in his mid-thirties. "I try to watch what I eat and stick to a workout, but it's tough."

Granted, the occasional overnighter—along with the requisite airline peanuts, fattening room service fare and missed evenings at the health club—won't pack a lot of excess baggage into your cargo hold. But for men like Brackett who travel for a living, the pitfalls can be profound.

"You're in a rush to get somewhere, so you don't have time to eat a decent meal. Or you might have a layover, where you'll be either bored or famished. Or you're arriving at odd hours, when there might not be a lot of good food choices open to you," says dietitian Patti Tveit Milligan, a nutrition columnist for *Selling* magazine, a publication devoted to men who travel for a living.

You may not be able to control flight schedules or check-in times, Milligan says, but you can still control what goes in your mouth.

Pack a snack. You skipped breakfast to make the first leg of your flight. Now you're stuck in a red plastic seat in an airport lounge far from anywhere, and your hurry-up morning has left you famished.

A bad situation, but easy to avoid. "Buy lots of little snack-size foods to pack in your briefcase or carry-on," says Milligan. She recommends miniature boxes of raisins or dry cereal. Fruit cups are also good, as are fig bars, crackers or those neat little boxes filled with juice.

"They keep for a long time, so once you pack them you don't have to worry about them. But they'll be on hand when you need to take the edge off your appetite," Milligan says. Fresh fruit is also a good traveling food, she adds.

Try terminal treats. Airports aren't exactly bastions of healthy eating, but when there's nothing else to nosh on, you can at least limit the damage. "The hot dog, burger and nacho kiosks are really bad choices—all of that food is very high in fat," says Milligan. "You're better off getting just a snack until you can have a decent meal."

She recommends assuaging the beast within with a more-or-less healthful snack—a bagel, say, or a soft pretzel with mustard. "A lot of the cafeterias have a bowl of fruit at the end of the line—that's a good choice. And if you go into some of the newsstands, you might even find a bag of dried fruit snacks."

Look for midair distractions. Once you're on board, avoiding midair collisions with food can be a tricky maneuver. "Airlines use food and alcohol to distract you from the fact that you're in a narrow metal tube, 35,000 feet up in the air," says Dr. Shaevitz. Look for less fattening distractions, he suggests. Pack a fast-paced novel or magazine. Watch the in-flight movie. Even catching a nap is better than wolfing peanuts—and asking your neighbor if you can have his, too.

If you don't see it, ask. When the meal cart rolls by, you may not have to settle for that Salisbury steak with the vegetables swimming in butter and the fudge brownie for dessert. Plenty of airlines offer special low-fat meals for passengers who call ahead. Even if you didn't call, ask anyway. The airlines typically keep a few special meals on hand and give them out to the first people who ask.

Be a two-fisted drinker. The air in

planes is extremely dry. "When we get thirsty, we often mistake thirst for hunger," Milligan says. So try to drink plenty of water during the flight.

Working Out at the Inn

Just because you've checked into a hotel for a few days doesn't mean you have to check out on healthy eating and exercise.

"Most hotels recognize that their guests are trying to be health-conscious," says Dr. Shaevitz. Many major hotel chains offer amenities such as exercise rooms or a pool, and low-fat fare on the room service menu. To stay in shape in your home away from home, try these tips.

Lodge yourself in the exercise room. If you're going to pay top dollar to stay at a hotel that has a pool and exercise room, you might as well get your money's worth. Even if you've had a long day, just 15 minutes on a stair machine can help you unwind. And a few laps in the pool can be the perfect relaxer before you hit the sack.

Pack your trunks. "I almost always stay at a hotel with a gym, but I never remember to bring clothes to work out in," says Brackett. It's a good idea to keep workout clothes, wrapped in plastic, in your suitcase. That way you're always ready to go—and the running shorts can double as swim trunks in a pinch.

Keeping the clothes wrapped in plastic helps ensure that you don't attend a sales conference in a suit smelling of tennis shoes.

Use your imagination. If your credit card's so worn out that you have to settle for a hotel with no exercise facilities, improvise. Do sit-ups and push-ups on the floor of your room. Go for a run—or even a brisk walk—around the hotel complex. Pretend you're back in high school and do sprints on the stairs.

We're not talking only about convenience: Stair climbing burns about 13.5 calories per minute, while pumping a stationary cycle in some smelly, mirrored room in the basement burns about 8 calories.

Skip your exercise. For a great on-the-road workout, take along a jump rope. "It's excellent exercise equipment for traveling. It fits easily in your suitcase or carry-on. You could jump rope for 10 or 15 minutes and get a good workout," says Art Mollen, D.O., director of the Southwest Health Institute in Phoenix. How good? In 10 minutes you'll skip about 800 times, burning about 130 calories in the process.

Just be considerate of the guy in the room beneath you and keep your rope-skipping to civilized hours.

Don't eat in your room. In the privacy of your hotel room, eating sensibly can be as tricky as figuring out the remote control. You're bored, no one's watching—hey, why not raid the honor bar or order a five-course meal from room service?

"Instead, go down to the hotel restaurant or walk to one nearby," suggests Milligan. For one thing, when we're in public instead of squirreled away in our rooms, we tend to eat less. Plus, just heading downstairs ensures you'll get at least a little exercise.

If you're getting in on the red-eye and all the eateries are closed, go ahead and eat in your room. "But order just a snack," says Dr. Shaevitz. Your best bets are lighter foods that won't keep you awake, such as fruit trays, salads (dressing on the side, of course), cereal or even a bagel and jelly.

Healthy Holidays

When guys go on vacation, they tend to take off from every kind of work—including the Herculean effort it takes to stay in shape. After all, it's not every week you get to lounge in some sun-dappled paradise, letting the cabana boys see to your every gustatory whim. It's vacation, for crying out loud. You're entitled to indulge a little.

You have a point. And if your vacation is the kind that includes plenty of physical activities, such as skiing, hiking or scuba diving, you can probably take a vacation from your usual workout routine.

"But if your trip is basically sedentary with lots of eating opportunities, such as a cruise or a visit to a resort, exercise should be mandatory," advises Dr. Shaevitz. You can still bask in the glories of surf and sun and squeak in time for fitness before the next round of margaritas.

Go ahead—live a little. One of the biggest joys of traveling is eating—just don't do it in a big way three or four times a day.

"I suggest that travelers have a couple of micro-meals and one bigger meal where they indulge a bit more," says Dr. Shaevitz. If you have cereal for breakfast and a salad for lunch, then have a four-course meal for dinner. This way, you can watch your food intake and still be a bit decadent.

Do as the natives do. Traveling isn't much fun if you can't sample some of the local cuisine. But that doesn't mean you have to eat the fattiest of foreign foods. If you're in an exotic locale, sample the indigenous fruits, vegetables and other local low-cal fare.

"When I went to Paris with my family, lunch often consisted of picking up three or four pieces of fruit at a local outdoor stand, a large bottle of sparkling water, a loaf of crusty French bread and just a few slices of cheese, which we'd share amongst the four of us," says Dr. Shaevitz. Avail yourself of the culture. Often as not, you'll find some pretty healthy choices.

When in Rome—roam. At least once a day on your vacation, get off your beach towel and do some sight-seeing. Stretch your muscles; expand your horizons. You'll have plenty of time later to lounge by the pool with a bottomless cocktail.

Staying on the Road to Fitness

You might think that a speeding ticket would be the worst thing you could pick up on a road trip, but ounce for ounce, fat is probably worse. For travelers who rely on ground transportation, riding the roads and rails is almost always an order-to-go proposition fraught with dietary perils.

"If you're driving or taking a bus or train somewhere, there's not much you can do except sit and eat. And when you do stop for meals, it's almost always at some roadside restaurant that offers fast—and not very healthy—food," says Milligan. Here are some ways to keep those excess pounds from hitching a lift with you.

Pack munchies for the miles. Instead of relying on the vending machine and bags of junk food in gas stations and rest stops, pack your own munchies for the road. "Fresh fruits and raw vegetables are the best choices, but you can also pack along low-fat crackers or dried fruit, or low-fat granola or sport bars," suggests Milligan.

Stretch your legs. After a few hours on the road, your butt is bound to fall asleep, and the rest of you may soon follow. A brisk walk around the rest area or truck stop will not only keep you awake, it will also help burn some of those calories you picked up at the last fast-food emporium.

Leave the station. Unlike airports, where you're usually stuck in the outlands, bus terminals and train stations are usually in the heart of town—and you don't have to mess with security checks to get in and out. So leave the vending machines behind and seek out a local restaurant or corner grocery. That way, you can eat well and also get a little sightseeing in.

Eating in Strange Places

When you're vacationing in some foreign paradise, you want to do as the locals do and eat their food. But deciphering a menu in the native tongue is tough enough without trying to figure out how fattening the dish you just ordered is. Here's a quick gastronomic review of world cuisine, helpful for the next time you dine in another country—or in the ethnic neighborhood near your hotel.

Cuisine	Good for You	Bad for You
Chinese	Wonton soup, steamed vegetables or rice, fish	Deep-fried egg rolls, barbecued pork ribs, fried rice
French	Consommé, vegetable salads, crusty bread (easy on the butter), anything grilled, broiled or roasted	Croissants, any creamy sauce
Greek	Pita bread, rice, fish, chicken, tzatziki (yogurt and cutcumbers)	Feta cheese, phyllo dough, nuts, olives, anchovies
Indian	Chapati (baked bread)	Poori (fried bread), samosa (fried pastries)
Italian	Pasta, tomato sauce with garlic, sherbet	Antipasto, parmigiana, Alfredo or other creamy sauces
Japanese	Natto soup, chicken teriyaki, sushi, anything yakimono (broiled) or nabemono (boiled)	Tempura, miso soup, anything agemono (deep-fried)
Mexican	Soft corn tortillas, grilled fish, chicken fajitas, salsa	Crispy tacos, chorizo, refried beans, tortilla chips, guacamole, sour cream

Snacking Strategies

No Need to Ax the Snacks

A hankering for a good snack can strike at any time—and often does. Between meals, before bed, in the middle of the night—sometimes your stomach just won't take no for an answer.

Maybe it doesn't have to. While experts once chastised mid-meal munchers for having weak characters (and rapidly expanding waistlines), they now agree that an occasional yes to snacks is in order.

The catch, of course, is that whatever your nosh of choice happens to be, it had better be at least relatively good for you. That's tough. The average guy, nine times out of ten, will bypass the celery or figs and reach instead for a beer and a large bag of chips. "What more is there?" asks Matt Marton, a 30-year-old newspaper photographer in Oshkosh, Wisconsin.

Cruel Comfort

Marton is hardly the only man who's misguided about munching. When it comes to snacks, our appetites are wide-ranging. For example, the Snack Food Association estimates that Americans consume about 5 billion pounds of salty snacks a year—more than 20 pounds per person.

Clearly, more is involved than just the occasional mid-morning hunger pang. Experts speculate that our urge to snack is also driven by some deep-seated psychological needs. "We might be bored or feel angry or depressed. Or we might feel we deserve a reward," explains Marcia Levin Pelchat, Ph.D., a food cravings expert at Monell Chemical Senses Center in Philadelphia. "Then we turn to certain foods that, in our experience, make us feel better."

To the woe of his waistline, however, a guy who craves comfort in the kitchen probably isn't setting his sights on broccoli spears. What he wants, Dr. Pelchat says, is fat: a quart of ice cream, say, or a pepperoni pizza. That's when snacking bites back.

New-Style Noshing

But snacking, experts now say, can also be good. Pause for a moment to let that sink in. What Mom never told you, and what more and more researchers are recommending, is noshing: eating several small meals—meals between meals, as it were—throughout the day. Forget the old rule of three squares a day. That went out with lava lamps.

"One of the most important stamina rules is that your body needs its fuel in moderate doses throughout the day to keep energy nutrients optimally available," says Dr. Peter M. Miller of the Hilton Head Health Institute. "I actually counsel people to eat four or five times a day."

At first, you might think that following this advice would make you a fat man rather than a healthy one. The idea isn't to stuff yourself, Dr. Miller adds. Nor do you want to fill up on junk food. "What I am suggesting," says Dr. Miller, "is that you reduce the amount of food you eat at any one time so that you can spread the same amount of calories more evenly over the day."

This type of snacking has a number of advantages. By eating smaller meals more often, you can help keep your metabolism more constant, leveling the energy peaks and valleys

Feed the Fat Tooth

Some call it a sweet tooth. Others refer to it as an uncontrollable case of the munchies. But regardless of the name, nearly everyone has experienced an occasional craving for some delectable, not-to-be-denied kind of food.

While men's food cravings are highly individual, they do have one thing in common: They're hardly ever healthy.

Research has shown that while men are more likely to crave salty, sour or spicy foods than sweet ones, "what you're really craving is fat," says Dr. Marcia Levin Pelchat of the Monell Chemical Senses Center. To prove the existence of the fat tooth, researchers at the University of Michigan in Ann Arbor asked obese men which foods they like the most. Here are their choices.

1. **Steaks and roasts**
2. **Ice cream and frozen desserts**
3. **Chicken or turkey**
4. **Doughnuts, cookies and cakes**
5. **Spagetti and pasta**
6. **White bread, rolls and crackers**
7. **Fish**
8. **Pizza**
9. **Cheese**
10. **Potatoes, excluding fried**

that even though you may be eating more than you did before, you'll be less likely to put on weight. "You end up burning calories very efficiently," says Dr. Miller.

It's important to note, however, that the benefits of grazing won't apply when your snacks of choice resemble photographer Marton's culinary bombs, like chips and beer.

Instead, when your stomach roars between meals, silence it with high-octane snacks such as fruits and vegetables. You should never again walk out of the house in the morning without stuffing an apple or a banana in your briefcase.

For that matter, carry a stash of carrot or celery sticks with you to handle the mid-afternoon slump, the time of day when you're most likely to fall prey to the siren call of the vending machine. Snacking on fruits and vegetables helps keep our pumps primed with a fuel mix that's rich in complex carbohydrates.

Dr. Miller says that our diets should be about 60 percent carbohydrates, 15 percent protein and no more than 25 percent fat daily. "Rather than having a steak and fries for lunch, for example, you would do much better ordering a fruit platter, salad or perhaps pasta primavera."

Putting Snacks on Track

While it's admirable—noble, even—to dedicate yourself to a healthy, five-or-more-a-day meal plan, you're bound to feel the need for some extracurricular eating now and again: an almond-studded chocolate bar, for example, or a bacon cheeseburger.

There's nothing wrong with enjoying the occasional sugary snack. The problem for most of us is that one serving has a way of

that dot the daily landscape. And because you're never letting your tank run completely empty, you'll be less tempted by whatever junk food happens to cross your line of sight—and your waistline.

An additional benefit is that eating more often—a better term might be *grazing*—keeps your metabolism running high. This means turning into two, which then becomes four. Naturally, this has consequences. Like when your cholesterol suddenly shoots higher than your bowling score. When your profile begins to resemble the Michelin tire man. When your afternoon slump lasts well into evening.

"Too much sugar is going to give you an energy high that won't last very long," warns Dr. Miller. Granted, if it's a mood-altering substance you're craving, you could do a lot worse than having an extra dessert now and again. But you can also do better. Here are some munchies that have the hallmarks of the great snacks: They're chewy, crispy, creamy or crunchy. And whether you need a sweet, sour or salty taste, one of these snacks will likely satisfy your craving—without putting on the pounds.

Give sweets to the sweet tooth. Although sugar has long been demonized as a dietary saboteur, by itself it's fairly innocuous, says Dr. Pelchat. It's when sugar is combined with calorie-laden fat, as in chocolate or buttery desserts, that it starts weighing in with trouble.

"If you have a balanced diet otherwise, it's really okay to indulge in something sweet once in a while," says Dr. Pelchat. To satisfy your sweet craving, you could try hard candies. They have zero fat and last longer than a sugary-sweet cookie. If you want something a bit more *al dente*, candies such as Gummi Bears, jelly beans and licorice will also satisfy the craving without the fat glut.

Shop for substitutes. When you do have a craving for something rich—a thick slice of German chocolate cake, for example—check out the low- or reduced-fat varieties in the grocery store. There are a lot available, and many actually taste pretty good.

Just don't eat the whole box. It's nice to think that a "reduced-fat" label somehow suspends the laws of reality, but fat or no fat, you're still consuming calories.

Don't be a cereal killer. Although the chocolate-covered sugar bombs you used to snarf while watching Saturday morning cartoons won't fit anyone's criteria for a healthy snack, there are a lot of good-tasting cereals that will keep you satisfied without pushing out your belt. A high-fiber wheat-flake cereal has minuscule amounts of fat. Add skim milk and fresh fruit or—what the hell—a sprinkling of sugar. You'll satisfy your urge for a nice, sweet, crunchy snack and get some valuable nutrients and grains all in the same bowl.

Top your popcorn. Air-popped popcorn is perhaps the least-appetizing staple of the weight-watching set. But with a little creativity, it can also be a taste treat, even without the butter. Try sprinkling a little grated cheese, or even hot spices like pepper or chili powder. You can even toss in some cinnamon or a handful of raisins.

Get the fat-free sensation. Real snacks provide more than just a sweet taste. There's also a certain texture—the chewiness of a caramel, for example, or the creaminess of a chocolate mousse—that adds to their charm. To combine both sweetness and the right sensory experience, try fig bars. Some have no fat at all, while even those that do are healthier than their cousins over in the candy aisle.

Scoop up some sherbet. One snack food that men love intensely is ice cream. To satisfy your ice-creamy cravings, try sherbet, which can contain about a third less fat than most ice creams. Some frozen yogurts are pretty low in fat, too. But check the labels: Some brands of frozen yogurt contain as much as eight grams of fat per serving. (As a rule, you should avoid desserts with more than three or four fat grams per serving, experts say.)

Say hello to Jell-O. Wonderfully squishy and eminently slurpable, flavored gelatin fits the mold when you're hankering for a sweet snack with zero fat. Or if your tastes lean to pudding, check the dairy section. Some are now made from low-fat milk. The whole-fat kind, by contrast, can have four times as much fat.

Stealth Snacks

To hear those sandal-wearing, granola-eating health nuts tell it, anything that's not organically grown or covered with ugly lumps is probably going to rot us from the inside out. That goes double for whatever you were planning to have for your afternoon snack.

It turns out, however, that their wholesome snack choices aren't so wholesome. Take granola. It may be rugged enough to withstand a two-month trek in Nepal, yet a single cup packs over 30 grams of fat. By comparison, a full-size Hershey bar has 13 grams. (Tell those nut-and-twig eaters to chew on that.)

Below are the grams of fat found in one serving of some common junk foods as well as in their "healthy" counterparts.

"Not-So-Healthy" Snack	Fat (g.)	"Healthy" Snack	Fat (g.)
French fries (20)	17	Bran muffin (4 oz.)	20
Peanut butter cup (2 large)	14	Sunflower seeds (1 oz.)	14
Potato chips (10)	7	Frozen yogurt (1 cup)	8
Chocolate mint patty (large)	4	Cottage cheese (4 oz.)	5

Go crackers. Much as you love those salty, cheesy, savory snack chips, try switching to something with more natural flavor and a lot less fat. For example, cracked wheat crackers, Ry-Krisps and even flavored rice cakes have plenty of the crunch and hearty taste guys want out of any self-respecting snack chip. The dividend is that they're healthy snacks with little sodium and fat.

Break bread before bed. While no one recommends cracking a loaf of French bread every night at bedtime, there are advantages to having a healthful late-night snack.

Your body starts processing carbohydrates—such as rice, potatoes and bread— immediately, so they don't hang around all night. Furthermore, they help speed tryptophan, a sleep-inducing amino acid, to the brain, says Judith Wurtman, Ph.D., nutrition researcher in the Department of Brain and Cognitive Science at the Massachusetts Institute of Technology in Cambridge. In other words, they'll fill you up and help you sleep.

"Diets that don't contain enough carbohydrates usually turn people into insomniacs," she adds.

But earlier is better. While a midnight carbo feed won't transform you overnight into the Hindenburg, insatiable nighttime gluttony can cause its own problems.

Many experts believe that food eaten at night has more of a chance of being stored as body fat than the same food eaten in the daytime. This is likely because there are fewer bodily functions occurring while you sleep that require energy, explains James O. Hill, Ph.D., an obesity researcher at the University of Colorado's Center for Human Nutrition in Denver. The net result: "More of the food you're eating is going into storage," he says.

Social Strategies

Ways to Eat Healthy and Still Keep Your Friends

Oscar Wilde once said he could resist anything except temptation. And as every man who has tried to lose weight knows, once you're out on the town, temptation abounds. Whether you're on a dinner date, at a party or out with the guys, there's going to be food. Good food. Food you don't want to say no to. Food you're not even aware you're snarfing until the bowl's empty.

Let's face it: Every invitation to go out includes a second, hidden invitation to eat fat. And as we all know from basic social etiquette, it's impolite to decline an invitation.

Maybe we should all be a little ruder.

"Socializing and eating often go hand in hand," says C. Peter Herman, Ph.D., professor of psychology at the University of Toronto who has studied the intricacies of social eating. "The problem is, when you're with your friends, you often don't pay attention to what you eat."

Or how much you eat. "You eat more at meals with friends than any other time. And if you have a drink or two—which is pretty likely—that makes keeping track of your food intake harder," adds Dr. Herman.

Sometimes it seems like there are only two options: Become a lean, fit man with no friends, or be a stand-up, eat-anything kind of guy who looks like a manatee on legs.

There's a third choice. With a few simple maneuvers, you can have a social life and evade fat— not only at restaurants and bars but wherever friends and food meet.

Dining Out—Not Pigging Out

Most restaurants do their best to provide the perfect space for a casual meal, a business lunch or maybe a candlelit dinner for two. But these same cafés and bistros also overdo it: They almost always give you way too much food, and that food almost always has way too much fat in it.

This doesn't mean you have to restrict yourself to water and a salad, either—eating should be a pleasure, after all. So here's an eight-course plan for cutting fat from your menu without sacrificing your social life.

Begin with the soup. When you're starving, the soup can seem more like an obstacle between you and the main course than something to be savored in its own right. Think again. That steaming bowl of consommé can get between you and another—and presumably fattier—appetizer.

"Soups do a good job of filling you up," says Dr. Steven Peikin of the University of Medicine and Dentistry of New Jersey Robert Wood Johnson Medical School and Cooper Hospital/University Medical Center. A study at Johns Hopkins University in Baltimore found that a tomato soup appetizer reduced overall calorie consumption during a meal by 25 percent.

While just about any clear soup or broth is low in fat, you may want to steer clear of the creamier variety. "They're pretty high in fat," Dr. Peikin warns.

Graze on some greens. Like soup, a green salad will take the edge off your appetite— meaning you'll be less likely to need a whole chicken and a side of ribs to feel satisfied. "Besides the vitamins and minerals, the fiber in the leafy greens and vegetables will be quite satisfying," says Dr. Peikin.

Be careful what you toss on the tossed salad, though. "You can ruin the healthiest salad with

Bar Chart

If you have a beer gut, don't blame it all on the beer. On any given night out, even the designated driver will toss back at least a few shots of fat—from nachos and peanuts to those little salted goldfish.

Just how bad is pub grub? See for yourself.

2 Beers with . . .	Calories	Fat (g.)
1 cup peanuts	1,146	72
7 Buffalo wings	1,028	44
8 nachos supreme	861	31
4 fried cheese sticks	512	12
30 corn chips	447	9
10 potato chips	397	7
1 pickled egg	382	5
1 cup popcorn	333	2
1 beef jerky stick	330	1

just a few sprinkles of some fatty toppings," cautions Dr. Peikin. These include sliced hard-boiled eggs, bacon bits and even seeds or nuts, any one of which can double the fat content of a salad.

Dress with discretion. Nothing is tackier than overdressing. That goes for something as elaborate as a dinner party or as simple as the salad in front of you. Most chefs agree that putting anything more than two tablespoons of dressing on your salad is like dumping ketchup on a filet mignon; it masks the true flavor of the food and shows that you're probably not ready to be taken out in public yet.

Of course, your good breeding isn't going to help if the waiter has a heavy hand. To make sure your salad doesn't arrive at the table already drenched, ask for the dressing to be brought on the side. That way you can control exactly how much goes on.

Incidentally, don't put all your faith in the vinegar-and-oil dressing: In a two-tablespoon serving, it has about as much fat—approximately

16 grams—as the blue cheese. It's best to order low-fat dressing, but don't feel guilty for getting the full-fat kind. If you don't overdo it, you're not going to move up a waist size regardless of the dressing you choose.

Read between the lines. That wonderful menu prose makes it easy to forget that "lightly kissed with our own savory sauce" usually means "slathered with butter." Anything described as batter-dipped, fried, sautéed or creamed is a giveaway there's gobs of fat in it. "The same goes for food that's described as having lots of gravy," adds dietitian Barbara Whedon of Thomas Jefferson University Hospital. "If you can't tell how much fat is in the sauce or gravy, you can always ask for it on the side."

Entrées that usually contain the least fat are those that have been grilled, broiled, baked, roasted or steamed. Don't hesitate to ask how a dish has been prepared. If restaurants want to print their menus in a foreign language, they should be willing to provide the translation.

Cast a wide net. It's hard to resist a hankering for a thick, juicy steak, but sometimes a fish steak will hit the spot just as well. "A nice piece of grilled salmon or tuna can be very satisfying," Whedon says. "It can be just as filling as the same portion of beef—and it's healthier for you."

Veg out. Even if you don't normally chew the parsley that comes stuck to your plate, the vegetables accompanying the meal are more than a colorful distraction. "A lot of meals come with a baked potato or another vegetable as a choice of side dish," says Dr. Peikin. A starchy spud or another high-fiber vegetable will be plenty filling. Keep in mind, however, that many restaurants serve their veggies dripping with butter or some other fatty sauce. "Ask them to serve it on the side, or leave it off entirely," Dr. Peikin says.

Don't desert dessert. "If you've been making good choices throughout the meal, it's okay to have some kind of dessert. And if you're out with someone, it's certainly very social to share the dessert with a date or a friend," Whedon says.

"Quite a few restaurants offer some kind of low-fat dessert, even if it's as simple as sherbet or sorbet," she adds.

Invite a like-minded friend. Experts have long recognized that people who eat their meals with others consume more chow than those who dine alone. Indeed, research has shown that buddies with gargantuan appetites have a way of encouraging—consciously or not—their tablemates to keep up.

This doesn't mean the only way to lose weight is to spend the rest of your life eating alone. Experts have noted that those who are diet-conscious are just as likely to imitate friends who eat with restraint as those who stuff it in with both fists. So go ahead and set the table for two. Just be sure to invite someone who eats at your pace.

Trimming Tactics at the Tavern

Be it bowling night, a post-game party or a down-and-dirty pub crawl, it seems like many male social activities involve at least some booze and a bowl of snacks.

Where there's alcohol, there's calories—seven per gram, to be precise. In many beers, that can add up to more than 150 calories—as much as in a handful of tortilla chips. And that's before you help yourself to any of the wonderful greasy, salty foods that go down so well with a couple of brews.

Preparing for the Main Event

Be it at the ballpark, bowling alley or beach, fun-spot food offerings will likely be fattening. As a golden rule, it's best to bring your own munchies. Besides saving money by avoiding extortionary concession stands, you'll also spare yourself unwanted calories.

At the movies. Movie popcorn smells great and tastes great. It's also made at some theaters with coconut oil, which is 86 percent saturated fat. Put another way, one medium-size bucket may contain 50 grams of fat—and that's before you add the butter.

In the bleachers. There's not much you can eat at the ballpark or stadium that isn't going to knock your diet over the center-field fence. Nachos, roasted peanuts, chili-cheese wieners—they're loaded with fat. They're also irresistible. So go ahead and have a hot dog with your light beer. Then make it a point to stick with pretzels the rest of the game.

At the bowling alley. Most bowling establishments stopped evolving in the early 1960s, which means the menu is pretty much limited to fatty snack bar and vending machine fare. About the best you can hope for is to find some pretzels in the machine or a turkey sandwich at the snack bar.

This isn't to say you have to become a teetotaler or wire your jaw closed every time someone passes the peanuts. But you can make smarter choices to ensure that when you belly up to the bar, your belly isn't resting on the bar.

Don't cruise on empty. When you're meeting friends after work, it's tempting to skip supper and make up for it with a round of Buffalo wings and some potato skins.

On the trail. **Hiking is one of the healthiest social activities you and your intrepid cronies could pick. You can make it one step healthier by booting the beef jerky and trail mix out of your pack—both have fat aplenty. For a trimmer trailside treat, try dried fruit, suggests dietitian Patti Tveit Milligan, a nutrition columnist for *Selling* magazine.**

At the ski lodge. **When you're trying to warm up after a morning of hotdogging on the black diamond slopes, it's tempting to snowplow into a big basket of fries or some steaming mozzarella sticks. For a better hot lunch, get a bracing cup of coffee, tea, cocoa or apple cider and a plate of pasta. If all else fails, treat yourself to a hamburger— that's right, a hamburger, without cheese. Yes, it has fat in it, but far less than those other fried goodies.**

At the beach. **Experts say that when we think we're hungry, we're often really thirsty—and despite all those waves, nothing dries you out like a day at the beach. So between volleyball games, while you're soaking up the rays and drinking in the view, take a minute to quench your thirst from that big jug of water you brought along. Or try a combination of half water and half juice, suggests Milligan.**

more than 70 grams of fat—before he's blown the foam off his first beer. Do yourself a favor and ask the barkeep if he has any other pub grub, such as pretzels and popcorn, which contain a lot less fat.

Beware the calories on tap. The average imported brew has about 170 calories per glass, while domestics weigh in at about 140 calories. "Some of the domestic light beers have even less—and they don't all taste as bad as guys think," comments Jim Horan of Boston's Statler-Hilton Hotel.

Be particularly wary of specialty brews: Some pack a serious punch. You can't spot them by their color, either. Brown, yellow, red— color doesn't make any difference in terms of either calorie count or alcohol content, says John Hansell, editor and publisher of *Malt Advocate,* a magazine for beer and whiskey aficionados.

Here's how to tell what you're getting into: Hold the brew up to the light and see how much light passes through. In general, the less translucent it is, the thicker it probably is. If it's thick, that means more barley went into creating it, thus more sugars and, inevitably, more calories.

You can also tell by tasting it. If it has a malty flavor, chances are it's a highly caloric beer. You don't have to give up your favorite brew. Just keep in mind that beers this rich are made to be savored in small quantities and not guzzled.

Mix drinks. Instead of guzzling your usual high-calorie brew or cocktail, try something lighter for a change, Horan suggests. "Some of the mixed drinks aren't so bad, especially ones with carbonated water in them." He recommends a wine spritzer. "Of course, not every guy wants to drink a spritzer with his buddies," Horan admits.

"Don't set yourself up to gorge on those fatty bar snacks," says Whedon. Instead, try to eat something low-fat before you start carousing. If your local tap doesn't serve meals, suggest meeting somewhere else for dinner first.

Skip the nuts. When you drink, your body naturally loses salt, which is why you readily reach for salted peanuts when you're drinking. The problem is, the average guy can down a couple of handfuls—which contain

Clothing Strategies

How to Dress for Excess

Those last ten pounds are taking longer to burn off than you'd hoped. Or maybe you have already lost ten pounds and are looking forward to flaunting your stuff. In either case, wearing proper duds can help make the most—or, since we're talking about size, the least—of your physical attributes.

It has been said that clothes make the man. But as any tailor can tell you, the wrong clothes make the man look fatter. Chances are your closet is filled with mistakes—clothes that looked good in the store but not on you. Take that Hawaiian shirt. You thought it would hide your gut, but instead it made you look bigger than a roast pig at a luau. Or those snug denims: They held everything in—until you bent over. Then they revealed a major crack in your fashion foundation.

On the other hangers are those special clothes that make you look 20 pounds lighter: a baggy sweater, those gray pleated pants, a jacket cut just so. If you could just put your finger on exactly what makes them work you would always look like a million bucks—without having to spend that much.

Sizing Up the Problem

In our society, women have a definite edge over men, fashion-wise. "Early on, women are taught to recognize which clothing styles look good on them, which ones make them look fat and why. Men aren't," says Keith Scott, general manager

for Giorgio Armani in New York City.

It's never too late for men to learn the sartorial sleights-of-hand that can make even less-than-perfect physiques look terrific. Here's what you need to know.

When in doubt, go big. Men sometimes buy too-tight clothes in the hope they'll hold the flab in. They don't. Stuffing yourself into smaller sizes will only make the fat more prominent. When shopping, look for clothes that feel comfortable or even roomy (but not baggy). If the item you're trying on feels snug, go to the next size up. In most cases, bigger will make you look thinner.

Keep your clothing quiet. "On jackets and shirts, large designs like paisleys, boxy patterns and wide horizontal stripes cause the eye to move from left to right," Scott notes. In other words, when someone looks at you in that checked shirt, they're going to focus on your girth, not your length. So stick with solids or small, subtle patterns.

Go vertical. While horizontal stripes make you look broader, vertical stripes coax the eyes to travel up and down. This will help you look tall and lean even if you're not. "In this case, a nice pinstripe shirt can really have a slimming effect," says Scott.

Tie one on. A tie can be a large man's best friend, giving a thin, vertical line to any outfit, Scott says. Keep your neckwear subdued and simple, he adds. "The trend has been toward solid, neutral colors, with maybe a faint pattern."

Live in layers. Paradoxically, some men look thinner when they pile on more clothes—a trick known as strategic layering.

"Basically, instead of one layer—say, a shirt and pants—you drape on something extra: a big sweater, for example, or a flannel button-down that you wear over a T-shirt," Scott says. The layering "distributes" your weight over the

Quick Cuts

There are a number of strategies clothiers use for "thinning" body parts, from double chins to big feet. Here's a quick primer.

Problem Area	Don't Wear	Do Wear
Double chin	Tight collars, which squeeze extra flesh upward	Pointed collars, which make the chin appear longer and thinner
Big waist	Narrow, tight jackets or pants that emphasize bulk	Pleated pants and jackets with shoulders broader than your hips, which create a slimmer profile
Large behind	Heavy, textured fabrics such as corduroy, which accentuate your bulk, or no-vent jackets that ride up and expose the seat	Thinner, flatter-looking gabardine or worsted wool pants, or a vented jacket
Fat feet	Light-colored shoes with thick soles, which make size 12s look like 24s	Dark shoes and thin soles, like a black or dark-brown oxford

body instead of making it look concentrated in the middle.

Don't tuck and cover. Wearing over-size shirts tucked in results in excess material inside your pants. This gives you a big bulge—and not the flattering kind, either. "Wear it untucked with a T-shirt underneath," advises Scott.

Wear high collars. Wide collars are right for the retro look, but when you're trying to look slim, go high, advises Marvin S. Piland, men's clothing consultant for Saks Fifth Avenue in New York City. Like stripes, high collars cause the eye to travel upward away from a thick neck or barrel chest.

Put your clothes on a diet. "As a matter of common sense, the heavier fabrics look heavier, the lighter fabrics are lighter," says Scott. So if you're trying to create the illusion of thinness, "cotton, twill, linens, even flannel can be much lighter-looking choices," says Scott.

Please with pleats. Pleated pants tend to make men look thinner by concealing the belly bulge, Scott says. "Plain-front pants are all right if you're thin, but they can be a

real problem on bigger men," he adds.

When wearing pleated pants, however, the pleats should lie flat. If they spread out or the pockets flare open while you're buttoning the pants, go for the next size up.

Beware of bold buckles. We all need to hold our pants up, but the last thing a big guy needs is a big belt with a matching buckle. For one thing, a big buckle acts like a bull's-eye, drawing everyone's gaze to your belly. Also, wearing a wide belt makes you look wider.

Use a thin belt—one not much wider than your thumb, Scott advises. It will keep your pants on without drawing attention to the equator.

Put yourself on suspension. If you're a big guy, wearing a belt cinches up flab and makes it more prominent. As an alternative, strap on some suspenders. They'll hold up your pants just as well and give you a smoother line. Limit your choice to subdued, solid colors, though. Rainbow suspenders won't lend you any character and will focus attention on the area you're trying to hide.

Part Five

Real-Life Scenarios

Quest for the Best
They're America's top talents: successful, celebrated and at the top of their games. Yet they face incredible demands on their time. Here are their secrets for staying in great shape.

You Can Do It!
Some things in a man's life (besides death and taxes) are universal. Like middle-age spread. Like wanting to get back in shape—but not knowing where to begin. These guys started over. So can you.

Male Makeovers
A century ago most guys worked for their food. Really worked—in factories, for example, or in the fields. Today, an eight-hour shift is as likely to be spent in a conference room as outdoors. Entertaining clients. Eating too much. Schmoozing in bars. For guys today, getting in shape is hard. Experts give their advice.

Postmortems
These men were big in every sense of the word. Not just in size, but in ability. Popularity. Lust for life. Yet the same appetites that made them household names also contributed to their downfalls. Here are their stories.

Quest for the Best

They're America's top talents: successful, celebrated and at the top of their games. Yet they face incredible demands on their time. Here are their secrets for staying in great shape.

Tom Brokaw, TV News Anchor

Exercise Anchors His Turbulent World

As he rounded a corner during his morning run, Tom Brokaw found himself face-to-face with a band of men brandishing weapons. In El Salvador during the war, surprising people with guns was not a great idea.

"It turned out to be a Salvadoran army patrol, thank God," Brokaw recalls. "They were heavily armed, and they were as startled to see me as I was to see them. I went back and confined my running to just around the hotel."

As anchor of the *NBC Nightly News* since 1983, Brokaw, who's in his mid-fifties, frequently finds himself in whatever corner of the world is ready to explode. And almost always, he finds a way to keep up his daily fitness regimen, which dates back long before the running boom of the late 1970s.

A Valuable Lesson

"I was a high school jock," says Brokaw, who grew up in Yankton, South Dakota. "Then I went to college, and I guess I thought that all the fitness I'd enjoyed through high school would be sustained, no matter what I did. So I kind of went on a beer and pizza diet and quickly ballooned up. I also started smoking."

After graduating from the University of South Dakota, Bro-

kaw landed a television news job in Omaha. Three years later, he was married and anchoring the late-evening news on an Atlanta station when he realized he had grown so overweight and out of shape that he could no longer take part in physical activities he once enjoyed. He kicked smoking and took up running.

"I found out how hard it was once you get out of shape to get back into shape," says the six-foot-tall Brokaw, who is now 185 pounds. "So I just kept working at it and working at it. And I finally got my weight down to an acceptable level. It became part of my mind-set. I've been doing it ever since."

Globetrotting

And he has done it all over the world. While reporting from China during the Cultural Revolution in 1974, Brokaw says, "I would get up very early in the morning and run in the streets of Beijing." Chairman Mao Tse-tung may have excoriated the running dogs of capitalism, but running proletarians were another matter. Mao had decreed that the masses should exercise, and they did—en masse.

"I had a blue running suit, just like the Chinese, and I would fall in with a group of Chinese who would be running down one of the main thoroughfares," Brokaw recalls. "Suddenly, they would realize there was this round-eye with them. And they would just veer off as one and go in the opposite direction. They didn't want to have anything to do with being around me."

Another time, in Warsaw,

Brokaw was running across a public square when he encountered an older couple. The man turned to the woman and, "with a real quizzical expression on his face, said something in Polish," Brokaw says. "She looked at me, then looked back at him and said 'Jogging.' So I guess it translates into every language."

Working Out

Brokaw usually starts his day with a 7:30 A.M. run through Central Park with his yellow Labrador, Sagebrush. After two to four miles, Brokaw returns home, works out with weights and does sit-ups and stretches.

In the afternoon, he goes to the NBC gym for a second workout on the equipment there. His favorite is the rowing machine. "What I can do on the ergometer is get into a very strong, fast rhythm and then spend a lot of time thinking about what we're going to be doing that night," he says.

One of the reasons Brokaw works out so faithfully is to stay in shape for what he calls "the other adventurous things I like to do." A self-described Walter Mitty, Brokaw loves mountain climbing, cross-country skiing, kayaking and hiking.

Brokaw has an additional reason for keeping fit. "I feel better mentally, as well as physically, if I work out. I'm able to come in here and deal with the day."

A Passion for Pasta

Brokaw watches what he eats, but confesses: "I'm not a fanatic. I succumb like everybody else does to the temptations of dessert. But I try to eat a pretty healthy diet. Pasta's a very large part of my diet."

True to his Midwestern roots, Brokaw

News for Travelers

When major news happens anywhere in the world, chances are Tom Brokaw is on the next plane there.

Over the years the network news anchor has come up with a number of strategies for staying healthy and fit while on the road.

Be prepared. "On every trip I always carry workout gear," Brokaw says. "And just like getting an aisle seat on the airplane, part of the routine here for my assistants is to get me into a hotel with a gym. No matter where I am, no matter how late I arrived the night before, I try to get up early enough to go to a hotel gym and work out for 30 minutes before I go out and start the day."

Keep moving. "I've been known to run the back staircases in hotels," he says. "When I have a long international flight and there's a fair amount of airport transfer and so on, I never take moving sidewalks. I never take escalators. I always run the stairs. And I always try to do something mid-flight—get up and stretch and move around a little bit."

Help yourself. "On airplanes, I have a standing order for a fruit plate or a vegetarian plate of some kind. That helps. Then, when I get where I'm going, I will often go out into the local marketplace and buy food—rice crackers or something like that, and a lot of fruit—and just keep it in the hotel room."

still enjoys an occasional steak, but most of his main meals are built around pasta, chicken or fish. When traveling to exotic locales, though, Brokaw indulges his adventurous streak. "I eat everything," he says. "I wouldn't give up that part of it. I try almost everything, and I've paid the price a couple of times, too."

Brokaw is living proof that being adventurous and fit are not mutually exclusive. Displaying the wry wit that has made him a nightly dinner companion for millions of Americans, Brokaw adds: "I like life, and I want to be around for a while."

Tom Monaghan, President and Chairman, Domino's Pizza

A Big Slice of Fitness

We promised to interview Tom Monaghan in 30 minutes or less—an appropriate offer for the president of Domino's Pizza. But when it comes to fitness, you can't limit Monaghan. His dedication knows no bounds.

A hearty commitment to health may seem strange for a man who has made millions as America's number-one pizza pusher. Monaghan, after all, could rest on his laurels and survey America from the apex of his career. He could, like countless other executives, enjoy the good life, sipping martinis and breaking a sweat only when stock prices drop. But instead, Monaghan—the king of a burgeoning $2 billion pizza empire—works every day to keep his five-foot-ten, 155-pound frame in shape. And with 16 percent body fat, his sleek physique is a tribute to his success.

"I usually run six days a week. I get up at 5:00 A.M. on weekdays and I run about seven miles," says Monaghan, who lives near Domino's corporate headquarters in Ann Arbor, Michigan. "On weekends, particularly Sunday, I run 12 to 24.5 miles—that's the most I've run."

When he's not pounding the pavement, this ex-Marine, who's now in his late fifties, is lifting heavy metal in the company gym or pumping out scores of punishing push-ups in motel rooms when he's on the road.

"I'll do 100 to 125 push-ups at one time, then I'll rest and do another 25 after," Monaghan says. "It's funny, but in the Marine Corps I never did more than 75."

Monaghan says he exercises so much because "it's easier than eating less." In fact, he cites a voracious appetite as his worst enemy in his fight against fat. "You're talking to a guy who has a world-class capacity for food," he laughs. "I can pile it away like you can't believe."

It's this appetite that 20 years ago pushed Monaghan to 200-plus pounds, the most he has ever weighed. Getting that heavy made such a negative impression that Monaghan lost 15 pounds almost immediately. He has been crusading against excessive weight gain ever since.

Monaghan today is meticulously careful about what he eats. He eschews sweets, alcohol and red meat and opts instead for lots of vegetables, pasta and beans. He drinks plenty of water and never eats until he's stuffed.

"I always want a little more when I'm done eating," he says. "I haven't tested my capacity in years."

The example Monaghan sets permeates Domino's corporate culture. The 450 employees at corporate headquarters have access to a gym and ongoing weight-loss programs. Monaghan himself once offered an obese top-level franchisee $50,000 if he finished a marathon.

"He was about 100 pounds overweight, and he was very impressed with the fact that I had just run my first marathon," Monaghan recalls. "I said, 'You could do that, but you'd have to train for it.' "

Monaghan's man did it. He lost about 100 pounds, ran the marathon and collected his 50 grand.

"The whole thing was great, it was very inspirational," Monaghan says. "I wish he kept it off. He's probably heavier now than ever."

In spite of that, or perhaps because of it, Monaghan will keep preaching the fitness gospel as long as he can.

"Most of us sit at a desk for a living. Our bodies aren't made for that, so we should do something to compensate," Monaghan says. "In the next 20 years, I don't want to start falling apart."

Galen Rowell, Adventure Photographer

In Shape to Get the Shot

Galen Rowell may have Jimmy Olson's job, but his body is more like Superman's.

Rowell, of Berkeley, California, owner of Mountain Light Photography, is one of the nation's premier adventure photographers and an expert mountain climber whose commitment to health has helped him conquer some of the world's most challenging peaks and rock faces. Now in his fifties, Rowell has led an expedition to Mount Everest and made the first one-day ascent of Mount McKinley in Alaska. Nearer to home, he has made over a thousand climbs on the rock faces of Yosemite and the High Sierra.

And if pictures are worth a thousand words, Rowell's photographs are the equivalent of the *Oxford English Dictionary*. His photos have graced the pages of *National Geographic*, *Life*, *Outside* and numerous calendars. His work is also featured in a dozen of his own books, including *My Tibet*, written with the Dalai Lama.

Yet Rowell credits much of his success to always staying in top shape. Without a fit five-foot-eight, 155-pound frame, climbing mountains while clicking shutters wouldn't be as easy, he says.

"I've always had a high degree of personal energy that empowers my work as well as my play," Rowell says. "When I stay fit, I can do things that others do and record them on film without getting left in the dust."

Rowell realized the advantages of being fit in 1974 during a 16-day, 80-mile cross-country ski trip through the White Mountains of California. Thirty-three at the time and a bit out of shape, Rowell and three friends set up camp in wind-packed snow at

13,000 feet. To his surprise, his 43-year-old camp mate got up in the morning and took off running to see how it felt. The older man had been consistently stronger than Rowell on the trail. He told Rowell that he ran daily in the city and offered to take him out sometime.

"When he later took me on a nine-mile hill run, I made it, but I was completely whipped," Rowell says. "I began running regularly then and dropped from a high of 185 pounds to 145 a year later at the end of a hard expedition. I eventually put on 10 pounds and have stayed about the same ever since.

"Fitness is important," he adds. "It allows me to stay active, do things I want to do, look good and eat big meals once in a while without feeling guilty."

Once a week, he'll run up to ten miles at full race pace. Other workouts include a nine-miler on Tuesday mornings and mountain biking on Fridays. He also does extensive rock climbing, for which he trains by climbing on local boulders or using a home climbing simulator in his garage.

Rowell prefers doing several high-intensity workouts a few times a week to daily workouts of lower intensity. He also "listens to his body" and backs off when he needs to.

Rowell limits fat and avoids red meat, but he never keeps a food journal or counts calories or fat grams.

"Moderation is key here," he says. "When I'm on the road, I'll sometimes eat a hamburger or slab of prime rib, and I'll have a beer or two with dinner, but rarely more."

And although he's at an age where most men start slowing down, relaxing and taking it easy isn't Rowell's style.

"When I'm in the mountains or on a long run, I rarely feel any different than I did at 30 or even 25," Rowell says. "For me, keeping fit is simply the best investment I can make in my future."

Story Musgrave, M.D., Astronaut

Peak Performance at Zero Gs

Some of Story Musgrave's workouts are literally out of this world. He has cycled around the globe at five miles a second. His idea of power-walking is striding several thousand miles above ground while carrying more than 400 pounds of space suit on his back.

A physician, an exercise physiologist and, since 1967, an astronaut, Dr. Musgrave has flown five missions and logged more than 850 hours in space. He helped design the Skylab space station and has flown on four space shuttles, including the ill-fated *Challenger*, which he rode during its maiden voyage. More recently, Dr. Musgrave thrilled earthbound viewers with his orbital acrobatics during the televised repair of the Hubble Space Telescope. On that jaunt, Dr. Musgrave went extravehicular—outside the ship—three times, successfully recalibrating the telescope so it could scan deep space.

"Let me tell you, weightless though you are in space, that 480-pound suit still has plenty of inertia. You've got to be in some kind of shape to deal with it," he says.

If anyone's in some kind of shape, it's Dr. Musgrave. When training for space missions—in his early sixties, he's still on NASA's short list for future launches—the five-foot-ten astronaut tries to keep his weight to 152 pounds. His strategy: a combination of low-fat eating and a variety of aerobic exercise.

"When I work out I try to mix it up a lot," says Dr. Musgrave. "I do 25 minutes on the stair machine, 20 minutes on the rowing machine, 30 minutes of high-grade fast-walking on the treadmill. Then I throw in circuit training." Outside, Dr. Musgrave runs three to four miles a day. "To get more of a workout, I run

on grass at the golf course near my home. And I run on my toes. It's less efficient in terms of speed, but it's a great toner."

That's his normal routine. "When I'm up for a mission, there's a lot of extra exercise thrown in," he says.

Dr. Musgrave's regimen emphasizes cardiovascular benefits, and with good reason. "At my age, good cardiovascular fitness is the one thing that has allowed me to keep going up in space and work long hours at mission control, decade after decade. It really helps me keep up endurance. And as an astronaut, in the shuttle or at mission control, you don't need to have a lot of muscle, but you've got to have the stamina. When I'm on the ground, communicating with a crew in orbit, I'm pulling 16-hour days and longer. I need to be in good shape in order to stay sharp and alert."

In these high-stress situations, Dr. Musgrave admits, he gives in to some down-to-earth weaknesses. "Long about midnight, I'll break down and just eat whatever junk food I can find. Anything with sugar—doughnuts and cinnamon rolls especially. I figure if I'm behaving the rest of the time, I'm allowed to have some junk when I really want it."

But in general, Dr. Musgrave says, he adheres to simple dietary rules. "I watch my fat intake. I watch the salt. I try to eat plenty of grains—the carbohydrates in them really keep you going for the long haul."

For physiological experiments, Dr. Musgrave has performed a number of exercises in space, including workouts on rowing ma-

chines and stationary bikes. But he's not so gung ho that he forgets where he is. "The way I figure it, my time in space averages out to about one day out of the year," he says. "When I've got time up there, I'm going to spend it at the window taking in the view, not sweating up a storm. I can work out on earth anytime."

Graham Thomas Chipperfield, Lion Tamer

Daring Feats of Fitness

Graham Thomas Chipperfield's life has a familiar ring. He finds eating on the road an ordeal. He tries to check his lust for burgers and steak. He works out to feel good and look good. And he has a high-stress job: One slip, and his co-workers will have him for lunch.

For Chipperfield, who's in his mid-twenties, that's no exaggeration. When you make your living in a cage full of feisty circus lions, falling down on the job can be fatal. When you let elephants stomp you off a teeter board, sending you airborne and somersaulting onto the back of another elephant, being fit and alert is everything.

"My job is very physical," says the 5-foot-11, 153-pound Chipperfield, animal trainer for Ringling Brothers and Barnum & Bailey Circus. "When the train stops in a town, we have to unload the elephants and walk them to the building we'll perform in. Yesterday I walked five miles and then did two shows."

The shows are an aerobic workout in themselves. Chipperfield's lions were selected for their tooth-baring, paw-swiping feistiness (which explains the hundreds of stitches he has received, including the 80 he got while breaking up a big cat fight). Shutting himself in a cage with ferocious felines inspires fancy footwork.

"My lion act is very fast-moving," Chipperfield says. "I'm moving around a lot and I have to be very careful. If I were to fall over, it could cause a lion to jump on me. I have to be really, definitely, 100 percent there—in mind as well as in body."

A lion would really attack?

"It might easily happen. Then that's all she wrote."

There's no backup plan?

"No sir. It's all up to the lions then. And it's never the animal's fault. A lion doesn't really want to take a bite out of you, but if you were to get into the wrong place at the wrong time, it's natural instinct for a lion to do that. It can't help it."

Chipperfield's routine with the elephants Kamela, Lechemie and Mena also keeps him on his toes. "The most precarious moment is definitely the backward somersault onto the back of another elephant," he says. To stay sharp, he practices the stunt up to 30 times every morning.

"If the animal hits the teeter board too hard, I fly over," he adds. "If she hits it too soft, I land on my head. She has to hit with just the right pressure. And I'm landing on a rounded surface with a spine down the middle. It's quite difficult. I've broken my leg doing that."

Chipperfield comes from a family of circus performers in England. He first stepped into the ring at age 11, but there's one trick he still hasn't mastered: eating on the road. "I eat only in restaurants, and finding the healthy restaurants is a very, very big problem. I try to stick to fish, but I also like steak. I know it's not very good for me, but it gives me a lot of energy. I definitely keep away from chocolate."

He's able to make up for some of his dietary excesses by eating a healthy breakfast with his business partners. "We have a lot of fruit that we deliver to the elephants—apples and bananas. So I have breakfast with the elephants, you might say. I steal a little bit of their food."

Backward somersaults are hell on the abdominals, so Chipperfield does stretches before every performance to prevent muscle tears. He also lifts weights daily. "I have to wear costumes where a lot of my body is showing, so I have to make sure my arms, chest and abdominals are well-exercised."

Bruce Beall, Olympic Rower

Oaring to New Heights

The odds were against Bruce Beall from the start. He was trying for a place in the 1984 Olympics, competing against the country's greatest young athletes—men who were a lot younger and at their physical peaks.

But any doubt about his ability to compete at this elite level evaporated as soon as he set his scull in the water. By day's end, he had charted a course to his life's greatest goal: winning a spot on the U.S. Olympic rowing team.

Although the team didn't medal, just getting a shot at the gold was enough for Beall—and an impressive accomplishment in its own right: At 32, he was the oldest oarsman on that year's team.

Now in his early forties, Beall still enjoys that competitive high, racing as often as he can in rowing and cross-country skiing events. Professionally, he has moved from an athletic position to an administrative one. After years as a rowing coach and then a fitness trainer, Beall is now executive director of the George Pocock Rowing Foundation in Seattle, an organization that promotes the sport of rowing.

"It sounds like a very athletic job, but it's purely administrative. I spend just as much time behind a desk as anyone else," he says.

Not surprisingly, Beall has discovered the dangers of a time-intensive but sedentary job. When the six-foot-five Beall raced in the Summer Games, he weighed about 206 pounds. Today, he tips the scales at 222.

"Part of me wishes I had more time to work out and get back in the shape I was. I know plenty of guys who feel the same way—they look back at

their college or high school playing days, and they know they'll never be in that good a shape again. They figure, what's the point of working out?"

Beall has taken a different tack. "Whenever I get a chance I try to work out—you'd be surprised how little physical activity will make you feel better. It's too time-consuming to get out in a boat and row every day. But if I have enough time, I'll run or use a rowing machine for 40 minutes a day, four days a week. When it's crunch time, I'll just do some stretches."

Beall's also looking at other ways to fit exercise into his day, such as commuting to work by bicycle. "I'm always looking at ways to sneak in some exercise—it just gives me a lot more energy, especially when my job demands late hours," he says.

He's also trying to watch his diet—not always with great success. "I have a real weakness for cheese. And I'll have a couple of beers once in a while, but otherwise I eat pretty well. For instance, I'm not a strict vegetarian, but I eat so little meat, I might as well be."

Beall's best advice for staying in shape? "Pick an upcoming event—a 10-K run, a cross-country ski race, whatever—and commit to it. Send in the entry fee—nothing commits guys faster than laying down their own money. And I found that if I choose an event that's a couple of months off, I've got something to focus on, to train for."

Plus, the Olympian-turned-executive is learning to always schedule his athletic commitments into his calendar, making them as important as an upcoming business meeting. "And the payoff for your exercise is great. Whenever you compete in these organized events, you usually get some type of medal at the end." As someone who has gone for the gold, Beall ought to know.

Tom McMillen, Former Congressman and Basketball Star

Electing to Exercise

As co-chairman of the President's Council on Physical Fitness and Sports in Washington, D.C., Tom McMillen's official mission is to encourage Americans to exercise and lead active lives.

And the former NBA star and three-term Democratic congressman from Maryland firmly believes in practicing what he preaches.

Instead of running for elective office— or running the hardwood in arenas nationwide—McMillen, now in his forties, can be seen almost every day running with his two Labrador retrievers.

"I run with them, or they run me," McMillen says with a chuckle. "They sometimes go off the beaten path and try to pull me here and there. That's a minor problem. I can usually adapt to that."

McMillen first became involved with the President's Council on Physical Fitness and Sports in 1970 when as a standout high school athlete, he was named to the organization by President Nixon. He went on to play basketball at the University of Maryland, and was a member of the 1972 Olympic basketball team. Along the way, he also picked up a Rhodes scholarship.

A first-round draft pick by the old Buffalo Braves in 1974, McMillen enjoyed an 11-year stint in the NBA before retiring in 1986. That year, voters in Maryland sent him to the U.S. House of Representatives for what was to be the first of three terms. Later, President Clinton named him to co-chair the fitness council along with Olympic

star Florence Griffith Joyner in 1993.

In addition to McMillen's work for the council, he's chairman and chief executive officer of Complete Wellness Centers, a health care clinic management company in Washington, D.C. Keeping a busy schedule and maintaining a healthy diet is tough, but he has made it a priority. A typical day starts with "a very light breakfast—a banana, toast, maybe some cereal, orange juice, coffee," McMillen says.

For lunch, he usually has a vegetable patty, turkey sandwich or salad. "At dinner I eat tomato-based pasta, fish or chicken," McMillen says. "Occasionally, once a month, I'll eat meat."

As a professional athlete, McMillen was always in great shape—running and lifting weights to help survive the grueling NBA schedule. What he learned on the road he continues to use. "I look for hotels that have health clubs," he says. "I look for hotels where there's an ease of exercise, where you can run nearby."

It was during his NBA days that McMillen started running the stairs at hotels when he was stuck in some frozen city during the dead of winter. "That's the way I would get a workout, because it was too cold to go outside," McMillen says. "Steps were a great way to do that.

"When I was a member of Congress, I had offices at various levels—the third, fourth and fifth floors. And I constantly used the steps because I thought it was one way to get some exercise."

In addition to aerobic workouts, McMillen hits the weight room about every other day. One thing he doesn't do much of is play basketball. "My regimen today isn't so much competitive sport–based as it is more individualistic," McMillen says. "I've evolved away from that, going out and playing a round of basketball. I just try to do something every day. That's the key, to just go out and exercise every day."

Doug Foreman, Entrepreneur and TV Personality

His Beat Is the Upbeat

Entrepreneur and TV personality Doug Foreman knows firsthand about motivation to lose weight. To make a new business venture fly, he had to jettison 25 pounds.

The story starts in 1990 when Foreman, now in his late thirties, founded Guiltless Gourmet, a food company specializing in the baked tortilla chip. "I started doing that in my oven at home," says Foreman of Austin, Texas. Foreman began with $200, and soon the company was doing in the neighborhood of $30 million in sales a year.

In the process of developing a health-related business, he concluded that Americans were hungry for information about diet and exercise. In the entrepreneurial spirit, he decided to fill that need.

He sold Guiltless Gourmet and started the television program now called *Good Living with Doug Foreman*, 90-second TV news inserts that cover a range of self-improvement topics, from eating low-fat food to bettering relationships. The show is syndicated in a number of southeastern and western states.

In the early days, however, one potential client had reservations about how Foreman looked on camera. "He said, 'Well gee, Doug is talking about how to live right—diet, exercise and health. But it looks like he may need to lose 25 pounds.'

"It was real motivating to me to hear people say they liked what I was doing, but I needed to lose a little bit of weight to come across on TV. The industry says TV adds ten pounds to you just when you get in front of the camera."

To shed pounds, Foreman began working out aerobically—biking and climbing stairs—one hour in the morning and again in the evening.

After a few months, he had dropped the offending 25 pounds—and got the client. Today, the 5-foot-11 TV host weighs 195 pounds and is generally satisfied with his physique. "I would still like to have that rippled stomach," he adds. "And who knows? Maybe by summer I will. When you're not out in the sun, when you're not out there exposed, you tend to let things go a little bit."

For the most part, he practices what he preaches. For breakfast he has orange juice, coffee and a bagel. "Breakfast is pretty steady, the monotonous routine. At lunch I have either a turkey sandwich—no cheese or mustard—or a breast of chicken with steamed vegetables. In the evening I try to stick with some type of pasta, or possibly chicken."

As an entrepreneur, Foreman thinks a lot about what motivates people. That inspired his idea for the M & M Diet.

"People would initially think that it's candy, but M & M would stand for Money Motivates," says Foreman. "I'd take 25 people and ask them to lose an average of two pounds a week over a two- or three-month period. I'd tell them that at the end of that period, I would give them $1,000 if they would lose the weight. And it's my contention that I would get a success rate as high or higher than any diet plan that's out there."

Foreman acknowledges that even M & M-ers—if he ever really put up the dough for such a diet—would still have to learn to eat responsibly if they wanted to keep the weight off long-term. "Yeah, that goes along with any diet," he says. "But it would at least get them started, and I think that's a big part of the whole thing—getting started."

You Can Do It! Some things in a man's life (besides death and taxes) are universal. Like middle-age spread. Like wanting to get back in shape—but not knowing where to begin. These guys started over. So can you.

On-the-Job Straining

Mark Donald, Dallas, Texas

Date of birth: September 8, 1950

Height and weight: 6 feet, 200 pounds

Profession: Freelance writer

Fitness accomplishment: Lost 30 pounds in eight months—and kept it off.

Favorite junk food: "Fried chicken. In Texas we have great fried chicken. Come to think of it, I haven't had any in over a year.... Well, hey, I gotta go...."

Favorite health food: "I don't know if mussels marinara is healthy, but if not, I'd say pasta in marinara sauce."

Call it serendipity. Call it good fortune. I call it a good gig: to lose weight, get in shape and get paid for it.

Men's Health magazine commissioned me to write an article chronicling how I dropped 30 pounds in eight months through proper diet and exercise.

Although it was tough, I'm glad I took the assignment. As a freelance writer, much of what I do is over the phone or on a computer—not what you'd call athletic. And since I work at home, it's easy to take snack breaks whenever I'm bored, so before I knew it, my weight had ballooned to 226 pounds.

Professional Help

The magazine paid for a nutritionist and a personal trainer to make sure I ate and exercised correctly. The nutritionist put me on a five-meal-a-day schedule, though two of those meals essentially were snacks. But by having those snacks, I didn't go hungry—and I don't like being hungry. In addition, the trainer put me on an aerobic workout three times a week for 30 minutes, and I worked up from there.

Today, I'm riding my bike for 25 miles once a week, jogging for 3 or 4 miles once or twice a week and lifting weights twice a week, an hour a clip. I also in-line skate with my son.

I call it eclectisizing, because I get bored easily and need a large variety of exercises to keep my interest. If I have to do something repeatedly, I don't enjoy it. This strategy keeps my exercise routine fun.

Mental Fitness

I've tried nearly every diet over the years and always managed to regain the weight I lost.

This time feels different. I have so much more nutritional awareness that to violate it and act in spite of it is not a healthy thing for me to do. When I do splurge, it's in moderation.

To me, the best part about getting in shape is measuring yourself by how you're fitting into your clothes. You're recomposing your body by adding muscle and losing fat. It feels great to tighten your belt a notch or two more and to buy new clothes because your old ones make you look like a fortysomething slacker.

Flying High

Jim Schwartz, Santa Cruz, California

Date of birth: March 5, 1950

Height and weight: 6-foot-1, 198 pounds

Profession: Pilot for Delta Airlines

Fitness accomplishment: Conquered an apathetic midlife crisis by taking up cycling, dropping 19 pounds and toning up. Now competes in triathlons.

Favorite junk food: "I really love chocolate, but I just try to limit myself."

Favorite health food: "We're big on pasta. Stay away from heavy sauces, and it's a great meal."

A couple of years ago, I reached a point where I felt restless and out of shape. My clothing had gotten tight and I felt heavy. It was real uncomfortable. The scary part is that it was so gradual. As my family grew to three wonderful daughters, my exercise became sporadic while my diet stayed the same. I gained maybe three pounds a year. Before I knew it, I weighed 217 when I was normally around 200.

Being out of shape bothered me because I had always been athletic in the past. I played lacrosse and football in college—those were in my twenties, when I could trash myself and bounce back every day. But here I was in my early forties. I went to bed one night thinking how uncomfortable I felt with my body. I vowed to get up the next day and do something athletic. I didn't have anything specific in mind, but I knew I was going to reclaim my health.

Taking Off

The next morning, I dusted off my 15-year-old ten-speed, filled the tires and took off. I felt like I was going to die after the first few miles, but I kept plugging away at it. I knew I couldn't ride away all the weight I gained in one day, but I didn't expect the ride to be as exhausting as it was. But I kept pedaling. And pedaling. And pedaling. And when I made it home, which I barely did, I actually felt good. I mean I really felt good. I was even smiling.

It grew from there—slowly but surely. Now, I've done a half-dozen triathlons, and my normal routine consists of swimming two to three times a week for an hour and a half, running four or five times a week for 3 to 8 miles and biking up to 200 miles on a good week.

As for diet, I avoid high-fat foods, like fast food. I make a conscious effort to do this because it seems everything in the world has too much sugar or fat. Since I'm a pilot and I travel a lot, it takes a little extra effort to be on guard for junk food. It's so easy to want to grab a burger on the run between flights, but I won't. Instead, I'll find the airport deli and get a turkey sandwich with no mayo. It's really pretty healthy, and if you're strapped for time, you don't have to settle for a greasy hot dog. For dessert, I'll usually pick up some nonfat yogurt. Together, those two really make a great meal.

Long-Term Rewards

I look back and can't believe how much I've gotten out of reclaiming my health. It's not just the tangible rewards, like losing weight or looking better. It's the sense of well-being. Sure, some days my workouts are crummy. Some days I quit midstream. But it doesn't stop me from going at it the next time, and that's important.

Exercise and fitness are a long-term deal. It's not a three-week program to make your friends envious; it's a commitment. But it's worth it, because when your body is unhealthy, it weighs on your mind. Being in shape calms your mind. It gives you a sense of control. When things are not quite organized at home, it's okay now, because I'm in a better place mentally and physically.

Staying on Track

Jeffrey Leon, Toronto, Canada

Date of birth: August 11, 1951

Height and weight: 5-foot-10, 180 pounds

Profession: Lawyer

Fitness accomplishment: Lost 150 pounds in one year through exercise and cutting fat from diet. Has since completed 11 marathons, with a best of 3:36 in 1993.

Favorite junk food: "I like them all. I really have trouble answering that."

Favorite health food: "I'm not sure what qualifies as health food. I enjoy pasta and bagels. But whether those are health foods depends on quantity."

Almost from as early as I can remember I was heavy. I can remember being teased as a kid. As things went along, I gradually kept getting heavier and heavier. At the stage when friends who were heavy slimmed down, I kept going.

There were times over the years when I did lose weight—through Weight Watchers, a protein diet and just eating less. But it wasn't combined with physical activity, and I generally put it back on right after I lost it. By October 1990 I weighed 323 pounds. I was 39, so 40 was looming closely. I was having increasing health problems—high blood pressure and chest pains. I kept getting bigger and bigger, and every time I needed new clothes, I was up yet another size. About the same time, I was referred to a nutritionist who had helped a number of people I knew. So it was a combination of factors that made me realize I had to do something.

Tough Beginnings

I started keeping a diary and wrote down everything I was eating. It kept me honest. I was going to a nutritionist on a twice-weekly basis to get weighed and review what I was eating. It was part of the discipline I was going through. For a while I was quite dedicated, almost fanatical, about the amount of fat I was eating in my diet. Over time, you get away from that. But basically, it's still a matter of being conscious of foods that have high fat content and trying to avoid foods that are high-calorie.

I joined a fitness club, and they gave me a program that basically was a combination of aerobics and weight training. I started on the exercise bike and StairMaster and lost weight fairly quickly—at the rate of about 20 pounds a month. Within a few months, I had lost enough weight to start doing a bit of running. I had friends who were doing some running, and it appealed to me quite a bit. Part of it was the challenge, because the idea of running— even the idea of walking—was something that had been so foreign to me.

When I first saw that I could run, it was really a demonstration of what I had accomplished. I started building up my mileage and, in June 1991, decided to enter a 10-K race. After I finished, someone jokingly said, "Next thing you know, you'll be running marathons." That got me thinking. So I talked to someone and asked what my chances would be of actually running a marathon. He said, "Well, it takes two or three months of training." So I got a program and stuck to it fairly religiously. I managed to do the Detroit Marathon in October 1991 and ran 3:47. That was a bit of beginner's luck. I've run ten marathons since that one, and I've beaten that time only once.

I think the most important key to keeping my weight down is continued physical exercise. Normally, I run between 40 and 50 miles a week. If I'm in active training, I'll run more. In the fall of 1994, though, I learned a valuable lesson. I was injured and wasn't able to run as much. I could see the whole thing starting over again as I put on a few extra pounds. So I don't think you can ever say the battle's over.

First-Class Success

Raul Cazares, Chicago, Illinois

Date of birth: June 3, 1957

Height and weight: 5-foot-11, 184 pounds

Profession: Mailroom supervisor

Fitness accomplishment: Lost 55 pounds in less than one year, mostly by cutting red meat from his diet.

Favorite junk food: "I still have pizza every Friday night. And I love my beers."

Favorite health food: "Fish. I try to have some type of fish at least a couple of times a week."

A bunch of co-workers and I went out to lunch a couple years ago. We were joking and picking on each other, and then one of them turned to me and said "You know, Raul, you got a really fat face."

And it stuck. For weeks after that they were calling me Fat Face. I didn't let on how hurt I was, but it really bugged me. That's when I decided to lose weight.

Stealth and Commitment

It would have helped if there had been people I could talk to, to get support. But I didn't mention it to the guys at work—that's the worst thing I could have done. You tell some people you're going on a diet, and suddenly they start teasing you, bringing you candy and cookies, and they just wear you down. So I kept my mouth shut.

It was tough to get started. I tried to go on one of those Slim Fast diets, but that didn't work. I did lose weight, but once I stopped, I actually put more weight back on.

Then I started asking my doctor and other people what they did. For just about everyone, diet seemed to play a big role. So I decided to cut out red meat. I was eating it three times a day, and once I found out how much fat was in red meat, I just cut it right out of my diet.

Right away I started eating a lot of fish and chicken. I'm big on salads, too—only I stay away from the dressing.

I also watched when I was eating. I tried to eat my biggest meal at lunch in the middle of the day and have just something light—even a bowl of cereal—for dinner. I still had evening snacks, but I kept them light and tried to eat them early at night. My doctor said the later I eat, the more likely that food will get stored as fat.

Easy Moves

Finally, I started exercising. I didn't lift weights or anything—that's too much work. I just started walking. I take at least a 20-minute walk every day. I take the stairs instead of the elevator. When I'm at the mall, I park as far away from the stores as possible to make myself walk extra.

The thing is, I still cheat. I never go to the gym. I sit around and watch TV a lot. I drink beer and eat all kinds of snacks. But I pay more attention, so I don't get out of control. I want to be in shape, but I don't want to go crazy getting there. If I've got a taste for a cupcake, I'll have one, but I'll eat it slow—I won't shove it down my mouth.

Even though the changes were a huge part of my life, it took months for the guys at work to notice—guys never notice this stuff. Besides, I hadn't bought any new clothes—I was still wearing my size 42 pants. But when I was down to size 34, I bought a bunch of new pants.

I came in wearing all these thin clothes, and that's when they noticed: I'd lost my double chin and all this flab in my arms and stomach. They couldn't believe it. Neither could I. You know what? I still keep one pair of size 42 pants to remind me of how fat I was—it's a real symbol of what I did.

Securing His Future

Tommy Saggus, North Augusta, South Carolina

Date of birth: December 13, 1946

Height and weight: 5-foot-8, 165 pounds

Profession: Security officer

Fitness accomplishment: Lost 25 pounds in one year.

Favorite junk food: "That'd have to be pizza with cheese and pepperoni."

Favorite health food: "I eat a lot of chicken—not the fried kind, either."

Not so long ago I was having some blood pressure problems. I went to see my doctor, and he really put the fear of God into me. I was carrying too much weight for a guy my size, I had a stressful job, and to top it off, my father had died of a heart attack.

That's three strikes against me, so I came out of that doctor's office determined to change things. They had to put me on blood pressure medicine for a while, and I felt like the next step was that I'd get a heart attack, too. I sure didn't want that. I didn't want to be on the medication, either—I wanted to find a way to control the problem on my own.

Exercising Control

I hadn't done much exercising before, so I started walking, then running. It was tough at first, but as I started getting in shape, it got a lot easier. I got to the point where I was up to three miles a day.

That's all I do. I don't need a lot of this heavy exercising with weights and so forth. Just a few warm-up exercises beforehand— and then I run. I'm never going to be hard-core, but being in better shape feels good.

It's good exercise, but I also found out it's a great way to blow off steam. I don't have much patience—I used to throw holy tantrums, and it didn't matter who it was in front of—but the exercise really calmed me down a lot and burned off the weight at the same time.

All of this made a big difference in my job. As a security officer, I've got to keep a cool head because I'm dealing with all sorts of people. Plus, in security, sometimes you spend a good bit of time sitting around—if you're not careful, you can get out of shape pretty fast. I don't have that problem so much anymore.

A Family Affair

I also started eating smarter and watching my fat intake. My wife has been real helpful on that end. I used to eat a lot of foods that weren't so good for me. Now I have things like wheat cereal for breakfast. I used to eat a lot of red meat and fried food for dinner, but we put a stop to that. I hardly ever eat anything fried or really fattening now—mostly it's the better meats, like chicken.

If there are snacks in the house, my wife makes sure they're low-fat. That has made all the difference right there. I could still do better—I still give in and have some pizza now and again, but only very infrequently. We're working on eating better all the time.

Since I dropped that weight I feel like a different man. I handle the stress of my job a lot better, and I've done real well in performance reviews. I had to take a physical for work not too long ago, and I ran my best half-mile ever—three minutes and 38 seconds, which is pretty good for a guy who'd never really exercised before. I've got a better temper, I'm more alert, and my blood pressure's down. That's a big relief to me—and I want to keep at it.

I have two daughters, and they are my life. I want to be around for them as long as I can. No sir, when I die, I don't want my lifestyle to have been a contributing factor.

Step-by-Step:
An Aerobic Recovery

Bill Buchholz,
Santa Rosa, California

Date of birth: June 25, 1944

Height and weight: 6-foot-4, 210 pounds

Profession: Sales manager for an automotive parts warehouse

Fitness accomplishment: Used aerobics to put back surgery behind him.

Favorite junk food: Hamburgers, french fries and chocolate shakes.

Favorite health food: Pasta with pesto sauce.

I had a serious back problem on the job when I was about 38 years old. I was lifting some stuff and I pinched a nerve, and I also had a bone spur lodged in my spine. When that happened I was paralyzed from the waist down. They hospitalized me and found that the only way to cure the problem was to operate.

They operated and removed the spur and some cartilage. There was a lot of physical therapy to get me back walking again. I have done 10 or 12 exercises, like pelvic tilts, every single morning since the operation. Without those exercises, it's a little tough to get going in the morning, but once I do them I'm fine.

I found that as soon as I started to gain any weight at all, it caused a lot of pain where the spur was removed. My girlfriend goes every day to a gym called Coach's Corner in Sebastopol, California. She was very instrumental in getting me to start aerobics there.

Aerobic Relief

Joanie Price was teaching a class on Mondays, Wednesdays and Fridays. I went in the early morning because I'm an early riser

anyway. We start at 6:00 A.M. and we're done at 7:00 A.M. Shower, and I'm at work at 7:30 or 7:45 A.M. So it works right into my schedule.

Joanie had written a small book about fitness and fat in the diet. I read it on a vacation in Maui, and when I came back, I started in on her regimen. I cut back on the fat and started working out three days a week. I like the music. The dancing part of it is great for me. Time flies by, and you're still getting a workout.

Our class does step aerobics, and usually one day a week we have weights involved in the workout. It's usually about 10 minutes of warm-up, about 5 minutes of step aerobics and then a few minutes of a small-weight workout, about two to five pounds per hand. It varies throughout the class for a total of 50 minutes, and we spend 10 minutes cooling down.

I've arranged my work schedule around this workout. The workout makes me feel better both physically and mentally. When I get on the scale after the holidays, when we've eaten all that good stuff, I can tell real quick. If I get up to 225, I can get back down to 210 or 212 in about two weeks if I just watch my diet and work out.

If I didn't have my girlfriend, I would probably be eating at Burger King every night. Honestly—that's it. She has been very instrumental in keeping me on a fat-free diet. We have very little red meat, chicken maybe two or three times a week, fish and a lot of pasta—angel hair. I've had a bout with gout, and red meat just raises hell with me, so I shouldn't eat it anyway.

After my back operation, I found out after trial and error that I couldn't continue my life the same. You have to learn a whole new lifestyle: what to lift, how to lift and what to do day-in and day-out.

I'm not Arnold Schwarzenegger by far, and I don't want to be, but my outlook on my daily routine is really up. There are too many people that go to work every day and hate their jobs. I can honestly say I love mine. I equate that with working out, you bet. If it takes exercise and diet to do that, fine.

The Wheel Thing

Brad Wade, San Jose, California

Date of birth: December 1, 1947

Height and weight: 6-foot-1, 180 pounds

Profession: Senior programmer, IBM Research

Fitness accomplishment: Rode bicycle from Los Angeles to Boston, covering 3,500 miles in 47 days.

Favorite junk food: "I'm a chocolate hound."

Favorite health food: "Potato and broccoli make a nice combination. I don't particularly go out of my way to buy anything that's called health food."

Robert Maynard Hutchins once said "Whenever I feel like exercising, I lie down until the feeling passes." That was sort of my theory when my doctor told me in 1979 that I needed to start exercising.

I had never done anything athletic that I particularly enjoyed or was good at, with the exception of badminton. When my doctor told me I needed to get some exercise, I said, "Well, I'm not particularly fond of jogging. I can handle myself in the water, but I don't particularly enjoy swimming." So he said, "Have you considered bicycling?"

Let the Good Times Roll

I went out that weekend and bought a reasonably nice bike, a Univega Sport Tour. Not having been on a bike in ten years, it took my bottom and my bicycle about a month to get used to each other. I went out for some long rides—at the time, 45 miles was a very long ride—and got totally exhausted. But I enjoyed it and kept at it.

I put 10,000 miles on that bike in five years. I rode to work one day a week because my car pool partner had another obligation on Wednesdays. I got more involved in the club, and they took me under their wing. I went on some longer rides, and within that very supportive environment, I progressed to my present level.

Riding for Life

In 1984, when I got an award at work for technical achievement that had a few dollars attached to it, I said, "Hey, I think I'm in this for the long term." So I went out and spent some of that money on a good custom bike, a Holdsworth. And I found that with a good bike, instantly, my riding went to 4,000 miles a year, simply because I enjoyed it so much more.

About the time I got the new bike, my car pool partner retired. I said, "Okay, this would be a good excuse to start riding my bike to work every day."

In May and June of 1992, I joined a fully supported cross-country tour given through the League of American Wheelmen called Pedal for Power. We rode from Los Angeles to Boston—about 3,500 miles—in 47 days.

I tell my friends that the important thing is to enjoy yourself. If you're interested in getting exercise, I will be glad to tell you about bicycling. But I'm not going to tell you that you ought to bicycle. I'm going to tell you that you should find something you enjoy doing. Because then you'll do it, by golly. If it's a chore and drudgery, you'll find all the excuses in the world for not doing it.

My diet is generally a bowl of cereal in the morning; low-fat yogurt, a banana and 1 percent milk for lunch; and dinners that alternate between something out of the freezer and a vegetable dish. By something out of the freezer, I mean some low-salt dish that I've cooked myself rather than anything I've bought prepared and ready to go from the grocery store.

Allow yourself an occasional celebration. When it gets to be Christmastime, you don't need to limit yourself to the carrot sticks and whatnot. Be a good sport and enjoy yourself, knowing that 360 out of the 365 days in the year, you're taking good care of yourself.

Marathon Man

Dave Dorff, Cincinnati, Ohio

Date of birth: February 1, 1956

Height and weight: 6-foot-1, 180 to 190 pounds

Profession: Executive vice-president and chief operating officer at U.S. Shoe Footwear Group

Fitness accomplishment: Dropped 100 pounds and has started running marathons.

Favorite junk food: Vegetable pizza. "Tortilla chips would be real close behind."

Favorite health food: Nonfat banana cream frozen yogurt.

The CEO of U.S. Shoe challenged four or five of us to a weight-loss contest. Whoever lost the largest amount of body weight, as a percentage of his total weight, would be the winner. On New Year's Day we all came to the office. The president brought the scales. I was at 290 pounds.

I'm fairly competitive, and there was no way I was going to lose. So I decided there were two things I was going to do: One, I was going to exercise. Two, I was going to change what I ate.

Table Topics

My typical eating pattern had been: If it was edible, I ate it. If there was no red meat at a meal, it was not a meal in my opinion.

I cut fat out of my diet. At the beginning, I limited myself to 10 to 15 grams of fat a day, although now I'm up to 30 to 40 grams a day, or about 15 percent of my total calories. No butter, no red meat. I went to fish and turkey and chicken. I went to pasta, rice and vegetables.

I eat three meals a day now, with two snacks—one mid-morning and one mid-afternoon. The largest meal is breakfast or lunch; dinner is good-sized but not excessive.

Before, I never ate breakfast unless it was a business meeting. Now, every morning for breakfast I have a bagel with nonfat cheese on top, nonfat sugar-free yogurt, two pieces of fruit, a vitamin supplement and a small glass of orange juice.

Lunches, I went to salads with nonfat dressings. I have fruit and occasionally a baked potato. I'll have pretzels and nonfat frozen yogurt, which is kind of my treat.

Healthy Strides

Before, the only exercise I did was play a little doubles tennis on the weekends. I decided to walk for exercise. January is not the best time of the year to start walking in Cincinnati, so I bought a treadmill. My first time on it I walked 1.97 miles in 30 minutes, and I was ready to die. For the first month I mixed walking and jogging. When I got to the point that I could jog for 30 minutes without stopping, I started jogging a bit faster. By March 17, I had lost 60 pounds and won the contest.

I ran my first 5-K and 10-K races that fall. I felt so good I decided to train for a marathon. I finished the Saint George Marathon in Utah in 3:40. I felt absolutely wonderful. I was a new man. I'd changed so much that when I ran into my old college roommate, who was best man at my wedding, he didn't recognize me.

The family support was critical. They did a lot of joking. My wife said it was nice to have my chins in the single digits. Once, I was lying on the bed after taking a shower. She came over and poked me in the chest and said "Oh, what are those—ribs?"

I'm very comfortable now with my body. I'm stable between 180 and 190 pounds. My waist has gone from a 48 to a 34. My chest size has gone from a 54 to a 40. My neck has gone from 18½ to 15½. My inseam has gone from a 30 to a 32, since I now wear pants across my belly button as opposed to below it.

Male Makeovers

A century ago most guys worked for their food. Really worked—in factories, for example, or in the fields. Today, an eight-hour shift is as likely to be spent in a conference room as outdoors. Entertaining clients. Eating too much. Schmoozing in bars. For guys today, getting in shape is hard. Experts give their advice.

The Full-Time Desk Jockey

The Scenario

Harry wrestled in college, but now he grapples with an overgrown gut. A desk job doesn't help his fleshy frame. A bigger problem is his wife, who lards her cooking with butter, salt and sugar. He desperately wants to drop weight and be athletic again without hurting his wife's feelings.

Solution 1

Harry could start by telling his wife he loves her so much that as an investment in their future together, they should both take steps toward better health.

Instead of making his healthy changes work at odds with his wife, he should encourage a teamwork approach. He should offer to prepare a big salad or low-fat soup to start their meals. He should eat smaller portions of any high-fat foods his wife prepares, use less butter and skip dessert.

Harry needs to take the initiative. If his wife refuses to join him in getting healthy, he should work on changing himself. He shouldn't preach or threaten her about her unhealthy habits—neither works—but he should stick to his decision and show her by example the benefits of changing bad habits.

—Joan Price, fitness instructor, owner of Unconventional Moves, a fitness consulting service in Sebastopol, California, and author of *The Honest Truth about Losing Weight and Keeping It Off*.

Solution 2

To start his plan, Harry should walk or jog a few miles each day. That shouldn't be asking too much of a guy his age. After he gets in shape a bit, he should continue with a regular exercise program that is heavy on aerobics and includes some resistance training. To reach his fitness goal of losing weight and being athletic again, he'll also need to focus on his diet and other lifestyle considerations. His wife simply needs to start learning about healthy cooking. She should cook less red meat and more beans, rice and pasta. The pasta doesn't have to be in cream sauce. Try a basil-and-tomato sauce that isn't high in calories. It'd be ideal if Harry's wife would join him in a healthy lifestyle, since a spouse or girlfriend can be a great motivator.

As for his lifestyle, Harry apparently is enjoying a well-to-do standard of living. Instead of taking vacations to the beach, he and his wife should plan vacations that are more athletic in nature. Instead of sunning themselves in Mexico, they could plan a hiking trip in the Grand Canyon or a back-roads wilderness hike. Ultimately, even if his wife doesn't join him, everyone has to be self-motivated, so Harry's own health should be his prime concern.

—Art Mollen, D.O., director of the Southwest Health Institute in Phoenix.

The Traveling Salesman

The Scenario

Sam has been a traveling salesman for a computer firm for more than ten years. He prides himself on being a good, solid employee—a hard worker who always puts a lot of himself into his job. Lately, however, it seems as though it's all coming back—with interest.

At six-foot-one and 234 pounds, Sam's carrying a bit too much software around the waist. It's no mystery how it happened, either. A big part of his job involves wining and dining wealthy clients. He's either in the office working at his desk or out on the town hustling business—usually while drinking in bars, devouring rich food in restaurants or grazing from buffets. Fact is, he can't even remember the last time he managed to eat a healthy quiet meal at home. For the past few years he has been nervously watching as his pants size gradually expands, but he's not sure how to go about reversing the trend. Back in high school and college he was naturally thin and active. These days, though, about the only exercise he gets is walking from the car to the office. But establishing a regular workout routine is difficult because he's always on the road. Sam's goal is to lose 35 to 40 pounds. Where does he begin?

Solution 1

This man is courting a heart attack. First, he needs to abstain from alcohol. I'm not saying he should quit entirely, but he can't drink three or four drinks a day to schmooze clients.

He should start a walking program, whether it's on a treadmill or outside. I'd recommend that he walk about two miles a day for 35 to 40 minutes.

He should eliminate red meat for the next 30 days. If he's going to eat chicken or fish, eat it only once a day. Otherwise, he should be eating more rice, beans, pasta and vegetables.

By doing all this, Sam could lose about ten pounds in a 30-day period. He should then focus on committing to another 30 days. After each month, he might wish to reward himself with new jogging shoes, a sweat suit or something like that.

—Art Mollen, D.O., director of the Southwest Health Institute in Phoenix.

Solution 2

Sam didn't develop poor fitness overnight, and he won't fix it overnight. He should exercise three to five days a week for 20 to 60 minutes per workout. He can split the workout into smaller sessions two or more times a day if it's easier. He should work out two to four times a week with resistance training.

Sam should ensure that the hotels where he stays have health clubs or other workout facilities, like a pool or tennis courts. He needs to select foods low in fat. That way, he can still eat heartily and lose weight over time. Instead of alcohol, he can opt for juice or water.

If he lives like this, he should be able to lose 35 pounds safely in about a year.

—L. Jerome Brandon, Ph.D., associate professor of kinesiology in the Department of Kinesiology and Health at Georgia State University in Atlanta.

The Power Schmoozer

The Scenario

Mike is a master of schmoozing. He's out with clients at least two or three nights a week, entertaining at one happy hour or another. Unfortunately, Mike has trouble watching his diet while he's glad-handing his guests. The fine wine, the prime rib, the beer, the appetizers, the buffet in the hospitality suite—it's adding up quickly. Fact is, Mike is in danger of becoming as big as the desk he sits behind. But to him, food and drink are necessary tools of his trade—they grease the wheels, they make him a favorite with his clients. How can Mike reconcile his business style with the necessity to start eating better and watching his weight?

Solution 1

Mike should realize that most people don't necessarily want big, heavy business meals anymore. He shouldn't feel the pressure to lavish a lot of food on his clients. If Mike lives in a big city, he should do some checking around to see what restaurants offer low-fat choices on the menu.

He needs to develop an arsenal of tips so that even when he is entertaining clients at meals, he's minimizing the effects of those meals. And they don't have to be very obvious things that might make Mike feel self-conscious in front of his clients. He can do very subtle things like order water instead of soda, eat his bread without butter or order his salad with dressing on the side. These tips help control little things

in a big meal, but those little things add up.

Since he schmoozes so well, he should spend a little time schmoozing with the maître d' and chef at the restaurants he takes his clients to, make them aware that he's trying to eat healthier. If he's a regular customer, I know of no restaurant that won't try to accommodate him.

—**Cheryl C. Marco, R.D., dietitian and manager of outpatient nutrition at Thomas Jefferson University Hospital in Philadelphia.**

Solution 2

If Mike's clients are health- and fitness-conscious, or if they actively participate in some sort of sport or game, taking his clients to the fitness center or playing that sport with them can be a healthy alternative to the restaurant route. If fitness and sports aren't Mike's clients' forte, Mike could at least try to entertain his clients in a way in which food is not the focus—taking his clients deep-sea fishing, for example.

Mike should also exercise. Aerobic exercise and proper nutrition are the ingredients needed to strengthen the heart and decrease body fat. Obviously, before starting any exercise program, he needs to obtain permission from his physician. Once he is cleared to exercise, he should probably start out slowly with a good low-impact exercise like walking, which he can do at any time.

With his busy schedule of entertaining, Mike should also look for a health club that has flexible hours to accommodate his schedule. Some fitness facilities—especially in cities—are open 24 hours. It might be even more convenient for Mike to invest in a piece of equipment, like a stationary bike or cross-country skier. This would provide Mike the opportunity to work out on a regular basis and at any time of the day his schedule would allow.

—**Mike Nishihara, director of the Center for Athletic Development at the National Institute for Fitness and Sport in Indianapolis.**

The Smoker

The Scenario

Peter has smoked two packs of cigarettes a day all his adult life. He never noticed adverse effects from his habit until he joined a health club and began working out. Five minutes into a session on the stair-climbing machine, he started coughing and hacking and had to quit. Another time, in the weight room, he became breathless in mid-rep and had to stop again. Every time Peter broke even a mild sweat, the symptoms would begin again—he'd start gasping for air and very quickly lose his energy. He knows he should stop smoking, but that's going to take some time. Meanwhile, he still wants to work out. What does he need to do?

Solution 1

The lay public puts a lot of emphasis on exercise—and it's certainly important—but it's not anywhere near as important as controlling your cholesterol or blood pressure. And absolutely, he's got to stop smoking. If he stops smoking, after five years his chances of coronary disease are as if he'd never smoked at all. After ten years his chances of lung cancer are as if he'd never smoked at all. It's important for men to know that, especially the ones who think that since they've smoked all their lives, no good will come of stopping now. They're wrong.

Peter also has to figure out whether he's having trouble exercising because he's out of shape or because he has lung trouble or a heart problem. It's a very serious question, but his doctor can tell pretty easily.

More importantly, nobody who has been indolent and smoking and is over the age of 35 should suddenly take up exercise without talking to a doctor first. Peter should have a simple stress test on a treadmill to see what his limits are. That's vital. If Peter has scarring on his lungs from all that smoking, or especially if he has a heart problem, just going out and exercising could be dangerous. But if he sees his doctor first, he can get on a very specific routine of exercise that, combined with lifestyle changes, can help him feel better and become more fit.

—Allen B. Weisse, M.D., professor of medicine and cardiology at the University of Medicine and Dentistry of New Jersey–New Jersey Medical School and University Hospital in Newark and author of *The Man's Guide to Good Health.*

Solution 2

Aerobic exercise will improve Peter's cardiovascular system, but he needs to learn how to do it properly. It appears that Peter was not doing exercises at appropriate intensity levels, since the exercises were causing him to gasp for air and eventually stop.

To work out aerobically, exercisers should exercise at a pace that keeps their heart rates at about 55 to 85 percent of their maximum heart rates. As Peter's heart rate approaches the upper limit of his aerobic training zone, breathing becomes labored—it becomes difficult to carry on a conversation without having to pause and take deep breaths—but he shouldn't be gasping. The exercise should utilize large muscle groups and should be done rhythmically and continuously for a minimum of 20 minutes nonstop.

If that's difficult for him, he could start out doing 5 or 10 minutes nonstop, whatever he can handle. Eventually, he can work his way up to 20 minutes. Peter needs to find himself an aerobic activity he enjoys, such as cycling, running, swimming or cross-country skiing.

—Mike Nishihara, director of the Center for Athletic Development at the National Institute for Fitness and Sport in Indianapolis.

The Former Athlete

The Scenario

Norman used to be a runner, and he figured he was destined to have a string bean physique. But the indisputable evidence is right there on his new driver's license: a round, fleshy face he hardly recognizes. His trousers are size 36, up from the 32s he used to wear. He usually eats three squares a day (his wife is a master with roasts). If he skips a meal at all, it's breakfast, and he makes up for that with a Danish at the office. Snacks include a doughnut in the afternoon, a bowl of ice cream before bed and—on weekends only—buttered popcorn at the movies. He is mystified by his weight gain and wants to return to his formerly trim self.

Solution 1

Norman is only 33, but he's the typical American heart attack waiting to happen.

He's probably not in shape to run track, but he could probably go for a mile walk. He could build up to a level where he is getting his muscles back in tone and burning some calories.

He should take a look at the type of meals he eats. Maybe he can cut down on the portions of the meat. If his wife is the main cook, maybe she could start cooking dishes where meat is more of an ingredient, like casseroles, pasta or Asian dishes.

The snack items—Danish, doughnuts, ice cream, buttered popcorn—all are things that are high in fat. Instead of a doughnut in the afternoon, a bagel or pretzels will help

satisfy his hunger but not contribute a lot of calories. About this ice cream before bed: Maybe he could switch to frozen yogurt or a lower-fat frozen dessert. A Popsicle or something like that would be low-fat or fat-free. When he goes to the movies, he could try not getting the popcorn buttered and choosing a smaller size rather than the jumbo.

Dietitians tell people not to ever skip breakfast. People usually pick up something in place of the meal like a Danish or doughnut, or they don't eat anything until lunch, and then they're ravenous. Breakfast is easy to do low-fat. He should switch to low-fat milk and cereals, bagels or English muffins.

—Martin Yadrick, R.D., a Los Angeles dietitian and spokesman for the American Dietetic Association.

Solution 2

I would encourage Norman to keep a diary of what he eats, so he can become aware of when he's doing most of his eating. Once people become aware of what they are doing, it becomes easier for them to find things they can gradually work on and change.

On a positive note, he eats on a regular schedule except for missing breakfast once in a while. He really likes to eat, so it sounds like there are a lot of opportunities to make substitutions. He should make a deal with himself to work on just one or two things at a time until it becomes a habit.

If he feels he has to have a snack at night, there are now frozen yogurts and low-fat ice creams. Popcorn doesn't have to have butter on it. He could also sprinkle on flavored seasoning.

I would really encourage some exercise. Maybe he could walk to work. Maybe there are stairs in his building. Maybe he and some of his buddies could play basketball at noon. I'd try to make it easy to fit exercise into his lifestyle

—Mary C. Winston, R.D., Ed.D, senior science consultant for the American Heart Association.

The Perpetual Eater

The Scenario

While Eugene is getting older, he still has an 18-year-old's appetite. Breakfast (when there isn't leftover pizza) is bacon and eggs. Lunch consists of a hoagie and chips, and dinner is something from the onion-ring-and-burger food group. He celebrates with filet mignon, and weekends call for ribs on the grill. And why drink water when you can have beer? Over the past 20 years, Eugene's waistline has expanded from slight "love handles" to a wide-track spare tire. He knows it's time to make substantial changes. But truth be known, he can't imagine a life that revolves around broccoli.

Solution 1

It's hard for a lot of men to realize that they can't keep eating the same way they did when they were 18. Eugene would have the most success if he made gradual changes. I call it the weaning method: to just gradually get used to lower-fat items in the diet.

He needs to expand his food repertoire. He could have the bacon and eggs two or three days a week and then the other days find something more healthful—cereal, toast and bagels. He could try cholesterol-free eggs one day. Or Canadian bacon instead of regular bacon. Just little changes.

There may be different versions of some of the foods that he likes. Pizza by itself isn't such a bad food. He could order one with fewer fatty toppings like pepperoni and sausage. This kind of guy wouldn't eat a vegetarian pizza, but maybe he would eat a Canadian bacon pizza.

He could switch to chicken or fish on the grill instead of ribs. Going to light beer is a good idea, and so is cutting down on the total number of beers.

As steaks go, filet mignon is a good choice because it's a leaner cut. The main things there are to have a smaller filet and to trim any visible fat. Or maybe there's something outside of a meal that he could do to celebrate: Go to a movie or rent a movie. Do something to celebrate that's not food-related.

—Martin Yadrick, R.D., a Los Angeles dietitian and spokesman for the American Dietetic Association.

Solution 2

Eugene has habits so firmly entrenched that they're not going to go away easily.

He needs the support of his family. It would be ideal if I could talk to Eugene and his wife together, because if he doesn't have the support of the person responsible for meals, he's not going to go anywhere. Sometimes you can start out by not changing any of the foods a person is eating but getting him to agree to cut back on the size of servings.

I would encourage him to get out and do some walking, some bicycling—to do something. He may drop a few pounds, and this would be encouraging to him.

There are plenty of lean meats now on the market that he could use for grilling. He might be willing to do away with the potato chips he eats at lunch. On the sandwich, he might tell the preparer to leave off the high-fat cold cuts. Even mozzarella or Swiss cheese wouldn't be as bad.

I would tell him not to think that he has to lose all these pounds right away. If he's active, he'll start to feel better. When that happens, he'll start to feel more pride and be off and running.

—Mary C. Winston, R.D., Ed.D, senior science consultant for the American Heart Association.

The Type A Overachiever

The Scenario

By the time Bill turned 40, he had worked his way up the corporate ladder to department head at the regional sales office. But the price has been steep. He routinely works 10- to 12-hour days. He grabs a doughnut for breakfast. At night, he'll hit a fast-food joint or fix something fast—and fattening—after he gets home. There never seems to be any time for R and R. He has gained 30 pounds and seems to always feel fatigued. What should he do?

Solution 1

From an exercise point of view, before he goes to work he should take a brisk walk or jog. If he cannot do that, he should walk or do his exercise at noon. If he cannot do that, he should find an exercise facility near his job and schedule some time during the day for exercise, just like he schedules his sales appointments. He should exercise a minimum of 30 to 60 minutes at least four times a week.

Before he leaves for work, he should eat a low-fat breakfast that is high in complex carbohydrates.

He should always bring his lunch from home. That could be a sandwich with low-fat cheese and lean ham with low-fat mayonnaise, lettuce and tomato. Lunch could also include pretzels, an apple and low-fat cookies, such as Fig Newtons, gingersnaps or graham crackers. The important cue here is that his lunch should be from home, so he has control over it.

Finally, whenever possible, his family should eat their main meal together. Examples would be lean meat, chicken or fish, baked or broiled; baked potatoes, brown rice or pasta; and salad and a vegetable.

—John P. Foreyt, Ph.D., director of the Nutrition Research Clinic at Baylor College of Medicine in Houston and co-author of *Living without Dieting*.

Solution 2

Because Bill is overweight and fatigued, what his body needs first is physical activity. He should seek out a gym near work and invest in a membership. He should engage in activities he enjoys, whether they be racquetball, tennis, swimming, walking, jogging or weight training. He should try to schedule time at the gym two or three days during the week and keep these appointments. It can be limited to an hour or so. The time he spends replenishing himself with exercise will pay off in increased energy and productivity both on and off the job. On the weekend, he should take advantage of opportunities to be active with his family, such as biking or taking walks in the park.

Despite Bill's busy schedule, one of the most important steps to take with diet is to eat regular meals and snacks. Eating on the run often means skimping on some meals, which can leave you craving desserts or snacks in between or overeating at other times because you've gone too long without eating. The simple step of bringing his lunch to work during the week can help to dramatically decrease both fat and calorie intake.

A low-fat late-afternoon snack can satisfy his appetite until he gets home rather than tempt him to stop at fast-food restaurants. Bill and his wife can purchase some new cookbooks to help them learn how to prepare low-fat, great-tasting meals. If all else fails, he should check into the increasing variety of low-fat, nutritious frozen entrées that are available.

—Paul R. Thomas, R.D., Ed.D., staff scientist with the National Academy of Sciences' Food and Nutrition Board in Washington, D.C.

The Beer-Bellied Pleasure Lover

The Scenario

Jimmy learned everything he knows about nutrition at his college fraternity. Then and now, he considered the main food groups to be beer, pizza and cheeseburgers. His exercise habits were also set in college: a couple of short runs during the week and spirited games of pickup basketball, touch football or softball on weekends. His weight has crept up slowly but surely. Jimmy now weighs some 30 pounds more than he did in college ten years ago. All of the added weight, it seems, is in a beer belly that has become a source of constant ribbing from his old buddies. How can Jimmy lose his beer gut?

Solution 1

I would say that any kind of behavioral change has got to be moderate, so a person sees it as something he can live with forever. So number one, I would say that Jimmy needs to get consistency in his exercise. He's exercising every once in a while, playing a little of this or that. I would shoot for a minimum of three days a week and have that be a top-priority time that doesn't get pushed aside or shoved behind some other priority that comes up.

Secondly, Jimmy should extend the length of his aerobic exercise sessions. If he's jogging only a couple of miles, that isn't going to take very long—probably somewhere between 15 and 20 minutes, even if he's out of shape. That's not enough. He should extend his aerobic exercise to at least 30 minutes.

My third suggestion would be to figure out a way to set reasonable limits on his beer, pizza and cheeseburger intake. Jimmy should look at what he can live with. If he's having cheeseburgers five days a week, can he cut back to one? Then, on the day he decides to have a cheeseburger, Jimmy can say "I'm not going to hell. I've planned for it, so I don't have to feel guilty about it. I've made a conscious decision that today's my cheeseburger day and I'm going to have it. But tomorrow I won't, because I've already had it for the week."

—Wayne C. Miller, Ph.D., assistant professor of kinesiology at Indiana University in Bloomington and director of the university's weight-loss clinic.

Solution 2

Jimmy should keep it fun. He shouldn't bother about counting calories. He should think about the fat content and bring it down slowly, not rapidly. In the exercise area, he should continue doing what he's doing that's fun. It would be good if he tried to increase his exercise and make it more consistent, but he should take out the feeling of guilt. That's when a lot of people stop exercising. There are a lot of little things he can do that will help. He should park his car a little farther away in the parking lot, so he walks more. He should use the stairs instead of the elevator. Walking up a flight of steps a day every day for a year equals one pound of weight lost.

If at the end of a softball game his buddies are going in for a pitcher of beer, he should at least look at how to cut down. If he's a regular beer drinker, he should go down to light beer. If he usually has 3 beers, he should go down to 2½. Instead of munching on potato chips, he should have pretzels. They have a lot less fat.

—Dale L. Anderson, M.D., head of the complementary medicine department at Park Nicollet Medical Center in Minneapolis.

Postmortems These men were big in every sense of the word. Not just in size, but in ability. Popularity. Lust for life. Yet the same appetites that made them household names also contributed to their downfalls. Here are their stories.

Theodore Roosevelt

The Rough Rider Went Downhill

When Teddy Roosevelt died of a heart attack in 1919 at the age of 60, he tipped the scales at about 200 pounds—a serious chunk of weight on a 5-foot-9 frame.

But the man who became our 26th president didn't start out that way. After suffering asthma, the sickly young Teddy set upon a vigorous course of exercise and outdoor activities, including bodybuilding, boxing, swimming, hiking, rowing and horseback riding. Later, he took up hunting and cattle-punching in the Dakota Territory.

"When he was police commissioner of New York City in the late 1890s, he had a crude stationary bicycle in his office. Since he was too busy then to get out and exercise as he used to, he'd just get on that bike and pedal," says John A. Gable, Ph.D., executive director of the Theodore Roosevelt Association in Oyster Bay, New York.

Executive Fitness

Roosevelt was the first U.S. president to play tennis. He studied judo in the White House and in winter was seen cross-country skiing on the streets of Washington, D.C.

"Like a lot of men then and now, he had a weight problem from his forties on," says Dr. Gable. "And as active as he was, throughout the course of his life he never regulated his diet." Roosevelt liked to eat—the richer the food, the better.

After becoming president, the demands of state ultimately proved too pressing for Roosevelt to maintain his athletic pursuits; the Rough Rider fell into a less active lifestyle. Without as much vigorous exercise to help burn off the fat and calories of his heavy diet, Roosevelt put on weight. His health gradually declined.

"Roosevelt can hardly be blamed for the diet he followed—he was a product of his time," adds Dr. Gable. Back then, health experts thought a thin man was a sick man. A round-bellied, robust gentleman with a hearty appetite was considered the picture of health and prosperity.

They were wrong, of course. Doctors now know that image paints a very different picture.

In 1919, Roosevelt died—possibly, experts say, because a blood clot from a leg injury broke loose and traveled upstream to his coronary artery, causing him to have a heart attack. But even if the embolism hadn't killed him, his lifestyle might have. That's because the dangerous combination of obesity and rich diet made him a poster boy for heart disease.

"If they knew then what we know now, Roosevelt certainly could have lived a longer and healthier life," says Dr. Gable. "But at the time, it was assumed that as you got older, you got heavier. That's how it was." And that's how it ended for Teddy Roosevelt.

Ernest Hemingway

The Bell Tolled for Him

When he wasn't writing about hunting in Africa, bullfighting in Spain or fishing in Big Two-Hearted River, Ernest Hemingway was living what men of his generation would consider the good life: a hedonistic adventure filled with wine and women, fine sport in the great outdoors and the celebrity that came with being the Nobel prize–winning father of modern fiction. What Hemingway's admirers didn't know was that he was slowly eating and drinking his way to the grave.

"His philosophy was that life is basically a tragedy, in the sense that you're going to die. So what do you do in the meanwhile?" says Hemingway scholar John Keats, professor emeritus of writing and editing at Syracuse University in New York. "Hemingway's answer was, do whatever the hell you want, eat whatever the hell you want."

Which he did, with style. He traveled widely—he lived in France and Spain and played in Hollywood and Manhattan—and always ate well. "That guy never ate poor," says Keats. "He ate at the best restaurants in the world. And no matter where he was, Hemingway was never far from a bottle of champagne, gin or whiskey."

A Gradual Decline

Despite Hemingway's active lifestyle as a globe-trotting hunter and sportsman, all the rich food and alcohol took its toll. "The fact is, near the end of his life he wasn't in very good shape, and he never got any better," says Keats.

Living in Paris in the 1920s, Hemingway probably weighed about 200 pounds. He enjoyed many of the physical pursuits he wrote about. Boxing,

skiing, fishing, safari hunting and bullfighting were just some of the sports that Hemingway made a part of his life. But even these activities weren't enough to offset the high-calorie intake from the writer's wining and dining.

Eventually, Hemingway discovered this for himself. According to one biographer, he began to worry about his weight and tried to keep it down: "(Hemingway) did exercises on the bed in the morning and ran along the road for about three miles."

It was a race he eventually lost. In his later years Hemingway sported a notable gut. His son described him as drinking "a quart of whiskey a day for the last 20 years of his life." Not surprisingly, Hemingway developed a host of physical ailments, along with serious mental problems. "He was slowly dying and he knew it," says Keats. "First his body deteriorated. He got fat. And he became ill.

"Hemingway had no use for doctors," says Keats. "He saw them as little as possible, and even when he did, he didn't pay any attention to what they said. His idea of life was to have fun and be a hedonist—and doctors had an annoying tendency to give you advice that precluded fun and hedonism."

But in the twilight of his life, Hemingway's ailments became so great that he began seeing doctors on a regular basis. He was diagnosed with a form of adult diabetes, the result of the excesses of his youth. The worst side effect of this illness was that he became impotent—a crushing blow for sybaritic Hemingway. According to Keats, these failures of his body began to prey on his mind. He couldn't bear the thought of slowly going crazy, so he ended it quickly.

One morning in 1961, Hemingway put a shotgun in his mouth and pulled the trigger. Had the master writer paid more attention to his health, the story of his life might not have come to such a dramatic end.

George Herman "Babe" Ruth

Legend Is Larger Than Life

In the most recent Hollywood treatment of his life, Babe Ruth is depicted as an incorrigible fat kid who was mercilessly teased by his schoolmates at St. Mary's Industrial School in Baltimore.

The teasing stopped only after the plump boy demonstrated an almost supernatural ability to knock baseballs out of the school yard. *The Babe*, starring the portly John Goodman in the title role, reinforced the popular notion of the hot dog–scarfing fat guy whose heart—and talent—was matched only by his appetite for food and women.

There's only one minor problem: It's not true.

"It's unfortunate that Hollywood can't keep its facts historically accurate," says Greg Schwalenberg, curator of the Babe Ruth Birthplace Museum in Baltimore.

In an article written for *Smithsonian* magazine marking the centennial of Ruth's birth, author Robert W. Creamer objected to the Goodman film, writing: "It depicted the Babe as a fat little boy who grew up to be a grossly fat man. Ruth wasn't fat when he was young, and even after he developed his famous paunch, he could still move with speed and grace.... He was a beautifully coordinated athlete, and that he could play so well even with a beer belly is evidence of that."

To be sure, Ruth was a man of voracious appetites. For baseball. For life. For food. For women. For drink. But some of his exploits doubtless have grown with constant retelling. "Definitely, there's a lot of exaggeration," Schwalenberg says.

In his 1974 book *Babe:*

The Legend Comes to Life—which Schwalenberg calls the bible of Babe biographies—Creamer meticulously documents Ruth's weight through his playing days.

When he left St. Mary's to sign with the Baltimore Orioles in 1914, the 19-year-old was a strapping six-foot-two, 185 pounds. His weight gradually crept up over 200 pounds, and after 1919 it rarely dipped below 220.

Some of the fantastic tales of Ruth's gluttony—eating an 18-egg omelet with three big slices of ham and a half-dozen pieces of buttered toast—probably have some grain of truth. The great Ty Cobb once said of Ruth: "I've seen him at midnight, propped up in bed, order six club sandwiches, a platter of pigs' knuckles and a pitcher of beer. He'd down all that while smoking a big black cigar. Next day, if he hit a homer, he'd trot around the bases complaining about gas pains and a bellyache."

In 1921, *Popular Science Monthly* set out to discover what made the Babe the greatest home run hitter of all time. He went to a laboratory at Columbia University in New York City, where he underwent tests measuring his dexterity, coordination and reaction time. "The secret of Babe Ruth's ability to hit is clearly revealed in these tests," the magazine concluded. "His eye, his ear, his brain, his nerves all function more rapidly than do those of the average person. Further, the coordination between eye, ear, brain and muscle is much nearer perfection than that of the normal healthy man."

Despite Ruth's occasional excesses, Schwalenberg says, there is evidence he worked hard to keep himself in condition to play the game he loved. But that isn't what people want to hear. "People want to think he never really kept in shape and he could walk out and hit a home run even after a night on the town," Schwalenberg says. "We want to think that's true because it adds to the whole mystique about Babe Ruth."

John Candy

Comedian's Bulk Weighed Him Down

Comedian John Candy made big waves with his breakthrough role in the 1984 hit film *Splash*. In her *New Yorker* review, critic Pauline Kael said: "He doesn't add weight, he adds bounce and imagination."

Throughout his career, Candy's roly-poly public persona helped set him apart from his peers. He hailed from a tradition of rotund funnymen that includes the likes of Oliver Hardy, Lou Costello and—among his contemporaries—the late Sam Kinison and Louie Anderson (who, in recent years, has become much thinner).

Behind Candy's beguiling smile, however, he was sensitive about his girth. In a 1989 *Playboy* interview, he was asked about several leading comedy stars who—like him—were overweight. The question—"Is fat funny?"—sparked a revealing reply.

"It's as funny as midgets. It's really in the eye of the beholder. Some choose to think that. I never dwell on it. I tend to look at people as people and not as tall, short, fat, skinny. Given the opportunity, I'm sure we could come up with a list of faults for everyone. We could find old people funny. People with big noses. People going bald. People with big ears. People with goiters. People who have face-lifts. People who have perfect teeth. You could cut anybody up.

"Roseanne is very funny, very talented. More power to her. Louie Anderson is funny. Sam Kinison is very talented. I think they're talented no matter what they look like. I don't judge people by how they look, and I try not to hang out with people who do."

Still, Candy didn't hestitate to joke about his weight. When asked to reveal a big man's sex secrets, he told *Playboy*: "Patience."

Playboy: "To what extent is size a love weapon?"

Candy: "The size of your wallet is very important. It should be bulging at all times. I think that usually speaks louder than anything else. Green stuff should be hanging all over the place."

But friends say he was extremely self-conscious about his weight. In 1981 he told *People* magazine: "I'm the one who has to look in the mirror, and after a while, it begins to eat at you."

Like many overweight men—he was six-foot-three and 330 pounds—Candy was capable of shedding pounds. He just couldn't keep them off. He spent a month at the Pritikin Institute in Santa Monica, California, in 1984 and promptly lost 75 pounds. But the weight came back.

In the 1989 *Playboy* interview, Candy said: "My weight fluctuates drastically. I'm trying to keep it on an even keel. My metabolism is slow, so exercise is very important for me to burn fat. I can eat a normal 1,500- to 2,000-calorie-a-day diet and put on lots of weight.

"I try to use the treadmill twice a day—at least an hour in the morning and an hour in the evening. A cardiovascular workout is very important for me. I work with weights now. My goal is to learn to discipline myself. It'll become a daily part of my life. I've never liked exercise. Pain was never fun for me. Some people get a real kick out of it, and I respect those people. I know what I have to do if I want to lose weight and stay healthy—eat a proper diet and exercise. All I've got to do is apply it. Therein lies the rub."

Candy was 43 when he suffered a heart attack and died in his sleep on location in Mexico in March 1994. He was still smoking up to a pack of cigarettes a day when he died.

Index

Note: Underscored page references indicate boxed text.